Financial Analysis and Business Decisions on the Pocket Calculator

WILEY SERIES ON SYSTEMS AND CONTROLS FOR FINANCIAL MANAGEMENT

Edited by Robert L. Shultis and Frank M. Mastromano

EDP Systems for Credit Management
Conan D. Whiteside

Profile for Profitability: Using Cost Control and Profitability Analysis
Thomas S. Dudick

Zero-Base Budgeting: A Practical Management Tool for Evaluating Expenses
Peter A. Pyhrr

Forecasting Methods for Management
Steven C. Wheelwright and Spyros Makridakis

Direct Cost and Contribution Accounting: An Integrated Management Accounting System
Germain Böer

The Corporate Memory: A Profitable and Practical Approach to Information Management and Retention Systems
Barbara N. Weaver and Wiley L. Bishop

Pricing Techniques for the Financial Executive
John C. Lere

The Strategy of Cash: A Liquidity Approach to Maximizing the Company's Profits
S. D. Slater

Fringe Benefits—The Depreciation, Obsolescence, and Transience of Man
Stanley M. Babson, Jr.

Competing for Capital—A Financial Relations Approach
Bruce W. Marcus

How to Improve Profitability Through More Effective Planning
Thomas S. Dudick

Financial Analysis and Business Decisions on the Pocket Calculator
Jon M. Smith

The Management System: Systems Are for People
Leslie H. Matthies

Financial Analysis and Business Decisions on the Pocket Calculator

JON M. SMITH

JMSA Business Systems Research and Analysis
St. Louis, Missouri

A Wiley-Interscience Publication

JOHN WILEY & SONS　　　New York　·　London　·　Sydney　·　Toronto

Copyright © 1976 by John Wiley & Sons, Inc.

All rights reserved. Published simultaneously in Canada.

No part of this book may be reproduced by any means, nor transmitted, nor translated into a machine language without the written permission of the publisher.

Library of Congress Cataloging in Publication Data:

Smith, Jon M   1938–
    Financial analysis and business decisions on the pocket calculator.

    (Wiley series on systems and controls for financial management)
    Includes index.
    1. Business mathematics—Problems, exercises, etc.
2. Calculating-machines. I. Title.

HF5695.S67   658.4'03'02854   76-5516
ISBN 0-471-80184-4

Printed in the United States of America

10 9 8 7 6 5 4 3

To
  Maurice Smith
  J. P. Johnson
  George LeCompte
  John Yardley
  Chuck Jacobson
  Fred Bradley
  Joe Goldstein
  Sara Goldstein
each of whom, in his or her own way, helped me attain a personal
financial goal and freedom.

SERIES PREFACE

No one needs to tell the reader that the world is changing. He sees it all too clearly. The immutable, the constant, the unchanging of a decade or two ago no longer represent the latest thinking—on *any* subject, whether morals, medicine, politics, economics, or religion. Change has always been with us, but the pace has been accelerating, especially in the postwar years.

Business, particularly with the advent of the electronic computer some 20 years ago, has also undergone change. New disciplines have sprung up. New professions are born. New skills are in demand. And the need is ever greater to blend the new skills with those of the older professions to meet the demands of modern business.

The accounting and financial functions certainly are no exception. The constancy of change is as pervasive in these fields as it is in any other. Industry is moving toward an integration of many of the information gathering, processing, and analyzing functions under the impetus of the so-called systems approach. Such corporate territory has been, traditionally, the responsibility of the accountant and the financial man. It still is, to a large extent—but times are changing.

Does this, then, spell the early demise of the accountant as we know him today? Does it augur a lessening of influence for the financial specialists in today's corporate hierarchy? We think not. We maintain, however, that it is incumbent upon today's accountant and today's financial man to learn *today's* thinking and to *use today's* skills. It is for this reason the Wiley Series on Systems and Controls for Financial Management is being developed.

Recognizing the broad spectrum of interests and activities that the series title encompasses, we plan a number of volumes, each representing the latest thinking, written by a recognized authority, on a particular facet of the financial man's responsibilities. The subjects contemplated for discussion within the series range from production accounting systems to planning, to corporate records, to control of cash. Each book is an in-depth study of one subject within this group. Each is intended to be a practical, working tool for the businessman in general and the financial man and accountant in particular.

ROBERT L. SHULTIS
FRANK M. MASTROMANO

PREFACE

This book is about making money. The money made or saved by applying the techniques and methods presented here can pay for the book many thousands of times over.

Keep a copy on your desk or in your briefcase or in your home. Refer to it when you want to reacquaint yourself with making business decisions based on financial analysis. Use this book for practicing business decisions. Use this book to find a business decision analogous to the ones you face **today**. Use this book to enjoy business decision making to its fullest. Use this book because it brings the full power of the pocket calculator to bear on your decisions and your business systems analysis.

This is not a book on "number crunching" on your pocket calculator, nor is it a book of "game playing" with your pocket calculator. This is a serious book on methods and techniques that are *sized* for pocket calculator analysis to assist you in making better business decisions through improved financial and business systems analysis.

This book will enable you to improve your earnings personally by improving the handling of your personal finances. It will help you to improve the earnings of the business for which you make business decisions, and it should improve your earnings by making you a more competent business manager and systems analyst for the organization you own or work with.

If you are an entrepreneur, this book will be important to you because your decisions must be made quickly and accurately. The entrepreneur's dealings are often characterized by fast cash movement on marginal information. Here the pocket calculator is an invaluable tool in making a quick "return versus risk" analysis of a business or other system of cash flow, to assist in deciding where your money should move next to maximize its rate of return.

The objective of this book is to make money for you, the reader. The approach to meeting this objective is to show how the pocket calculator can help you make better business decisions through faster, better financial analyses in a number of business areas.

When you have finished reading this book, you will have learned that many financial analyses that impact business decisions reduce calculations involving **only five numbers:**

- Present value.
- Future value.
- Payments.
- Interest.
- Number of compounding periods.

Many forms of systems analysis for business, banking, finance, and real estate involve only these five parameters, and there are only **twelve basically different types of problems** to be solved. The first part of this book shows you how to set up and solve these twelve financial problems in the **simplest** possible keystroke sequences for pocket calculators in general and for five of the most commonly used business calculators in particular. By examining both the general procedures and the specific keystroke sequences, you will be able to grasp both the financial concept and the details of financial calculations.

You will also understand that many financial analyses for many different fields use the same basic mathematics—only the *language* is different. In this sense the pocket calculator is a *teaching machine*. The pocket calculator casebook examples will teach you (*a*) how to extend your expertise beyond your field, and (*b*) how to encompass other disciplines that you may have thought were beyond your reach. **Broadening your business horizon will increase the opportunities for making money**. Working the casebook examples will show that the keystroke sequences are identical for seemingly different problems in obviously different disciplines. The casebook examples are prepared to enable the reader to relate the *language* of the financial analysis in his own field to other fields in a *learn-by-doing* mode of instruction.

This book will help you make money because the casebook examples are of real-world financial calculations and business decisions that managers and executives face every day. The problems presented in this book are not academic. They represent situations encountered by the author and his associates as they have conducted day-to-day business operations. These real-world examples demonstrate how to make money by quantifying and analyzing the "yield versus risk" of business decisions with your pocket calculator. The case histories also discuss the subtle or "interacting" effects of business decisions based on financial analysis, making clear the issues that are "black and white" and those that are not.

This book will also help you make money by showing how the pocket calculator is used in *business systems analysis*. The emphasis is on pocket calculator analyses supporting business decisions that are couched in uncertainty and involve significant penalties for a bad decision. Some of the toughest business decisions are those made in the face of uncertainty and at high risk but with high payoff. These include bid decisions, product development decisions, product termination decisions, capital investment decisions, and corporate start-up decisions, to name a few. Part 2 of this book deals exclusively with this type of business problem. The approach is to discuss the practical analytical techniques that are useful in making such business decisions.

This book will also help you improve your intuitive judgment about financial matters. Business is largely intuitive and certainly as much art as science. This is particularly true with respect to corporate policy making, new business decisions, business start-up activities, and entrepreneurial activities. The author has found that **intuitive business decision making improves** as more decisions are made and as experience is gained in the decision-making process. Thus perhaps the single most important contribution the pocket calculator makes to you, the business manager, is allowing you to examine a number of case studies and alternatives and to *practice* decision making based on financial analysis. Your business calculator can, at a keystroke, conduct the more laborious and tedious calculations associated with financial analysis, thus freeing you to *invent* better business methods. Figure 1 illustrates the point that what at first seems *counterintuitive* becomes *intuitive* as the individual acquires more insight and understanding. Here a number of counterintuitive findings about one of the author's businesses are plotted as a function of the number of days from receipt of his business pocket calculator. The period from one to six days was the most intense period of experimentation: three hours an evening were spent going over financial analyses and business decisions made in 1972 and 1973, the key start-up years for that business. The "surprises" found during this period of pocket calculator experimentation are due to the following factors:

- The financial findings that the calculator analysis uncovered.
- Findings about the characteristics and nature of the business system itself.

The period from 6 to 11 days is probably more typical of the learning

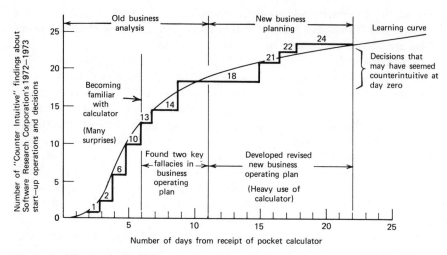

Figure 1. The pocket calculator can improve a businessman's intuition. Chart taken unrevised from *SRC Business Diary*.

curve of one who is analyzing a business that is long past the start-up stage and is fairly well understood. Finally the period from 11 to 22 days is characterized by the findings associated with the discovery of new ways to alter the business system as a result of the financial and business system analysis conducted in the first 12 days. In a sense, some of the findings at day 22 that would be considered intuitively obvious would certainly have been counterintuitive on "day zero." These data are presented to illustrate that the pocket calculator can be used to improve business decisions that are based on intuition.

Now a few words about the organization of this book. Financial and business systems analyses for each casebook example usually include:

- A computational procedure that can be used on any pocket calculator.
- Keystroke sequences for the simple four-function calculators.
- Keystroke sequences for business calculators that use a reverse-Polish calculator language.
- Keystroke sequences for business calculators that use an algebraic calculator language.

Those not yet familiar with the algebraic and reverse-Polish concepts in pocket calculator languages will find Chapter 1 particularly interesting because it makes clear the differences in calculator *languages*, helping the novice to decide which type of calculating machine best suits his needs.

This book is about business operations during a period of dramatic changes in the world's economic systems, when fast, accurate consideration of the time value of money is impacting even the local merchant and small businessman. The examples are drawn from *current* businesses and financial decisions with which the author is intimately familiar. These include the development of investment corporations, real estate investments, new product development decisions, capital investments, tax shelter analysis, major program bid decisions, and new business funds resource allocation.

The chapter on business statistics is a practical and pragmatic discussion of the statistical methods useful for analyzing the revenues, costs, risks, and returns of a business venture.

Throughout the book, more attention has been given to subjects of greater interest to the business practitioner than to the business theorist. Although the treatment of this material is mathematical, *only useful formulas are presented* in the text and casebook examples. The derivation of or elaboration on formulas is reserved for the appendices. Only the key formulas, procedures, and keystroke sequences are shown in each chapter. The author has not tried to achieve conciseness or rigor beyond that required for pocket calculator analysis.

The material for this book was developed over a decade of engineering and business systems analysis and entrepreneurial business ventures. Some of the business analysis concepts presented here have been discussed in the *Harvard Business Review*, in business mathematics books, or to some slight degree in books previously published on pocket calculator analysis. This material, however, is couched in the form of concrete financial calculations that are useful for making daily business decisions.

I would like to close this preface with an opinion on business decisions: all of us make business decisions. They improve with insight into the art and *science* of business operations. The science of business operations is closely tied to the basic concepts of financial analysis. Thus improving the ability to make business decisions involves improved understanding of the basic concepts of financial analyses. Better decision making follows directly from more extensive use of the principles of business finance to business problems faced from day to day. In this sense the pocket calculator becomes a useful tool to improve business decisions because (*a*) it electronically automates the tedious calculations of business and financial analysis, and (*b*) it constitutes a reasonable tradeoff between the fully automatic "hands-off" computerized analysis and the fully manual analysis, which though slow and laborious, allows the decision maker to get closer to his problem.

In short, the pocket calculator allows the business decision maker to stay close to the financial consequences of his decision by doing the tedious financial calculations with keystroke ease, thus freeing him to explore more ways to improve the yield of his decision.

I am deeply indebted to my associates in JMSA Business Systems Research and Analysis, Software Research Corporation, Calculator Technology Services, Executive Pilot Training Corporation, and the McDonnell Douglas Corporation. They have shared with me many of their techniques for business management, proposal bid strategies, and business systems analysis. I am particularly indebted to Fred E. Bradley, of the McDonnell Douglas Corporation, who taught me certain systems analysis techniques that I applied to the analysis of business systems and business ventures with uniformly profitable results, even during depressed economic times.

Finally I would like to thank one of my business partners, William B. Cunningham, Jr., for his help as we wrestled one business venture from near disaster to a successful low-risk business with 28% ROI in a short but intensive six-month period of very tough decision making and equally tough cash-flow manipulation (an exercise that convinced me that a book like this could help other businessmen).

My thanks to the people at Hewlett-Packard, Rockwell International, and National Semiconductor Corporation who reviewed and critiqued the manuscript, and in particular to the Hewlett-Packard marketing staff, including Glen Theodore and A. J. Laymon. Also, I would like to thank Chung Tung, the HP-65 Chief Engineer, for reviewing the section on the programmable pocket calculator.

To my wife Laurie, my special appreciation for putting up with my writing schedule.

Finally, my thanks go again to Mrs. Florence Piaget who typed the manuscript and helped me prepare it for publication.

J. M. Smith

St. Louis, Missouri
September 1975

CONTENTS

APPENDICES

CASEBOOK EXAMPLES

5 PAYMENTS AND NUMBER OF PERIODS IN BUSINESS DECISIONS

6 CONSUMER FINANCE

7 MERCHANDISING CALCULATIONS

8 REAL ESTATE CALCULATIONS

10 BUSINESS SYSTEMS ANALYSIS

GLOSSARY OF TERMS

Accrued Interest   Interest earned (but not yet collected).

Add-on Interest Rate   A year's simple interest that is "added on" to the principal amount for each year of the life of the loan.

Amortization   The gradual reduction of any amount over a period of time.

Annuity   A series of equal payments at fixed time intervals.

Chain Discount   A series of discount percentages.

Compound Interest   Interest resulting from the periodic addition of simple interest to principal.

Costs   Sum of all costs in a venture (see *Profit*).

Declining Balance Depreciation   A method of computing the annual charge for depreciation when the amount of depreciation is computed as a percentage of the balance of the asset value.

Declining Factor   The factor that determines the fixed percentage to be applied in the *Declining Balance Depreciation* method.

Depreciation   (See *Sum-of-the-Digits Amortization, Declining Balance Depreciation, Declining Factor.*)

Direct Reduction Loan   A loan in which the interest is computed on the amount of the principal base for that period. The principal base for the next period is then established by subtracting the remaining part of the loan payment amount.

Discount   The difference between the value of a future benefit and its present value.

Discounted Cash Flow   A cash flow occurring some time in the future which has been discounted on a compounded basis.

Discounted Note   An instrument of indebtedness specifying the full repayment amount as par or face value; the note's proceeds are less than the face value by the discount amount.

Effective Rate   The ratio of income, periodically realized, to market value of an investment or to a sum invested; usually expressed on an annual basis and as a percentage.

Effective Yield   (See *Effective Rate.*)

Finance Charge   Cost of consumer loan; the difference between amount borrowed and total amount to be repaid.

Future Value   The amount yielded after compounding for a number of periods at a given interest rate per period.

Interest   The amount paid for the use of money or its equivalent. (See *Simple Interest* and *Compound Interest.*)

Markdown   The amount subtracted from a selling price for the purpose of determining a new selling price.

Markup   The amount added to a base price for the purpose of determining selling price.

Mortgage   A lien on land, buildings, equipment, or other real property, given by a borrower to a lender as security for his loan.

Note   A written promise by a debtor to pay to a creditor a stated sum of money on a specified date.

Periodic Payment   The discharge of a financial obligation by a periodic payment of money or its equivalent.

Present Value   The present sum that will yield a stated future value if compounded at a given rate of interest per period over a given number of periods.

Principal   An amount on which interest accrues.

Profit   Revenues minus costs.

Rebate   A partial refund of the price paid for a commodity.

Revenues   Earnings from all sources. (See *Profit.*)

Rule of 78   A method of amortizing a consumer finance charge using the *Sum-of-the-months' digits* technique.

Simple Interest   The charge for the loan of money or for a deferment of the collection of an account.

Sinking Fund   An annuity and the interest it earns.

Standard Deviation   A measure of dispersion of a distribution.

Sum-of-the-Digits' Amortization   A method of amortizing whereby the amount reduced each period is obtained by multiplying the total amount to be amortized by a fraction whose numerator is the digit representing the remaining number of amortization periods and whose denominator is the sum of the digits representing the number of periods of amortization.

Sum-of-the-Digits' Depreciation   Depreciation method utilizing *Sum-of-the-digits'* amortization technique.

Financial Analysis and Business
Decisions on the Pocket Calculator

PART 1

POCKET CALCULATORS
FOR FINANCIAL ANALYSIS
AND BUSINESS DECISIONS

CHAPTER 1

POCKET CALCULATOR INTRODUCTION

Throughout this book there are **casebook decisions** and **casebook examples** illustrating the use of the pocket calculator as an aid to making business decisions. Most present the decision or example problem, the computational procedure to be used in the financial analyses, the keystroke sequences needed to solve the decision problem, and the final decision. For example:

CASEBOOK DECISION 1

As a business manager, you are required to set high standards for your business operation. These high standards apply to the big-picture decisions involving product development and growth, as well as ensuring that the *detailed decisions* within your organization are made in a competent manner. Your business has $10,000 of surplus cash in its working capital fund. You have asked your youngest finance officer to identify investment alternatives and select a good *5-year investment* for your surplus. He has found two alternatives that appear attractive. First, to invest in a $10,000 corporate bond issue that returns 10% compounded annually on a 5-year investment; and second, to invest in a subdivision of your company, permitting it to make a capital investment whose cash flow will return $2000 in the second year, $3000 in the third year, $5000 in the fourth year, and $5000 in the fifth year. The current return on investment in the subdivision is only 7%. If the capital investment were made, the subdivision's yield would rise to 9%, which is good although less than the bond yield. The 9% yield would apply to all the returns the subdivision realizes on the investment.

Your finance officer's decision is to invest in the bonds. Did he make the right decision?

This problem is not trivial. Every business manager, at every level in every organization, must test the capabilities of the people under him. The test of rightness or wrongness of a decision is independent of the significance of the decision. The decision test just described is typical of those given to junior financial analysts before promoting them to manage increasingly greater investments, involving larger payoffs (and penalties). We use this example to introduce our approach to casebook examples throughout the book.

1.1 CASEBOOK DECISION PROCEDURES*

The following general procedure applies to any pocket calculator for analyzing the typical financial problem just outlined.

Procedure and Approach

Step 1. Convert the rate of return to decimal equivalent, call it r_1.

Step 2. Add 1 to r_1, call it r_2.

Step 3. Compute $r_2 \times r_2 \times r_2 \cdots n$ times (here n is the number of periods over which the investment is escalated), call this r_3 (equivalent to r_2 raised to the nth power).

Step 4. Multiply the present value of the investment by r_3 to compute the future value of the investment.

This four-step procedure is used to escalate the $10,000 at 10% over a 5-year period to determine the return from the bond investment. This procedure is also used to escalate each of the return cash flows on a 9% return to determine the net 5-year return from investment in your own business. Then a comparison is made of the escalated values of the alternative investments to determine which has the greatest future value.

When the $10,000 bond investment is escalated at 10% per year for 5 years, it returns $16,105.10. The return on the money invested in the subdivision of your own business which yields 9% per year is as follows:

- $2590.06 on the $2000 returned in the second year.
- $3564.30 on the $3000 returned in the third year.
- $5450.00 on the $5000 returned in the fourth year.
- $5000.00 returned in the fifth year.

Thus a total of $16,604.36 is earned by investing in your own business. In

*Those not familiar with the concepts of time and money will benefit by reading Appendix A.

short, $499.26 more can be earned by investing in your own business than by investing in the corporate bonds.

In this case you would call in the financial analyst and point out this error, thereby (a) showing by example the high standard you expect from your financial analyst, (b) earning this extra money for your business, and (c) getting an equivalent 10.67% return on your 5-year investment, compared with the 10% return on the government bonds.

Not only is the procedure just described applicable to any pocket calculator; significantly, it is a short procedure that applies to what appear on the surface to be dissimilar investments. Similar procedures are given for all casebook examples in the book.

Although this example is fairly straightforward, in many cases a simple procedure can be used to unravel complicated financial analyses associated with sophisticated business decisions. We will see that many financial analyses that appear to be completely different problems in different fields are in fact the same problem, disguised only by the *language barrier* of different business disciplines. Indeed, a great many business decisions hinge on financial analysis involving **only five parameters** that, when all possible combinations of financial calculations are considered, **reduce to only twelve basically different types of financial problem.**

Starting with Chapter 3, the first part of this book deals with establishing the time value of money based on these five parameters and twelve basically different arithmetic problems. The procedures presented will illustrate the proper order in which the twelve types of financial calculations are conducted. The objective is to clarify financial analysis for the business manager in such a way that he can fearlessly challenge tough financial problems, secure in the knowledge that there are only five terms involved in most financial calculations that support most business decisions, and at most twelve ways of arranging them in most financial analyses. Quoting from Chapter 5:

"Virtually all the financial calculations of interest to the business manager are combinations of only five parameters. These parameters are:

1. The number of conversion periods.
2. The interest rate per period.
3. The payment per period.
4. The present value of the money in the calculation.
5. The future value of the money in the calculation.

"Although some financial analysts are aware of this fact, most are accustomed to manipulating these relationships only *in their specific disciplines.* Less common is the analyst who can manipulate these factors in many financial disciplines. In fact, it is unusual to find an interdisciplinary analyst who knows that a number of financial disciplines that appear to be quite different are based on the same financial concept and use identical mathematics."

Chapter 5 then presents a detailed illustration (pp. 105-109) of the significance of these five parameters and their applicability across disciplines.

1.2 CASEBOOK EXAMPLE KEYSTROKE SEQUENCES

The keystroke sequences* for analyzing two investment alternatives are given in Table 1-1 for the more popular "business" calculators. A quick glance indicates that the workloads for different types of calculations are quite different. Comparing Table 1-1 with a hand or slide-rule calculation makes the point that any calculator is certainly better than none. Besides, in financial transactions you should make the calculation twice, no matter what calculator you use, to be sure that the keystroke sequence has been

Table 1-1a   Typical Business Reverse-Polish (HP-22/HP-70/HP-80 Type) Keystroke Sequences for Analyzing Casebook Decision 1 Investment Alternatives

	Alternative 2			
Alternative 1	Second Year	Third Year	Fourth Year	Fifth Year
(10)	(9)			
i	i			
(5)	(3)	(2)	(1)	(5000)
n	n	n	n	$\Sigma +^b$
(10,000)	(2000)	(3000)	(5000)	RCL
PV	PV	PV	PV	9
FV	FV	FV	FV	
	$\Sigma +^a$	$\Sigma +^b$	$\Sigma +^b$	

[a]For the HP-70 calculator, replace with $\left\{ \begin{array}{c} \text{STO} \\ \text{M} \end{array} \right\}$.

[b]For the HP-70 calculator, replace with M+.

*Care has been taken throughout this book to use keystroke sequences that work on most pocket calculators. More than 100 pocket calculators were considered in preparing the keystroke sequences. In some cases the keystrokes given may not be *the* most efficient for certain calculators. They should, however, be near the optimum.

Table 1-1b Typical Business Algebraic (RI-204 Type) Keystroke Sequences for Analyzing Casebook Decision 1 Investment Alternatives

Alternative 1	Alternative 2			
(10)	(9)	(9)	(9)	(5000)
ET	ET	ET	ET	TA
i	i	i	i	Σ
(5)	(3)	(2)	(1)	ET
ET	ET	ET	ET	READ
n	n	n	n	PMT
(10,000)	(2000)	(3000)	(5000)	
ET	ET	ET	ET	
PV	PV	PV	PV	
AT	TA	TA	TA	
FV	FV	FV	FV	
	TA	TA	TA	
	Σ	Σ	Σ	

Table 1-1c Typical Simple Four-Function Algebraic Calculator with Chain Multiply Keystroke Sequences for Analyzing Casebook Decision 1 Investment Alternatives

Alternative 1	Alternative 2		
(10)	(9)	(5000)	(2000)
÷	÷	=	=
(100)	(100)	×	M+[a]
+	+	×	(5000)
(1)	(1)	(3000)	M+[a]
=	=	=	RCL-M[a]
×	×	M+[a]	
×	(5000)	÷	
×	=	(3000)	
×	STO-M[a]	×	
×	÷	×	
(10,000)		×	
=			

[a]Abbreviations: STO-M = store in memory or on scratch pad, M+ = add to memory or scratch pad, RCL-M = recall and display contents of memory or scratch pad.

done correctly. The "business" calculators offer speed, convenience and, most importantly, easy error recovery. Business calculators do the intermediate steps in a financial calculation flawlessly, since the calculation is built into the electronic chip. At most the analyst will make a mistake on the input or reading the output. The calculator does the intermediate steps in the computational procedure correctly. Generally speaking, the fewer the keystrokes, the less the chance for error.

1.3 POCKET CALCULATOR LANGUAGES CONSIDERED IN THE CASEBOOK EXAMPLES

Of more than 400 combinations or ways to design and build a pocket calculator, there are about 50 distinguishable types. The differences arise from the varieties of input/output methods and languages used by the calculator, the types of displays built into the calculator, the extent to which memory is built into the calculator, and other factors.

Of all the possibilities in calculator design, only a few are of importance to the business analyst. One of these is the type of language used. There are two types commonly available in business pocket calculators: algebraic and reverse-Polish.* In the algebraic language machines the data and arithmetic instructions are *input* exactly in the order of a simplified algebraic equation. In the reverse-Polish language machines (so named because the notation was developed by the Polish mathematician Lukasiewic), the data and arithmetic instructions can be *input* in many different orders—the most unusual being that all numbers are entered first and then the instructions telling what to do with the numbers are entered. For example, the calculation $a + b = c$ is entered into the algebraic calculator in that order, and the keystroke sequence is

number	a
instruction	$+$
number	b
instruction	$=$
result	$\boxed{c}$ displayed in calculator window

Calculators using reverse-Polish language solve the same problem with the following sequence of keystrokes:

*Sometimes the term reverse-Polish notation is abbreviated RPN.

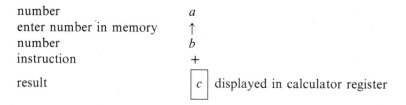

number	a
enter number in memory	↑
number	b
instruction	+
result	$\boxed{c}$ displayed in calculator register

It is interesting to note that the reverse-Polish sequence does not involve stroking an "equals" key. Also it is clear that the algebraic implementation is "natural," whereas the reverse-Polish is "different" (although not unnatural). The obvious question is, why did mathematicians go to the trouble of inventing such a different mathematical language? The mathematicians' answer is that the reverse-Polish language is somewhat more efficient from a computer design viewpoint. The pocket calculator designers say that reverse-Polish becomes a more *flexible* language as more difficult problems are encountered. Also, reverse-Polish notation is a *human-engineered language* in that unlike the algebraic language, it is quite forgiving of intermediate mistakes made in a complicated calculation.

Table 1-2 illustrates this point with keystroke sequences for typical algebraic and reverse-Polish machines for some arithmetic tasks often encountered in business calculations. A number of insights to analysis on various pocket calculators can be derived by examining Table 1-2. The most obvious is that the algebraic language programs the calculation of simple series arithmetic calculations exactly as they would be written as an algebraic expression reduced to its simplest form. It is equally obvious that even simple series arithmetic calculations can be performed in a number of different ways when using reverse-Polish language (except for the simplest operations of adding and multiplying two numbers). In a sense then, for these simple arithmetic tasks, the algebraic language has one unique sequence of keystrokes for performing the task and reverse-Polish does not. The algebraic language enthusiast considers this ambiguity in ways of solving simple series arithmetic problems in reverse-Polish to be a possible confusion factor for the pocket calculator user. The reverse-Polish language enthusiast views the same property as a measure of the flexibility of the reverse-Polish notation—that is, the user has greater flexibility in the number of ways a problem can be solved. He could argue further that the first form shown in each of the series calculations in Table 1-2 is close to the algebraic language keystrokes, and only the second and last keystrokes are different.

It is interesting that this distinction even arises, since the mixed arithmetic of the last two examples in Table 1-2 shows the many ways in which the sum of products can be evaluated with algebraic and reverse-Polish

Table 1-2   Arithmetic in Algebraic and Reverse-Polish Languages

	Keystroke Sequence	
Task	Algebraic	Reverse-Polish
Sum $A \& B$	$A + B =$	$A \uparrow B +$
Sum $A \& B \& C$	$A + B + C =$	$A \uparrow B + C +$ $A \uparrow B \uparrow C + +$
Sum $A \& B \& C \& D$	$A + B + C + D =$	$A \uparrow B + C + D +$ $A \uparrow B \uparrow C + + D +$ $A \uparrow B \uparrow C + D + +$ $A \uparrow B \uparrow C \uparrow D + + +$
Multiply $A \& B$	$A \times B =$	$A \uparrow B \times$
Multiply $A \& B \& C$	$A \times B \times C =$	$A \uparrow B \times C \times$ $A \uparrow B \uparrow C \times \times$
Multiply $A \& B \& C \& D$	$A \times B \times C \times D =$	$A \uparrow B \times C \times D \times$ $A \uparrow B \uparrow C \times \times D \times$ $A \uparrow B \uparrow C \times D \times \times$ $A \uparrow B \uparrow C \uparrow D \times \times \times$
Compute $(A \times B) + (C \times D)$	$A \times B \div D + C \times D$ $= \text{(no memory)}$ $A \times B + C \times D$ $= \text{(with hierarchy)}$ $A \times B \text{STO} C \times D \text{RCL} +$ $= \text{(with memory)}$	$A \uparrow B \times C \uparrow D \times +$ $A \uparrow B \uparrow C \uparrow D \times R \downarrow \times R \uparrow + ^a$ $\vdots$ $\vdots$
Compute $(A + B) \times (C + D)$	$A \times B \text{STO} C + D \times \text{RCL} =$	$A \uparrow B + C \uparrow D + \times$ $A \uparrow B \uparrow C \uparrow D + R \downarrow + R \uparrow \times$ $\vdots$ $\vdots$

[a]See page 24 for a definition of $R\downarrow$ and $R\uparrow$.

languages. Note that the first example of the use of algebraic language to evaluate the sum of products illustrates rewriting the algebraic form as

$$(A \times B) + (C \times D) \equiv \left(\frac{A \times B}{D} + C \right) D \qquad (1\text{-}1)$$

We see from the sequence of keystrokes that the sum of products can be evaluated without memory. This form of evaluating the sum of products is ideal for use in the simplest four-function calculators, since it requires no "scratch pad" memory and is within the set of operations available. This is not the case for the product of sums as shown in the last example of Table 1-2, where the symbols STO and RCL symbolize putting the numbers appearing in the display register into memory and then recalling them.

The importance of rewriting the expressions in forms that are easily evaluated on the pocket calculator is obvious. However it is difficult to imagine businessmen manipulating algebraic expressions into forms that are most conveniently analyzed on the simpler pocket calculators. Thus most pocket calculators have memory, enabling intermediate calculations to be stored and later recalled without the need for manual scratch pad storage. Also, for even more complicated analyses such as those encountered in scientific analyses, the algebraic machines include a *hierarchy* of arithmetic operations. This means that certain algebraic pocket calculators accept numbers in a keystroke sequence and "multiply" operations are conducted before the "add" operations. For example, a pocket calculator would solve the equation

$$(a \times b) + (c \times d)$$

as shown in Table 1-2 with no memory [but requiring the expressions to be rewritten as in (1-1), with hierarchy and with memory].

1.4 BUSINESS CALCULATOR KEYBOARD INSTRUCTIONS

The basic four-function calculator has keys for instructing the calculator to add, subtract, multiply, and divide. What is amazing is that these small four-function machines, purchased at relatively low cost, can provide tremendous computing power. Examples of the use of the four-function pocket calculator for evaluating some of the most sophisticated business analysis are presented later. The four-function machine is also capable of computing powers of a given variable through repetitive multiply operations. Whereas squaring a number involves only two multiplies, the number must be double entered. Thus the simplest additional instruction that can be added to a pocket calculator that reduces the number of keystrokes is the squaring operation or modifying the multiply instruction to square a number when only one data entry has been made.

Entirely new capabilities are added when square root and reciprocal instructions are added to the calculator instruction set. There is no single-stroke way for a four-function calculator user to numerically invert a number without using a scratch pad and double data entry. A similar situation holds for the square root. Thus we find the next most sophisticated pocket calculator to be a seven-function machine including square,

square root, and reciprocal functions implementable with a single keystroke. Beyond this, instructions are added to aid in special-purpose computing in a variety of ways. The underlying purpose of adding functions to a pocket calculator keyboard is to reduce the number of keystrokes associated with data input.

Because we will be continually referring to instructions found on most business calculators, let us define the instruction sets.

Key Symbol	Key Name	Key Instruction
CL	Clear	Clears information in the calculator and display and sets the calculator at zero
CLχ	Clear entry	Clears the last keyboard entry
CA	Clear all	Clears all memories (Rockwell 204 only)
0 1 ⋯ 9	Digit	Enter numbers 0 through 9 to a limit of an eight-digit mantissa and a two-digit exponent
·	Decimal point	Enters a decimal point
CHS +/−	Change sign	Instructs the calculator to change the sign of the mantissa or exponent appearing in the display
+	Add	Instructs the calculator to add
−	Subtract	Instructs the calculator to subtract
×	Multiply	Instructs the calculator to multiply
÷	Divide	Instructs the calculator to divide
x^2	Square	Instructs the calculator to find the square of the number displayed
$\sqrt{x}$	Square root	Instructs the calculator to find the square root of the number displayed

(*Continued*)

Key Symbol	Key Name	Key Instruction
$\boxed{1/x}$	Reciprocal	Instructs the calculator to find the reciprocal of the number displayed
$\boxed{y^x}$	y to the x power	Instructs the calculator to raise y, the first entered number, to the power of x, the second entered number
$\boxed{\text{STO}}$ $\left.\begin{array}{c}\boxed{\text{STO}} \\ \boxed{5}\end{array}\right\}$	Store	Instructs the calculator to store the displayed number in memory (location 5, e.g., if the calculator has addressable memory by using the numeric keys); the HP-22 has nine storage registers addressable from the keyboard.
$\boxed{\text{RCL}}$ $\left.\begin{array}{c}\boxed{\text{RCL}} \\ \boxed{5}\end{array}\right\}$	Recall	Instructs the calculator to retrieve stored data from memory (location 5, e.g., if the calculator has addressable memory such as the HP-22)
$\boxed{M}$ $\boxed{K}$	Storage registers	Store the contents of the display register in the M or K location
$\boxed{\Sigma}$ $\boxed{M+}$ $\boxed{\Sigma+}$	Sum and store	Instructs the calculator to retrieve stored data from the memory
$\boxed{=}$	Equals	Instructs the calculator to complete the previously entered operation to provide the desired calculation result (algebraic entry method only)
$\boxed{\text{ENTER}\uparrow}$ $\boxed{\text{ENT}\uparrow}$	Enter	Loads contents of X register into Y register and retains contents of X register in X register

(*Continued*)

Key Symbol	Key Name	Key Instruction
TO ANS * Called TA in keystroke sequences	To answer	Instructs the calculator to compute and display the next (secondary) keystroke function
ENT TO † Called ET in keystroke sequences	Enter to	Instructs calculator to use the contents of the X register as the variable indicated by the next keystroke
n	Total number of compounding periods	Computes the number of periods in a financial analysis when the payment, present value, and interest are known, when the payment, future value, and interest are known, or when the present and future values and interest are known
i i/yr	Interest rate per period	Computes the interest when the number of periods in the present value and future value are known, when the number of periods and the present value and payment are known, or when the number of periods and the future value and payment are known
FV	Future value	Computes the future value when the number of periods, the interest, and the present value are known, or computes the future value when the number of periods, the interest, and the payment are known
PV	Present value	Computes the present value when the number of periods, the interest, and the future value are known, or computes the present value when the number of periods, the interest, and the payment are known

*Called CPT (compute) on some calculators.
†Called ENT (enter) on some calculators.

(*Continued*)

Key Symbol	Key Name	Key Instruction
PMT	Payment	Computes the payment when the number of periods, the interest, and the future value are known, or computes the payment when the number of periods, the interest, and the present value are known
i INT	Interest	Computes the interest in a financial calculation
SELL	Sell	Enters contents of display into memory
COST	Cost	Enters contents of display into memory
MARGIN	Margin	$\dfrac{SELL - COST}{SELL} \times 100$
%	Percent	Converts percentage to its decimal equivalent
Δ% % CHG	Delta percent	Finds the percentage difference between two numbers
DSP DS	Display; Decimal display	Fixes the decimal place by depressing this key, followed by any number key 0 through 9 (on the Hewlett-Packard calculators). The display is then rounded to the number of decimal places corresponding to the number key pressed. The display is usually left-justified and may include trailing zeros within the setting specified. When this key is followed by the decimal-point key, the number is converted from decimal notation to scientific notation. In scientific notation, a convenient way of expressing very large or very small numbers, a

(*Continued*)

Key Symbol	Key Name	Key Instruction
		number might have form $N \times 10^n$, where N is a number having a magnitude between 1 and 10 and n is a positive or negative integer.
		$\boxed{\begin{array}{c}\text{TO}\\\text{ANS}\end{array}}$ followed by $\boxed{\text{DS}}$ and $\boxed{4}$ will display a number to four places past the decimal point on the Rockwell 204.
$\boxed{\text{F}}$	Double function access key	Instructs calculator to recognize the secondary function of the next key stroked
$\boxed{\text{MR}}$ MR/MC	Memory recall	Instructs the calculator to recall the contents of the memory register to the display register
$\boxed{\text{MS}}$	Memory store	Instructs the calculator to store the contents of the display register in the memory register
$\boxed{\begin{array}{c}\text{ENT}\\\text{TO}\end{array}}$ $\boxed{\text{READ}}$ Called ET ET in the keystroke sequences	Read memory	Instructs the calculator to read the memory location indicated by the next keystroke
$\boxed{\text{READ}}$ $\boxed{\text{DSP}}$	Read; display	Reads or displays the contents of the registers where data are indicated by the next key to be stroked
$\boxed{12 \times}$	Monthly conversion for number of periods	Converts yearly periods to monthly payment periods
$\boxed{12 \div}$	Monthly conversion for interest rates	Converts annual interest rate to interest rate per month

(*Continued*)

Key Symbol	Key Name	Key Instruction
ACC	Accumulated interest	Computes accumulated interest between any two time periods of a loan
INT	Simple interest	Computes simple interest on basis of both 360 and 365 days
BAL	Remaining balance	Computes the remaining balance of a loan at any point in time
L.R.	Linear regression	Calculates the best straight line through a group of correlated data pairs
$\bar{X}$	Average	Calculates the mean or arithmetic average of a group of data
S	Standard deviation	Calculates the standard deviation of a group of data
Begin End	Annuity switch (SW)	Instructs calculator to calculate annuity based on payment at the end of the conversion period (End, for ordinary annuity) or at the beginning of the conversion period (Begin, for annuity-due)

1.5   THE CALCULATORS DISCUSSED IN THIS BOOK

As mentioned previously, there are numerous entry methods, types of memory, and kinds of numbers that can be implemented in any of the three kinds of pocket calculators with four types of function sets and two types of input/output. This results in some 400 combinations of calculators that could be made from different combinations of these electronic hardware alternatives. Although the number of reasonable combinations is somewhat smaller, about 50, the number of possible types of pocket calculators is still too large to be covered in one book. Only four hypothetical pocket calculators are therefore defined and discussed here:

- A simple four-function algebraic calculator.
- An algebraic business calculator.
- A reverse-Polish business calculator.
- A reverse-Polish programmable calculator.

Typical keystroke sequences for the first three types are provided in Parts 1 and 2, and the programmable pocket calculator is discussed in Part 3. These hypothetical calculators are representative of the Texas Instruments SR-10, SR-11, 1500 and 2550 Series, the HP-22, HP-70, and HP-80 Series,* the Bowmar "Brain" Series, the Kingspoint KP200 Series, the Sinclair "Cambridge" and 101 Series, and the NOVUS 6020 "Financier,"* the Rockwell 204 "Financier,"* and the CORVUS "Financier."

The fourth type is the programmable pocket calculator, which we assume to have a four-register stack with addressable storage and 50 to 100 keystroke sequence memory. This hypothetical calculator is representative of the HP-25, HP-55, HP-65, NOVUS "Financier 6023," or Sinclair

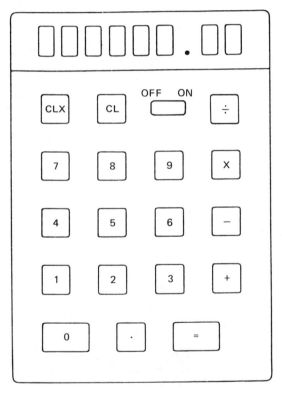

Figure 1-1.   A hypothetical four-function pocket calculator keyboard.

*Calculators are not characterized so much by their keyboard as by the type of electronic chip used to do the computing. Three popular chips are those of Hewlett-Packard, Rockwell Semiconductor, and National Semiconductor.

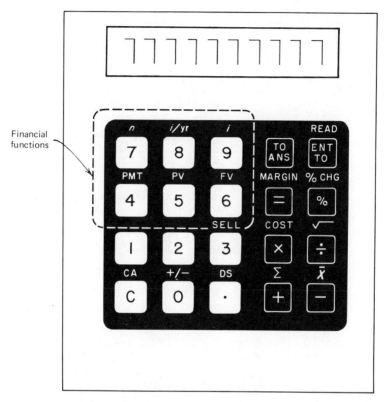

Figure 1-2.   Hypothetical business pocket calculator keyboards. (a) Algebraic (Rockwell-Corvus type).

Scientific Programmable. The properties of this hypothetical machine are defined in the context of the discussion.

Of these four hypothetical pocket calculator types, **we stress the business-type calculator with its usual complement of business functions**. Also, because the simple four-function machine is now available at very little cost, **emphasis is given to providing instructions for performing business analysis** on the basic four function machine when the instructions are applicable to the problem being solved. For all these machines we limit ourselves to at most a 10-digit register using floating-point arithmetic with exponential notation. The keyboard for the hypothetical four-function calculator to be discussed is sketched in Figure 1-1. The keyboard functions for the business pocket calculators and for the programmable pocket calculator appear in Figures 1-2 and 1-3, respectively. It is reasonable to expect these hypothetical calculators to be representative of the calculators that are available now and will be available in the foreseeable future. The

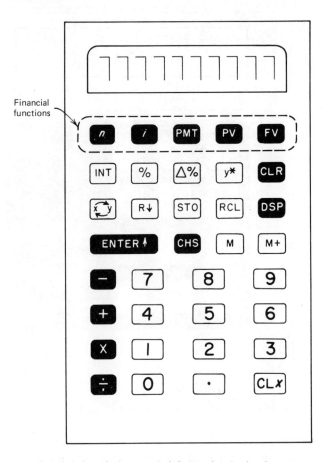

Figure 1-2. (b) Reverse-Polish (Hewlett-Packard type).

display details for all calculators discussed here (Figure 1-4) include the following:

Decimal point	Assumed to be to the right of any number entered unless positioned in another sequence with the $\boxed{\cdot}$ key
Minus sign	Appears to the left of the 10-digit mantissa for negative numbers and to the left of the exponent for negative exponents

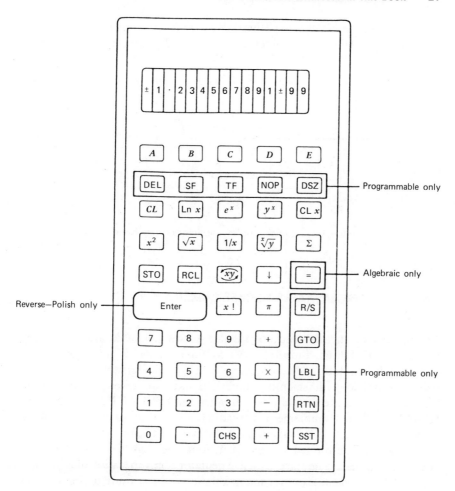

Figure 1-3.   A hypothetical advanced business calculator keyboard (mixed algebraic and reverse-Polish and programmable functions).

Overflow indication	In most pocket calculators the largest number that can be entered without an overflow when a function is pressed is $\pm 9.999999999 \times 10^{99}$; if a calculation result is larger than this value, the display will flash or give some other indication of overflow
Underflow indication	If a number closer to zero than to $\pm 1.0 \times 10^{-99}$ is entered in the calculator, the display will flash or indicate an underflow

We concentrate on the hypothetical machines just mentioned, but we comment on particular machines with slightly different keyboards when appropriate.

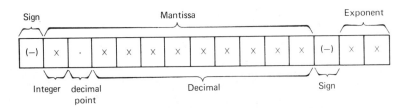

Figure 1-4. Typical pocket calculator display format.

1.6   THE PROGRAMMABLE POCKET CALCULATOR

The more sophisticated pocket calculators now available are the SR-52, HP-25, HP-55, HP-65, and the NOVUS "Financier 6025." Most operate in reverse-Polish notation, have memory stacks and registers, use floating-point arithmetic with scientific notation, have an extensive three-level function set, and are programmable. Since the HP-25, HP-55, SR-52, and HP-65 calculators implement logical (Boolean) equations as well as algebraic equations, can make logical decisions, and are able to iteratively execute a preprogrammed set of instructions, they can be correctly called pocket computers. They are called calculators only because they do not satisfy the United States government's import/export trade definition of a computer. It is generally accepted that the definition of a computer (or calculator) changes as the state of the art of computer design changes. Thus it is also acknowledged that in 1955 these programmable pocket calculators would have been called computers.

Programmable calculators provide a quantum jump in pocket computing capability by making libraries of program listings and prerecorded magnetic tape programs available to the analyst at relatively low cost. These libraries can be compiled by the user himself or can be purchased from the manufacturer or from pocket calculator users clubs.*

---

*The HP-65 users club address is *65 Notes*, 2541 West Camden Place, Santa Ana, Calif. 92704.

1.7 DATA MANIPULATION*

The use of memory in pocket calculators is sometimes overlooked in manufacturers' manuals. Rather, the keystroke sequences given "get the user up to speed in a hurry" but can leave him on something less than firm ground when it comes to data manipulation in the calculator's memory. This omission can lead to loss of interest and eventual nonuse (or at best limited use) of the calculator's memory. Most pocket calculator users quickly learn how to take full advantage of the machine's arithmetic capability, but they then struggle because they do not know precisely how the memory is implemented. We depart from the mainstream of financial analysis and business decisions for the next few pages to clarify data manipulation among the data storage and memory registers for both the reverse-Polish and the advanced algebraic machines. This is probably the only point at which the nonmathematician reader must knuckle down to learn a little about data handling. The effort is worthwhile, however, to ensure that our business and financial analyses are not confused by the language of data processing on the pocket calculator. These discussions are already complicated enough, since many business disciplines use different languages even though they are actually solving the same types of problems. The objective then is to clarify the data handling operations in the pocket calculator and establish the language, style, and format of the arithmetic discussions to follow.

When we speak of a calculator with stacks, a single stack is understood to consist of registers for storing numbers. First we discuss the reverse-Polish pocket calculator. Following Hewlett-Packard notation, we call the stack registers X, Y, Z, and T. Register X is at the bottom of the stack, T is at the top of the stack, and the display always shows the number in the X register. We designate the number in the register by the same letter in *italic* type. Thus X, Y, Z, and T are the contents of registers X, Y, Z, and T. When a number key is stroked, the number enters the X register, which is displayed. The number is repeated in the Y register when the "enter" key

$\boxed{\uparrow}$ is stroked. Whatever is in the Y register is "pushed up" into the Z

register. The contents of the Z register are moved into the T register and the contents of the T register are lost (Figure 1-5). As data are entered into the Y register from the X register, the data in the other registers are

---

*The book can be understood without reading this section. It is an important section, however, for those who want to get the most out of a pocket calculator. Much of the material in this section is drawn from "Scientific Analysis on the Pocket Calculator," J. M. Smith, 1975, by permission of John Wiley & Sons. Inc.

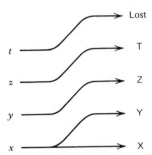

Figure 1-5.   Data flow associated with data entry.

"pushed up" automatically, and the only data lost are those in the T register. Data in the Y register can be viewed in the display by rolling the data from the Y register down to the X register by stroking the "roll-down" key $\boxed{R\downarrow}$. The data in the X register are then worked backward in the stack to move to the top register (T), the data in the top register move to the Z register, the data in the Z register move to the Y register, and, again, the data in the Y register move into the X register where they are displayed. Stroking the "roll-down" key once more causes the data that were formerly in the Z register, which have been moved to the Y register, to move down to the X register where they can be seen in the display. All other data are moved to a neighboring register in the direction in which the roll is made. It follows that after four "roll-down" keystrokes, the stack will be arranged in the original order, where X is in its original location and is displayed in the X register, Y is in its original location, Z is in its original location, and T is in its original location. Stroking the "roll-down" key moves the data in the registers in the direction from the Y register to the X register. Stroking the "roll-up" key $\boxed{R\uparrow}$ moves the data in the direction from the X register to the Y register. The data flow associated

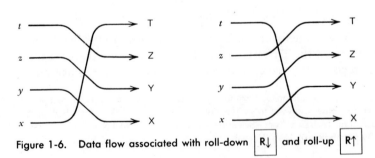

Figure 1-6.   Data flow associated with roll-down $\boxed{R\downarrow}$ and roll-up $\boxed{R\uparrow}$

with the data entry and "roll-down" and "roll-up" operations can be seen in Figure 1-6.

Another commonly used stack manipulation is the replacement of the data in the X register with the data in the Y register, and vice versa. The data flow associated with stroking the "X-Y exchange" key $\boxed{x \circlearrowright y}$ is sketched in Figure 1.7.

From the data flow associated with the stack operations when performing addition, subtraction, multiplication and division, (Figure 1-8), we see the following:

1. For summation, the contents of the Y and X registers are added and displayed in the X register.

2. For subtraction, the contents of the X register are subtracted from the contents of the Y register and displayed in the X register.

3. For multiplication, the contents of the X register are multiplied by the contents of the Y register and displayed in the X register.

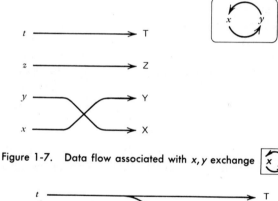

Figure 1-7.   Data flow associated with x, y exchange $\boxed{x\;y}$

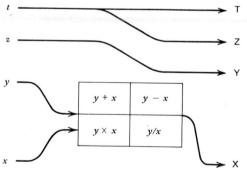

Figure 1-8.   Data flow associated with $+$, $-$, $\times$, and $\div$.

4. For division, the contents of the Y register are divided by the contents of the X register and displayed in the X register.

For these basic four functions, the contents of the T register are always retained and never lost. This feature of the operational stack is very useful for certain repeated calculations.

Tables 1-3 and 1-4 illustrate the typical data flow in the stacks when the product of two sums and the sum of two products are evaluated using reverse-Polish with stacks. The usual procedure for evaluating the sum of products (Table 1-3a) does not involve the use of the top register. To illustrate the flexibility of reverse-Polish with stacks and operations associated with the top register, Table 1-3b shows the same calculations using the "roll-up" and "roll-down" features of the stack manipulations. Figure 1-9 and Table 1-5 present the typical data flow associated with keyboard functions and a calculation of the product of two sums using algebraic languages with memory. A comparison of Tables 1-3 to 1-5 and Figure 1-9 indicates clearly that the greater the memory storage capacity in a pocket calculator, the greater the flexibility in its use.

The question of which language is "best" for pocket calculators is akin to that in minicomputers or large computers, or different nationalities for that matter—the language you know the best is the language you like the most, unless you have sufficient multilingual skills to recognize the subtle advantages of one language over another. **What matters least is the type of language or size of memory associated with any specific pocket calculator, what matters most is to begin to use some pocket calculator in business analysis.** The solid-state revolution has enabled the analyst to perform fairly sophisticated analysis at his desk, in his home, or on a trip, without requiring access to a computing facility. **Simply stated, those who capitalize on the calculator solid-state revolution and keep current with the development of pocket computing machines will have a tremendous advantage over those who do not.**

Table 1-3a Data Flow Associated with the Sum of Two Products $(A \times B)+(C \times D)$ Using Keystrokes $A \uparrow B \times C \uparrow D \times +$ on a Reverse-Polish Machine

T									
Z						$(A \times B)$	$(A \times B)$		
Y		A	A		$(A \times B)$	C	C	$(A \times B)$	
X	A	A	B	$(A \times B)$	C	C	D	$(C \times D)$	$(A \times B)+(C \times D)$ | Display register
Key	A	$\uparrow$	B	$\times$	C	$\uparrow$	D	$\times$	$+$
Step	1	2	3	4	5	6	7	8	9

Table 1-3b Data Flow Associated with the Sum of Two Products $(A \times B)+(C \times D)$ Using Keystrokes $A \uparrow B \uparrow C \uparrow D \times R \downarrow \times R \uparrow +$

T						A	A		$(C \times D)$	$(C \times D)$	A	A
Z				A	A	B	B	A	A	A	$(A \times B)$	
Y		A	A	B	B	C	C	B	A		$(A \times B)$	
X	A	A	B	B	C	C	D	$(C \times D)$	B	$(A \times B)$	$(C \times D)$	$(A \times B)+(C \times D)$ | Display register
Key	A	$\uparrow$	B	$\uparrow$	C	$\uparrow$	D	$\times$	$R \downarrow$	$\times$	$R \uparrow$	$+$
Step	1	2	3	4	5	6	7	8	9	10	11	12

Table 1-4 Data Flow Associated with $(A+B)\times(C+D)$ Using Keystrokes $A\uparrow B + C\uparrow D + \times$ on a Reverse-Polish Machine

	Step 1	2	3	4	5	6	7	8	9	
	Key A	$\uparrow$	B	$+$	C	$\uparrow$	D	$+$	$\times$	
T										
Z						$(A+B)$	$(A+B)$			
Y		A	A		$(A+B)$	C	C	$(A+B)$		
X	A	A	B	$(A+B)$	C	C	D	$(C+D)$	$(A+B)\times(C+D)$	Display register

Table 1.5 Data Flow Associated with $(A+B)\times(C+D)$ Using Keystrokes $A+B=\text{STO }C+D=\times\text{RCL}=$ on an Algebraic Machine with Memory and Hierarchy ("Multiply Before Add")

	Step 1	2	3	4	5	6	7	8	9	10	11	12	
	Key A	$+$	B	$=$	STO	C	$+$	D	$=$	$\times$	RCL	$=$	
M					$(A+B)$	$(A+B)$	$(A+B)$	$(A+B)$	$(A+B)$		$(A+B)$		
Z													
Y		A	A				C	C		$(C+D)$	$(C+D)$		
X	A	A	B	$(A+B)$	$(A+B)$	C	C	D	$(C+D)$	$(C+D)$	$(A+B)$	$(A+B)\times(C+D)$	Display register

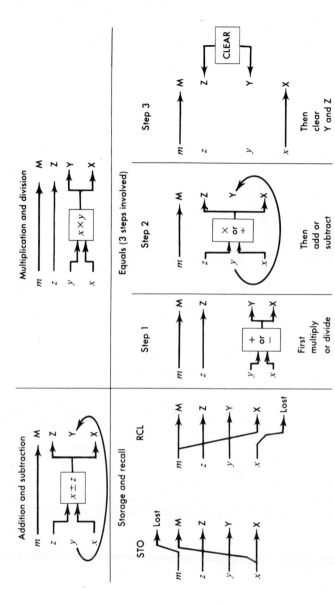

Figure 1-9. Data flow associated with keyboard functions of an algebraic machine with memory and hierarchy ("multiply before add").

CHAPTER 2

AN INTRODUCTION TO BUSINESS DECISIONS AND FINANCIAL ANALYSIS ON THE POCKET CALCULATOR

Decisions are the bread and butter of the businessman. He faces many each day, and virtually all involve those business operations that result in revenues or costs. It follows that many business decisions can be analyzed completely in terms of their effect on the return on investment (ROI) and the financial statement of the business. It also follows that one way to become a better business manager is to be able to quantify the consequences of business decisions more quickly and accurately in terms of their effect on the financial position of the business. Eventually every business decision directly or indirectly affects the profit and loss statement.

To clarify these general statements, consider the following specific examples of a commonly encountered business decision.

CASEBOOK DECISION 2

Your company has decided to bid on a government contract. Its main competitor, the incumbent on the job, has already worked for more than a year on the first phase of the job. You are asked to manage the bid strategy. Your marketing staff informs you that your competitor does not plan to team with any subcontractors on this job. You see this as a weakness on his part and would like to capitalize on it by teaming with subcontractors for your company's bid. You find that the subcontractors are willing to team with your company, but they want a sizable part of the winnings (profits). Your decision boils down to a choice between (*a*) bid teamed—lowest risk/lowest profit, and (*b*) bid alone—highest risk/highest profit.

The Decision Tree

The *decision tree** for this process (Figure 2-1) summarizes qualitatively the decision process, making clear the following factors:

1. The elements of the decision process you control.
2. The elements of the decision process you do not control.

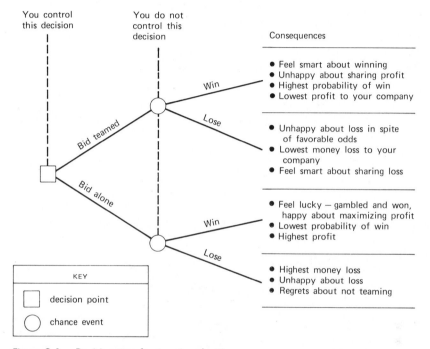

You control
this decision

You do not
control this
decision

Consequences

Bid teamed

Win
- Feel smart about winning
- Unhappy about sharing profit
- Highest probability of win
- Lowest profit to your company

Lose
- Unhappy about loss in spite of favorable odds
- Lowest money loss to your company
- Feel smart about sharing loss

Bid alone

Win
- Feel lucky — gambled and won, happy about maximizing profit
- Lowest probability of win
- Highest profit

Lose
- Highest money loss
- Unhappy about loss
- Regrets about not teaming

KEY

☐ decision point

◯ chance event

Figure 2-1.   Decision tree for teaming decision.

*Those not familiar with decision trees should read the outstanding article entitled "Decision Trees for Decision Making" (John F. Magee) in the July–August 1964 issue of the *Harvard Business Review*. Decision trees are useful for three major reasons.

- **At a minimum**—documenting your decisions in a clear way so you can review your judgments and analyses long after the decision is made; an ideal way to "log" your decisions with a minimum of writing; very useful for people who make many decisions and need to stay on top of them all, or for those who make only a few decisions of sufficient importance to necessitate clear documentation.
- **Nominally**—aids the decision maker in the systematic quantification of his decision and its consequences.
- **At a maximum**—leads to the discovery of counterintuitive insights into the decision that might have been overlooked if the decision tree had not been prepared.

3. The risks and costs you must consider in your decision.

4. A judgment of the consequences of traversing both success paths and failure paths.

Quantifying the Decision Tree: Intangible Factors

The probabilities for winning and losing based on your decision are shown on the decision tree in Figure 2-2. Usually these numbers are based on subjective judgments gathered in discussions with your staff and in toying with ways to compute probability of win that eventually coincide with your judgment—or your judgment coincides with the method (depending on your viewpoints and beliefs about the degree to which you can quantify business judgment). All other factors being equal,

probability of win = 1 ÷ number of bidders = POW

probability of loss = 1 − POW = POL

In this decision tree analysis there are two bidders. The POW (for bidding

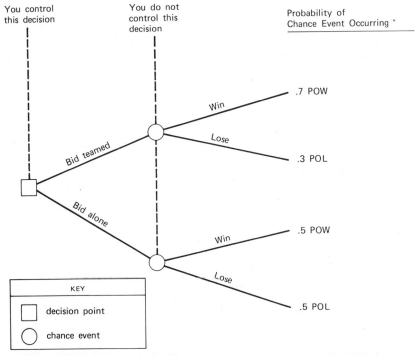

Figure 2-2. Decision tree for teaming decision with probabilities. Asterisk indicates intangible, judgment-based factor.

alone) is thus .50. By teaming, you expect to improve your chances of winning by 20%, thus elevating the POW by .20.

Tangible Factors

On the other hand, your teammates ask that you give them 40% of the job, permitting them to earn 40% of the profits. Assuming the value of the contract is $1 million and that the fee is 10%, the maximum profit your company can earn is $100,000. If you bid teamed, the maximum profit is $60,000. Another piece of useful financial information that can be conveniently calculated is the probable profit, which is computed by multiplying the maximum profit by the probability of win. The maximum probable profits for this venture are tabulated for this decision tree in Figure 2-3. The maximum probable profit is a useful financial indicator of the profitability of a new venture in that it is a combination of both quantitative tangible factors in the decision and the quantitative intangible factors all expressed in a single number. In a sense it is a measure of the

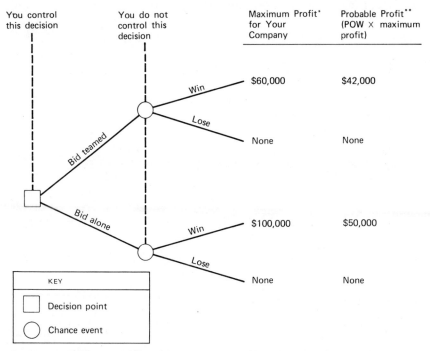

Figure 2-3. Decision tree for teaming decision with profit potential. Asterisk indicates tangible, quantifiable factor; double asterisk, a combination of tangible and intangible factors.

value of the decision choice if one does not take into account the cost associated with the decision choice.

Finally, the cost of making the bid is negotiated with your teammates and it is agreed that the bid will cost $20,000 of which your company will contribute $12,000. Based on this division of costs, you can now calculate the probable profit return on investment according to the formula

$$\text{ROI} = \frac{\text{probable profit} - \text{bid and proposal cost}}{\text{bid and proposal cost}}$$

which gives, for this million dollar venture,

$$\text{ROI} = 2.5 \text{ when bid teamed}$$

$$\text{ROI} = 1.5 \text{ when bid alone}$$

The data are summarized on the decision tree appearing in Figure 2-4.

The Payoff Table

A *payoff table* (Table 2-1) for this teaming decision now can be prepared, displaying in a summary form all decision choices and all chance events

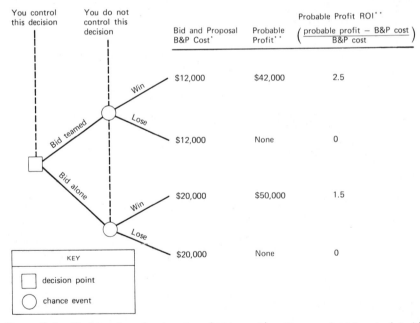

Figure 2-4. Decision tree for teaming decision with return on investment. Asterisk indicates quantifiable, tangible factor; double asterisk, a combination of tangible and intangible factors.

and their consequences, as a means of putting all the decision findings in a form that is convenient for review.

Table 2-1   Payoff Table for Teaming Decision

Events and Consequences	Win	Lose

Bid teamed	Can be accused of being too conservative
	Generally satisfied—smart bid
	Maximum profit—$60,000
	Probability of win = 70%
	Maximum return = $60,000 − $12,000 = $48,000
	Probable return = $42,000 − $12,000 = $30,000
	Probable profit ROI = 2.5
		Lose $12,000 of B&P money
		No regrets on teaming
		Can be accused of
		    poor bid management—
		    lost in spite of favorable
		    odds

Bid alone	Happy—gambled and won—shrewd bid
	Maximum profit—$100,000
	Probability of win = 60%
	Maximum return = $100,000 − $20,000 = $80,000
	Probable return = $50,000 − $20,000 = $30,000
	Probable profit ROI = 1.5
		Can be accused of be-
		    ing too liberal but is
		    usually considered
		    acceptable because in-
		    dicates "tiger" attitude
		Lose $20,000 of B&P money
		Regrets for not teaming

The Decision

Table 2-1 shows three things clearly.

1. That **there is no one way to go in making the decision!** What would you do? The decision is almost manager-attitude dependent.

Attitude	Decision
Tiger (maximize profit)	Bid alone
Winner (maximize POW)	Bid teamed
Survivor (minimize personal risk)	Bid alone
Buck sniffer* (maximize ROI)	Bid teamed
.	.
.	.
.	.

*Read "The Big Buck and The New Business Breed," Butler, Macmillan, 1972.

2. That a manager cannot embrace all these attitudes simultaneously (have his cake and eat it too).

3. That a number of careful financial calculations are required to fill in

the financial data to quantify the tangible factors in the decision tree. Here the pocket calculator becomes a valuable tool to aid in understanding, making, and documenting the decision process. The pocket calculator effortlessly does virtually error free, repeatable calculations "to the cent."

This book is not primarily about making decision trees. Every manager uses some process for preparing his decisions. Usually the process involves at least all the considerations needed for making a decision tree discussed in Casebook Decision 2. In almost all decisions, however, calculations of the financial consequences associated with the final choice are usually made at some point in the decision-making process. It is at this point that the pocket calculator conveniently enters the decision-making process as a significant new tool. For one thing, the pocket calculator allows the decision maker to consider many more choices in his decision trees and to evaluate many more consequences in the same period of time that he would have needed to do the calculations on a smaller tree by hand. In short, the pocket calculator does the arithmetic that frees the decision maker to expand the scope of his decision analysis.

In addition to expanding the scope of the decision analysis, the modern business calculator allows the decision maker to extend the depth of the analysis by making more involved calculations, again at the stroke of a single key. The modern business calculators conveniently calculate the time value of money, thus allowing the dimension of time to enter the decision maker's problem-solving approach. Given a changing economic structure characterized by inflation rates and interest rates that are continuously varying, it is essential that the time value of money be considered in every business decision. The business pocket calculator makes this conveniently possible by performing time/money calculations with keystroke ease. It is an interesting coincidence that the personal business calculator has become available in the global marketplace at such a time in our economic history. Fortunately the spinoffs from military and civilian high technology developments have supplied this very convenient tool to support business and commerce throughout the world.

The foregoing financial calculations purposely did not involve the time value of money, since that discussion is deserving of special consideration. The casebook decision was intended to demonstrate that one way to become a better business manager is to learn to quantify more quickly and accurately the consequences of business decisions in terms of their financial impact. To make good business decisions, it is necessary to have a good understanding of the basic concepts of business finance, and an objective of this book is to set forth these concepts in the simplest possible form, making them immediately useful in helping arrive at business decisions. Another objective is to present the concepts of business finance in such a way that the financial analysis can be conducted quickly and efficiently on the pocket calculator. Too often complex financial formulas are presented to the business or financial analyst with the expectation that he will unravel the best way to use them. By contrast, in this material the keystroke sequences have been developed in a way that enables the financial calculations to be conducted quickly and efficiently with a minimum of work by the decision maker, business manager, or financial analyst. Now let us delve into the concepts of business finance.

The first and perhaps most important concept of modern business finance is that the value of money changes with time. This concept is the basis of our credit economy and the credit capitalism on which American business is built.

2.1   THE TIME VALUE OF MONEY *

Money is the medium of exchange of one product or service for another product or service. The value of money changes with time. An understanding of the specific and direct relationship between time and money is the key to modern financial analysis and business decisions that lead to stable, steady economic growth.

Certain business decisions result in loss of return simply because of a lack of understanding of the relationship between time, money, and the nature of the decision. A business can go broke on 5-year investments by not properly forecasting the value of the money invested and the effects that inflation and the cost of capital will have on the products developed and/or services rendered. Clearly, understanding the time value of money is important, but this relationship becomes relevant only in the context of how a manager's decisions affect it. Thus all businessmen must understand how their decisions affect return if they are to capitalize on the pocket calculator to improve their decision-making capability.

No matter where a business manager resides in an organization, he affects the return on the company's investment in some way, and the proper performance of his duties requires him to understand how *his decisions* affect ROI. He must bring the maximum possible return at his level: failure to do so may cost the company money, and that obviously is the result of poor decision making. To determine where decisions and the time value of money interact, it is first necessary to consider certain particulars in the time/money relationship. The time value of money is quite obvious when one examines the simple money loan.

2.2   INTEREST: THE COST OF CAPITAL

Consider the case of money borrowed from a lending agency, such as a bank, a finance organization, or a venture capital organization. The money

---

*If you haven't already, read Appendix A now.

paid to the lender for the use of his money capital is *interest*. The longer
the borrowing period, the more the interest. Thus interest is a measure of
the time value of money and is specified in terms of the amount of money
paid for a given period of time during which capital is loaned.* Two types
of interest are considered in this book—simple interest and compound
interest.

Simple interest is the amount of money that is calculated as a percentage
of the original principal only. Compound interest is the amount of money
that is calculated as a percentage of both the original principal and the
interest that has previously accrued. Thus the amount of compound
interest depends on the number of times the interest is compounded (the
number of time increments or periods of the loan). Many types of loan
periods are considered in this book, but we deal most frequently with the
monthly and annual compounding periods. Occasionally reference is made
to a daily compounding period.

Simple Interest

The following example illustrates simple interest calculations and makes
clear the definition of terms used in discussing simple interest loans.
Suppose you lend $10,000 that earns simple interest at the rate of 10% per
year. At the end of 5 years, you would receive $10,000 plus $1000 for each
year that the money is loaned, for a total interest of $5000, a total payback
to you of $15,000.

Compound Interest

If the same $10,000 loan earns compound interest and the 10% interest is
compounded annually, at the end of the first year the interest would be
$1000 (10% of $10,000). At the end of the second year 10% would be paid
on $11,000—that is, on both the principal and the interest that was earned
at the end of the first year. Interest earned in the second year is $1100. The
total interest earned at the end of the second year is $2100. At the end of
the third year the total interest earned is $3310. At the end of the fourth
year the total interest earned is $4641. Finally, at the end of the fifth year
the total compounded interest is $6105.10, for a total payback of $16,105.
10. Obviously compound interest grows faster than simple interest.

Now consider the case of interest compounded on a monthly basis. The
interest per month is 10% divided by 12, or 0.83%. Compounding this over
the 60 months that make up the 5-year investment period, we find that the
interest earned on the $10,000 is $6453.09. In the case of a 10% annual rate

*Interest is usually expressed as a percentage of the amount loaned.

compounded on a daily basis, the interest earned is $6468.07. Now let us summarize this analysis. In all these cases the interest rate per year is the same but the interest earned is different. Furthermore, compound interest earns more than simple interest. Also, the more frequently the interest is compounded, the greater the interest earned. Here the interest on the loan is computed for the 5-year period. It is also apparent that a law of diminishing returns becomes effective as the compounding frequency is increased. In fact it is found that the upper limit of the interest earned occurs when it is compounded continuously, a common concept in computer savings account interest calculations. These examples illustrate four of the fundamental parameters always found in financial calculations. The initial value of the money loaned (the $10,000) is called the **present value** of the investment. The amount received at the end of the investment period is called the **future value** of the $10,000 invested, and the difference between the two is the interest. In this sense the interest represents the increase in the time value of $10,000 for the 5-year period. The present and future values represent two of the parameters always found in financial analyses. Another parameter we used was the **interest rate** per compounding period (for compound interest). The fourth parameter was the **number of compounding periods**.

A fifth parameter encountered in financial calculations is the **periodic payment amount**. Payments are made into investments such as savings accounts, trust annuities, and sinking funds, or a mortgage or loan amortization.

A sixth parameter discussed in this section is the **simple interest amount**. Simple interest is treated in detail, since it is important in business finance. However, because much of today's business economics involves compound interest, more emphasis is given to the compounded time value of money (exponential growth) than to the simple time value of money (linear growth). Thus the five parameters: payment (**PMT**), present value (**PV**), future value (**FV**), interest rate per period (i), and number of compounding periods (n) are stressed throughout this book. These parameters and the formulas relating them are built into the business pocket calculators. In fact, the calculators have special keys for these five financial parameters, and it is the keys that visually differentiate the business pocket calculators from the simpler four-function calculators or the scientific calculators (Figure 2-5).

2.3   CASH FLOW

The value of any investment is constantly changing with time, whether the money is in a bank, in a business, in bonds, or elsewhere. The comparison of two investment alternatives involving costs or revenues at different

Figure 2-5. Typical business calculator keyboard.

times and in different amounts is usually not straightforward because the *values* of the monies are different at different times. Obviously then it is necessary to compare investment alternatives simultaneously. This amounts to either (*a*) forecasting and comparing the future values of all monies in a cash flow or (*b*) computing the present value of all monies in a cash flow (discounting), to determine and compare the present values of the alternatives. Of course any intermediate time could be used, but all investment alternatives must be considered at the same time. Bringing future value investment cash flows (cf = cash flow = − investments + revenues − costs) to present value is sometimes referred to as the **real value** of an investment. The total of the present values of all investments, revenues, and costs in a venture is usually called its **net present value**.

Present Value

The relationships between certain types of business decisions and the time value of money are clear. For example, would you rather have accounts

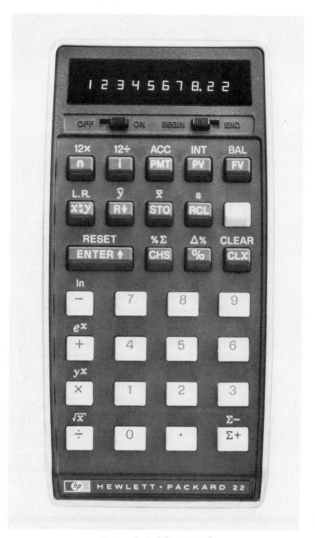

Figure 2-5. (*Continued*)

receivable paid when due or in the future (say 30 days)? Obviously the sooner the payment is received, the sooner you can earn interest on the money collected. Money put into a savings account will earn 4 to 9%, depending on the account. If you invest the money in your own business, you probably will realize a greater return, say 15 to 25%. If you hold your accounts receivable longer than a month, you are probably charging interest (if the law allows) that equals or exceeds the return on investment in your own business. This decision example is straightforward.

Figure 2-5. (*Continued*)

Less straightforward is a case involving two alternatives in paying for a capital investment. Suppose you buy a minicomputer from the XYZ Corporation for $20,000. The payment options are payment on delivery or $20,500 at the end of 90 days. Which alternative would you select if your business has an earnings rate of return of 15% per year? To make a correct decision, compare the present value of the $20,500 delayed payment and the $20,000 present payment. The present value of the $20,500 future payment is $19,750.08. Said another way, $19,750.08 will grow to $20,500 in 90 days (if you retain it in your business for this period). If you pay for the minicomputer outright, it will cost you $20,000 of today's money. We see that approximately $250 can be saved by deferring payment for 90 days. Suppose, now, that you are going to remove the money from your business and put it into a savings account with an effective 7% per year rate of return, compounded monthly. The $20,500 delayed payment has a present value of $20,145.40 when discounted at 7% per year and compounded monthly. In other words, $20,145.40 would be the required principal in a 7% per year savings account to grow to $20,500 in 90 days. The alternatives for paying for the minicomputer are summarized in Figure 2-6.

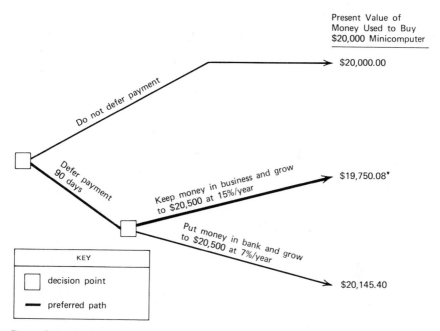

Present Value of
Money Used to Buy
$20,000 Minicomputer

Do not defer payment $20,000.00

Defer
90 days payment

Keep money in business and grow
to $20,500 at 15%/year $19,750.08*

Put money in bank and grow
to $20,500 at 7%/year

KEY

□ decision point

— preferred path $20,145.40

Figure 2-6.   Decision tree for minicomputer payoff method decision. Asterisk indicates decision to defer payment 90 days and retain money in business.

This example indicates that investment alternatives involving cash flows distributed over time must be brought to the same time (in this case, present time) if an effective comparison is to be made. This calls for the specification of the interest rate per period (rate of return), which in turn depends on whether your money remains in your business or is put into a savings account or other money-generating system. Thus an understanding of rate of return is essential to responsible business decision making. Chapter 3 presents ways to identify the rate of return for a business, a department within a business, a personal economic system, and many other money-generating financial systems.

The technique used in the foregoing example is called present value analysis. It requires discounting future values by the interest rate per period. Discounting is, in a sense, computing interest in reverse. Instead of starting with the present value of capital and asking, "What will be its future value?", the concept is to take a given future value and discount it "backward" to the present value.

Up to now we have examined only the present and future values of investments. In the more typical financial arrangements there is a series of cash payments. Many investments, if not most, involve periodic handling of cash revenues and costs over a period of time. This is known as cash flow. Probably the most familiar examples of cash flow are the payments made on a home mortgage or an amortized loan repayment schedule. Instead of borrowing the money for a home and paying it off in a single payment at the end of the loan period, you are asked to repay it in monthly installments. These payments are the cash flow received by the lending agency as its return on its investment in your mortgage. Financial analysis in the area of cash flow becomes more sophisticated, and the alternatives of payoff are less clear. As an example, again consider the $20,000 minicomputer purchase, but with three payoff options: the $20,000 is paid on delivery, a single payment of $32,906.18 is made 5 years from the date of delivery, or a monthly payment of $424.94 is made for a period of 60 months (the total of all payments being $25,496.45). Assume your business has a 10% annual rate of return. Which alternative is best?

Twenty seconds of analysis on a business pocket calculator will show that the net present values of *all these alternatives are identical*, even though significantly different cash flows and total cash outlays are involved in each. Surprised? From a present value analysis, any one of the alternatives is as attractive as any other. Thus the management decision must be based on *other factors*. (If the present $20,000 value of all three alternatives is the same, what about the future value of these alternatives? The answer to this naturally occurring question is that the future values are identical as well.)

The amazing fact about the analysis on the business pocket calculator of this particular problem is that only eleven keystrokes (10 seconds) are required to compute the present value of either the amortized loan or the final payment alternative. Chapters 3 and 5 deal with such calculations. Once you master these time-value-of-money calculations you will probably use them with increasing frequency to better understand the financial consequences of your business decisions.

2.4   RATE OF RETURN ON INVESTMENT

Perhaps the single most informative financial parameter to calculate when making investment decisions is the return on investment. No matter how investment alternatives are specified—whether in terms of present value, future value, or periodic cash flow—the internal rate of return for the investment can be computed, and this gives a single common denominator for comparing investment alternatives. To illustrate this point, consider two $100,000 investments. Project A would return a cash flow of $27,000 per year for 5 years, a total of $135,000. Project B would return no cash flow during the first 4 years but would pay $150,000 at the end of the fifth year. Which offers the better return on investment?

A manager lacking a good understanding of the rate of return on investment might conclude that project B is better because of the apparent additional return of $15,000. However, when the rate of return for project A is computed, it is found to be 10.9% per year, whereas that of project B is only 8.5% per year—a whopping 28% difference in yields. The keystroke sequences in Chapter 3 can solve this type of problem in *six keystrokes*. Think of it—six keystrokes. Six steps to compare such different types of investments without using

- Tables.
- Scratch-pad arithmetic.
- "Casting out nines" to check arithmetic.
- Waiting for computer runs that could distract you from analyzing investment alternatives.

2.5   INFLATION

In this period of transition to global economic equilibrium, inflation is varying significantly. For a long while, the United States Department of Defense used an inflation rate of between 4 and 5% to compute the growth in the value of their major systems' alternatives. In 1974 they switched to the schedule of inflation rates shown in Table 2.2. This table served as the basis for escalating the present values of the *life cycle* cash flows of their programs to future value dollars (to compute the budget Congress must approve for procurement of a system). The difference in the total DOD projected budget using a 4 to 5% inflation rate and the projected budget with the inflation schedule of Table 2-2 was on the order of $16 billion.* The message is clear that whether you are in the government or in business, inflation must now be considered in all time and money calculations. This is particularly true for those who work for or with the government, and social discounts are applied by the Federal General Accounting Office in comparing programs vying for a place in the nation's annual budget. Previously dollars were inflated at a constant rate and discounted at a constant rate, a simple calculation. Now the inflation must be considered on a scheduled basis. In a word, one must escalate before discounting when computing the costs of programs seeking congressional funding. The concepts of social discount rates, inflation escalation rates, and business discount rates are treated in Chapter 10, "Business Systems Analysis." Although these concepts are not pocket calculator subjects, they are so important in our new economy that a book on financial analysis would be incomplete without them.

---

*Aviation Week, Aug., 1974, McGraw-Hill, N.Y.

Table 2-2   Price Escalation Index, August 20, 1974[a,]

Year	Procurement		Construction		Labor	
	Indices	Annual Rate of Change (%)	Indices	Annual Rate of Change (%)	Indices	Annual Rate of Change (%)
1974	100.0				100.0	
1975	111.0	11.00	100.0		108.2	8.20
1976	119.9	8.00	112.0	12.00	115.8	7.00
1977	128.3	7.00	122.08	9.00	112.7	6.00
1978	134.7	5.00	130.63	7.00	128.9	5.05
1979	140.6	4.38	138.46	6.00	134.6	4.42
1980	146.7	4.33	145.39	5.00	140.4	4.30
1981	152.1	3.68	152.66	5.00	146.3	4.20
1982	157.8	3.75	160.29	5.00	152.4	4.20
1983	163.6	3.67	168.30	5.00	158.8	4.20
1984	169.6	3.67	176.71	5.00	165.5	4.20
1985	175.9	3.71	185.56	5.00	172.5	4.20

[a]Source: Directive from the Office of the Assistant Secretary of Defense.

Table 2-3   The Twelve Financial Functions and Five Financial Variables Most Frequently Used in Business Pocket Calculator Analysis

	Input Parameters[a]		Output Parameters	Typical Uses	Financial Functions Used in Business Pocket Calculator
1	n PV	FV[+]	i	Investment	$i = \sqrt[n]{\dfrac{FV}{PV}} - 1$
2	n PV	PMT[+]	i	yield	$i = \dfrac{PMT}{PV}[1 - (1+i)^{-n}]^*$
3	n FV	PMT[+]	i	comparisons	$i = \dfrac{PMT}{FV}[(1+i)^n - 1]^*$
4	i PF	FV[+]	n	Investment	$n = \dfrac{\log \dfrac{FV}{PV}}{\log(1+i)}$
5	i PMT	PV[+•]	n	horizon	$n = \dfrac{\log \dfrac{1}{1 + iPV/PMT}}{\log(1+i)}$
6	i PMT	FV[+]	n	comparisons	$n = \dfrac{\log\left[1 + \dfrac{iFV}{PMT}\right]}{\log(1+i)}$

Table 2-3 (*Continued*)

Input Parameters[a]			Output Parameters	Typical Uses	Financial Functions Used in Business Pocket Calculator[b]
7	n	i $FV^{+\bullet\circ}$	PV	Net present value	$PV = \dfrac{FV}{(1+i)^n}$
8	n	i $PMT^{+\bullet\circ}$	PV	analysis	$PV = PMT\dfrac{1+(1+i)^{-n}}{i}$
9	n	i $PV^{+\bullet\circ}$	FV	Growth comparison	$FV = PV(1+i)^n$
10	n	i $PMT^{+\bullet\circ}$	FV	analysis	$FV = PMT\dfrac{(1+i)^n - 1}{i}$
11	n	i $FV^{+\bullet\circ}$	PMT	Affordability	$PMT = FV\dfrac{i}{(1+i)^n - 1}$
12	n	i $PV^{+\bullet\circ}$	PMT	analysis	$PMT = PV\dfrac{i}{1+(1+i)^{-n}}$

[a] Symbols as follows:
   +   available on HP-22/70/80 type calculators
   ●   available on Rockwell 204 type calculators
   ○   available on NOVUS 6020 type calculators.

[b] Definitions as follows:
   i = interest rate per compounding period
   n = number of compounding periods
   PV = present value of money
   FV = future value of money
PMT = amount of equal periodic payments when payments are made at the end of the compounding period. When equal periodic payments are made at the beginning of each compounding period, as with an annuity-due, the inputs to calculators which only solve ordinary annuity problems can be easily modified to account for the effect of the advanced payment schedule. The modifications are tabulated as follows:

ORDINARY ANNUITY PARAMETER	ANNUITY-DUE ADJUSTMENT	ANNUITY-DUE PARAMETER
n	multiply PMT by (1+i)	PMT′=PMT(1+i)
i	subtract PTM from PV	PV′=PV−PMT
PMT	divide PV by (1+i)	PV′+PV÷(1+i)
PV	multiply PMT by (1+i)	PMT′=PMT(1+i)
FV	multiply PMT by (1+i)	PMT′=PMT(1+i)

This factor is conveniently accounted for on the HP-22 calculator with a switch to correctly calculate the annuity parameters depending on whether the annuity is an ordinary type annuity (rents, leases, insurance payments, etc.).
   *   solved iteratively with the pocket calculator electronics

2.6   THE FIVE PARAMETERS OF FINANCIAL ANALYSIS

As mentioned earlier in this chapter, only five parameters are required to analyze problems involving most decisions on cash flow alternatives. It is even more startling to realize that there are really only twelve types of financial calculations needed to do most business financial analysis, and these calculations involve at most nine different types of input data. This would appear to be a small combination of problems in light of the fact that five variables taken three at a time result in twenty different ways of making the calculations. It is found however that about half of these are simply the same problem stated differently, with the result that there are only twelve basically different financial calculations.* The dozen possible calculations and the inputs are shown in Table 2-3. Note that the first six are straightforward calculations of future value, interest rate, pay periods, and present value, whereas the last three involve cash flow when payment schedules are part of the financial analysis. The equations that are used to perform these calculations are set forth in Appendix A. The temptation is great to include the equations at this point and to discuss their derivation and interpretation, but they are not necessary to acquaint the reader with financial analysis on the pocket calculator for business decisions. Both the novice and the reader trained in business mathematics will benefit from Appendix A. The novice will find that the keystroke sequences presented throughout the remainder of the book are straightforward, and although they are based on the financial formulas given in Appendix A, their derivation need not be understood. The formulas are typical of the financial functions that are used in financial analysis computer programs by commercial credit organizations, businesses, and lending, banking, and other institutions. Suffice it to say that the procedures and keystroke sequences appearing in this book are solidly founded on financial functions used by business and money handling institutions.

Finally, this book contains numerous examples of calculations involving groups or combinations of these financial functions. The sequence of formulas to be so solved to conduct a complex financial analysis is not important; what is important is to recognize that no matter how complex financial calculations become, they can often be reduced to these twelve fairly simple functions. Even more important, these financial functions are built into many of the business pocket calculators available today.

---

*Complex financial calculations involve the sequencing of the twelve types of calculations in a manner that models the economic system of a business.

CHAPTER 3

CALCULATING INTEREST, INTEREST RATES, AND RATES OF RETURN FOR BUSINESS DECISIONS

Interest is the price paid for the use of money and can be expressed in terms of an amount of money or as a rate of payment. As mentioned in Chapter 1, interest is also a measure of the time value of money. Interest rate is an agreed-upon percentage of the amount borrowed for an agreed-upon period of time. Generally the interest rate is related directly to the risks the lender takes and to competition in the money marketplace. Interest varies as the economy and the demand for and supply of money vary. Through its control of the prime interest rate, the Federal Reserve Bank in large measure regulates explicitly the interest rates for loans to big business and implicitly those made to small business.

We discuss here two types of interest. In simple interest the agreed-to percentage is based only on the amount borrowed or loaned; in compound interest the agreed-to percentage is based both on the amount borrowed or loaned and on the interest that accrues. Thus it is apparent that interest depends on the following:

1. The amount borrowed or loaned.
2. The agreed-upon interest rate.
3. The time for which the money is used.

The time is usually expressed in days, months, or years. Compound interest is usually compounded on daily, monthly, or yearly periods. Some financial institutions today are offering continuous compounding. In what follows, the interest rate or percentage agreed to is the charge per annum unless otherwise specifically stated.

3.1 SIMPLE INTEREST

Simple interest is the amount paid on money borrowed where the amount borrowed remains unchanged for the period of time the money is in use. The amount borrowed is called the principal.

There are three types of simple interest: ordinary simple interest, commercial interest (or bankers' interest), and accurate interest. Ordinary simple interest, based on a *30-day month* and a 360-day year, is frequently used on simple real estate loans, installment loans, and periodic repayment personal loans. Commercial interest is based on a 360-day year and an *exactly specified number of days*. When no statement is made by a lending institution in a loan agreement, the latter type of interest is generally used. Commercial interest, as might be expected, is the method that results in the greatest return for the lender. Accurate interest is based on a 365-day year and *an exact number of days*. This method is becoming more frequently used in commercial dealings but is most often encountered in dealing with the federal government. In a number of business and finance books and manuals, accurate interest is referred to as "exact interest." Both terms are used in this chapter. The bases for ordinary simple interest and commercial interest might suggest that another method for calculating simple interest would be on a 365-day year and/or a 30-day month. This method is sometimes discussed, but it has been the author's experience that agreements are seldom entered into on this basis. It is reasonable to expect that this method would be chosen under special circumstances, the terms being negotiated between the parties.

The basis for a loan determines the way in which time is calculated for computing simple interest. Obviously the time calculation is different depending on whether a 30-day month or an exact number of days is used. When the 30-day month method is used, it is necessary to determine only the number of months over which the loan is based and to multiply by 30 days. If there are days to either side of an even month, they are accounted for by simple addition. Remember that 30-day month calculations are used only for ordinary simple interest.

The exact-time basis is used for commercial or bankers' interest and requires determining exactly the number of days during the life of the loan. The count usually includes the last day but excludes the first day. If the month of February is included in the time period, an extra day must be added when accounting for leap year. Counting the number of days between two dates on which a loan is made is a tedious process. It must be carefully done, of course, to realize the most return. Tables have been developed (e.g., Table 3-1) for calculating the exact number of days between two dates. Hewlett-Packard's HP-80 pocket calculator has a

Table 3-1   Table for Calculating Exact Number of Days Between Two Dates

Number of Each Day of the Year

Day of Month	Jan.	Feb.[a]	Mar.	Apr.	May	June	July	Aug.	Sept.	Oct.	Nov.	Dec.	Day of Month
1	1	32	60	91	121	152	182	213	244	274	305	335	1
2	2	33	61	92	122	153	183	214	245	275	306	336	2
3	3	34	62	93	123	154	184	215	246	276	307	337	3
4	4	35	63	94	124	155	185	216	247	277	308	338	4
5	5	36	64	95	125	156	186	217	248	278	309	339	5
6	6	37	65	96	126	157	187	218	249	279	310	340	6
7	7	38	66	97	127	158	188	219	250	280	311	341	7
8	8	39	67	98	128	159	189	220	251	281	312	342	8
9	9	40	68	99	129	160	190	221	252	282	313	343	9
10	10	41	69	100	130	161	191	222	253	283	314	344	10
11	11	42	70	101	131	162	192	223	254	284	315	345	11
12	12	43	71	102	132	163	193	224	255	285	316	346	12
13	13	44	72	103	133	164	194	225	256	286	317	347	13
14	14	45	73	104	134	165	195	226	257	287	318	348	14
15	15	46	74	105	135	166	196	227	258	288	319	349	15
16	16	47	75	106	136	167	197	228	259	289	320	350	16
17	17	48	76	107	137	168	198	229	260	290	321	351	17
18	18	49	77	108	138	169	199	230	261	291	322	352	18
19	19	50	78	109	139	170	200	231	262	292	323	353	19
20	20	51	79	110	140	171	201	232	263	293	324	354	20
21	21	52	80	111	141	172	202	233	264	294	325	355	21
22	22	53	81	112	142	173	203	234	265	295	326	356	22
23	23	54	82	113	143	174	204	235	266	296	327	357	23
24	24	55	83	114	144	175	205	236	267	297	328	358	24
25	25	56	84	115	145	176	206	237	268	298	329	359	25
26	26	57	85	116	146	177	207	238	269	299	330	360	26
27	27	58	86	117	147	178	208	239	270	300	331	361	27
28	28	59	87	118	148	179	209	240	271	301	332	362	28
29	29		88	119	149	180	210	241	272	302	333	363	29
30	30		89	120	150	181	211	242	273	303	334	364	30
31	31		90		151		212	243		304		365	31

[a]For leap years add 1 after February 28.
Source. Flora M. Locke, *Business Mathematics*, Wiley, 1972.

built-in calendar that permits the number of days between two dates to be calculated. This calculator has another convenient calendar feature that computes and displays a payoff date when the starting date and the exact number of days of a loan are given.

On business calculators not having the calendar feature, the *sum and store key* can be used and the months counted off, remembering how many days in each month. When the number of days does not begin or end exactly on an even month, the additional days are computed separately (remembering to exclude the first day and include the last day).

3.2   CALCULATING INTEREST

The formula for computing simple interest is

$$\text{interest} = \text{principal} \times \text{interest rate} \times \text{time}$$

or

$$\text{INT} = \text{PV} \times i \times n$$

where PV is the principal present value or amount loaned (or borrowed), INT is interest, i is the interest rate per period, and n is the number of days the money is loaned. Since it is common practice to specify the interest rate in terms of an annual rate, if the agreed-to compounding period is one month, the annual rate must be divided by 12. If the compounding period is in days, the annual rate must be divided by either 360 (ordinary and bankers' interest) or 365 (accurate interest, as when dealing with the federal government).

To illustrate the difference between bankers', accurate, and ordinary interest, consider the case of $10,000 loaned at 9% from June 1 to November 1. Bankers' interest would be calculated as

$$\text{INT} = 10{,}000 \times 0.09 \times \frac{153}{360} = 382.50$$

The same calculation to determine accurate interest would be

$$\text{INT} = 10{,}000 \times 0.09 \times \frac{153}{365} = 377.26$$

Ordinary interest would be calculated according to the formula*

$$\text{INT} = 10{,}000 \times 0.09 \times \frac{150}{360} = 375.00$$

The Hewlett-Packard HP-22, HP-70, and HP-80 have both the 360-day and 365-day interest calculations built in. The HP-80 will compute the exact number of days, given the date of the loan and the payoff date, using its built-in calendar. Neither the HP-22 nor the HP-70 has such a calendar feature. However the exact number of days may be determined by a

*Five 30-day months

separate but easy calculation using the "sum and store" key. The procedure is as follows:

Step 1. Remember the exact days in the months and accumulate them in the "sum and store" register in the calculator.

Step 2. Calculate and sum the additional days if the loan does not begin or end on an even month.

Step 3. Add an extra day if it is a leap year and the loan period includes February.

3.3 COMPOUND INTEREST

Compound interest is computed on the basis of a principal that changes at the compounding intervals. The principal at each compounding period is the sum of interest earned over the *preceding* compounding period and the previous principal. Compound interest is usually computed annually, semi-annually, quarterly, monthly, daily, or continuously. In this book we consider it to be compounded annually unless otherwise stated.

Interest is said to be *converted* when it becomes part of the principal; that is, when the interest is computed for a compounding period, it is computed on the basis of simple interest and converted to principal. The number of conversion periods or compounding periods is the number of times the interest is converted during a year. The present value of the original principal grows to its future value at the end of the loan period. The difference between the original principal or present value of the loan and its future value is the compound interest. The longhand computation of compound interest is an iterative calculation of simple interest. To see this, assume that $100 is to be compounded (or converted) annually for 4 years at 10%. The compound interest can be computed as follows:

$100.00	Present value (equals original principal)
10.00	Interest for first year
$110.00	Principal at end of first year
11.00	Interest for second year
$121.00	Principal at end of second year
12.10	Interest for third year
$133.10	Principal at end of third year
13.31	Interest for fourth year
$146.41	Principal at end of fourth year

The compound interest is equal to $146.41 minus $100.00, that is, $46.41.

This process would be quite tedious if the compounding periods were in days or even months and the calculations had to be done manually. On a pocket calculator the process is simple, particularly when the compounding periods are in months; and the business pocket calculator very easily handles compounding periods of days. The business calculators require only four keystrokes to compute the interest, whether simple or compound, using the financial function keys and the built-in electronic circuitry. Also most of the business calculators, when computing simple interest, do the calculation on the basis of both 360 and 365 days and conveniently store both figures. Heretofore interest calculations have been made with the aid of interest tables. A pocket calculator **eliminates the need for all tables**, since it can compute the calculations quickly and as accurately as any prepared tables.

3.4 EFFECTIVE INTEREST RATES

In business and finance, interest rates per period are quoted in a number of ways. All these different interest rates can be reduced to an effective annual interest rate in a manner similar to that in which different cash flows are related to present value. The effective rate generally accepted by most businessmen is **the annual interest rate that will produce in a single conversion the same interest as an agreed-to rate**. For example, $100 loaned at 10% interest and converted annually returns $10 on the $100. Its annual interest rate identically equals its effective interest rate of 10%. If, however, the $100 loan is converted semiannually, the interest is converted twice during the year and the $100 will earn $10.25, for an effective annual rate of 10.25%. Another way of thinking of this is that 10% compounded semiannually yields 10.25% on an annual basis.

3.5 DISCOUNTING INTEREST–BEARING NOTES

As pointed out in Chapter 1, discounts* are similar to interest working in reverse. Discounts on interest-bearing drafts and promissory notes can sometimes be confusing, and it is worth taking a few moments to refresh the reader's memory on concepts in financial discounting.

Let us start with the simplest case—the promissory note. Promissory notes are negotiable instruments. As such, both their purchase and sale are based on their face value. They are the documented evidence of a debt by the borrower. Remember that a negotiable note must meet four criteria:

*Cash and trade discounts in merchandising are discussed in Chapter 7.

1. It must be signed by the borrower.
2. It must specify the exact due date.
3. It must clearly state that it is payable to order or to the bearer of the note.
4. It must be an unconditional promise to pay a definite sum of money.

Notes may be interest bearing or non-interest bearing. If a note bears no interest, this must also be stated on the instrument.

Since notes are negotiable instruments, they can be sold to banks or other parties. When a bank buys a note, whether from the borrower or from an intermediate party, a *bank charge*, sometimes called a *bank discount*, is made. This bank discount is calculated on the maturity value (not on the principal) of the note. That is, the discount is calculated on the note's future value, not on its present value. If the note bears interest, the future value must include the interest. The bank discount is then computed on the principal plus the interest. In a sense bank discounts can be considered to be "interest in advance."

Discount rates are quoted in terms of an annual percentage of the future value of the note. Remember that notes are usually given for short periods of time (the most common being for 30 to 90 days) and are computed on an exact-day basis. That is, commercial notes are on the 360 exact-day basis similar to the commercial interest discussed previously. Of course different time bases for discounts can be arranged, but these are usually negotiated as particular cases. Notes are usually discounted on a 360 exact-day basis.

The *proceeds* of a note (the amount paid to the holder of a note by the bank) is the future value of the note minus the bank discount. If the note is non-interest bearing, the future value is equal to the present value and the proceeds are the maturity value minus the bank discount—a net loss to the holder of the note. If you wish to lend money on a minimum interest basis, it follows that a note should bear at least enough interest to cover a bank discount if you anticipate having to recover your money earlier than the note due date.

An example of a simple discounted promissory note is a non-interest-bearing note for $10,000 sold to a bank at an 8% discount rate for a period of 90 days. In this case the bank discount would be

$$\$10,000 \times 0.08 \times \frac{90}{360} = \$200$$

The proceeds of the note paid by the bank would then be

$$\$10,000 - \$200 = \$9800$$

An important point to remember here is that the annual effective interest rate is not really 8% but 8.163% because the actual money available to the maker (or borrower) is $9800, the 8% discount rate having been computed on $10,000. From the borrower's viewpoint, the effective interest rate is

interest rate = interest divided by (principal times time)

$$\text{interest rate} = \$200 \div \left(\$9800 \times \frac{1}{4} \text{ year} \right)$$

$$8.163\% = \frac{\$200}{\$9800} \times 4 \times 100$$

The foregoing example deals with a note whose originator was the borrower. Often an interest-bearing note is sold to a bank or other institution by the lender. If a business holds a note in payment of an obligation, it may sell the note to a bank at a date earlier than the maturity date of the note (a process ambiguously called "discounting"). In this case the bank holds the note to maturity and collects from the borrower.* Assume that a note is for 90 days, has been held for 60 days, and the note holder cannot wait the additional 30 days for the cash. He sells the note to a bank and accepts the bank's discount as a penalty. When a note is discounted, the time is computed in exact days from the date "sold" to the maturity date: this is called the *term of discount*. Again consider the $10,000 note bearing 8% interest for 90 days. The maturity value of the note would be

$$\$10,000 \times 0.08 \times \frac{90}{360} + 10,000 = \$10,200$$

Here the term of discount would be 30 days, and assuming a 7% discount rate, the discount value would be

$$\$10,200 \times 0.07 \times \frac{30}{360} = \$59.50$$

The proceeds received by the note holder would then be

$$\$10,200 - \$59.50 = \$10,140.50$$

Drafts are also negotiable instruments used primarily in commerce. They generally serve the specific purpose of buying and selling goods and

*Of course if the borrower fails to meet the payoff obligation, the lender who has sold the note to the bank is held responsible by the bank for the mature or future value of the note.

are drawn by the seller on the buyer (drawer and drawee, respectively). Examples of drafts are *bills of exchange* and *trade acceptances*. There are both interest-bearing and non-interest-bearing drafts, usually of two varieties: sight drafts and time drafts. Sight drafts are payable on presentation. Time drafts are payable at the maturity date or due date. Time drafts can also be written "after sight"; that is, a draft can be made payable at a specified period after it is accepted. For example, if a draft dated September 6 is due 30 days after sight and is accepted on September 10, the maturity date is 30 days after September 10, which is October 10. If a time draft is specified in months, the months are usually considered to be 30-day months.

Drafts may be sold to a bank and the discount penalty assumed by the seller, in the same way as promissory notes. Generally, however, a bank also charges a collection fee that is a percentage of the mature (future) value of the draft. In most cases the proceeds of a draft are

$$\text{face value} - \text{discount} - \text{collection fee}$$

Consider the example of computing the proceeds of an interest-bearing draft for $20,000. The draft, for the purchase of a minicomputer, is payable to the manufacturer 90 days after the date of September 6 and bears an interest rate of 7%. If the draft is discounted on October 13 at 6% and the bank charges a collection fee of 0.02%, the proceeds on the note received by the minicomputer manufacturer would be computed as follows:

Face of note	$20,000
Interest on note (7% of $20,000 for 90 days)	$350
Future (or maturity) value of note	$20,350
90 days after September 6	December 5
Term of discount (October 13 to December 5)	53 days
Discount (6% of future value for 53 days)	$179.76
Collection fee (0.02% on future value of $20,350)	$40.70
Proceeds	$20,350 - $179.76 $-\,$40.70 = $20,129.54

3.6 INTEREST RATE AND YIELD CALCULATIONS

Interest rate is the ratio of the interest earned to the principal for a given corresponding period. For example, if $10 is earned on the loan of $100 for one year, we say the interest rate is $10/$100 per year or 0.1 per year or 10% per year. Interest rate is a near-term measure of how fast the value of money is changing with time. As such, it is a useful measure of the difference between investment alternatives. For example, an 11% per year yield investment is better than a 10% per year yield investment, *all other things being the same.*

Yield, though a key parameter in business decisions, is definitely not useful as the sole parameter because it gives little indication of risk. It is one of the most commonly used measures of a venture. Certainly one would not explore the risk parameters without the yield. Thus yield calculations are essential for investment comparisons. Pocket calculators permit the calculation of yield with but a few keystrokes, and thus are very useful for investment comparison analysis.

Since in this discussion "yield" is used synonymously with "interest rate," it is logical to ask, "Are yield and interest rate the same?" The answer is both yes and no. *Yes* in the sense that the same mathematical formula is used to calculate the two. *No* in the sense that interest rate per year specifically applies to money, whereas yield can apply both to money and to *money's worth*. Yield is usually applied to the growth rate per year of money, corporate worth, personal worth, and so on. Yield is simply a measure of the rate of growth of processes that grow or decline in a compound way.

The interest rate per period can be calculated (*a*) for the simple growth of a present value to a future value, (*b*) for the growth in the value of a series of money payments where the payments are made at the end of the compounding period, and (*c*) for the growth in the value of a series of money payments where the payments are made at the beginning of the compounding period.

And that's about it. If the payments are all the same amount, we call the payment program an annuity. If the payments are made at the beginning of the compounding period, we call the program an annuity due. If the payments are made at the end of the compounding period, we say it is an ordinary annuity.*

Examples of ordinary annuities include

- Mortgages.
- Personal loans.
- Sinking funds (corporate bonds).

*If these annuity terms are new to you, be sure to read Appendix A.

Examples of annuities due are

- Rents.
- Leases.
- Personal savings.

Most pocket calculators implement only the ordinary annuity formulas. They can be easily adapted to calculate annuity-due problems, however, since this type differs only in the treatment of the first and last payments. The casebook examples make clear the distinction and illustrate the modified keystrokes. At present only the Hewlett-Packard HP-22 can solve both ordinary annuity and annuity-due calculations without modifying the payment time. Hewlett-Packard's approach is to provide a switch that can be set to indicate whether the payments are made at the beginning or end of the compounding period. The *annuity switch* can be seen at the top of the HP-22 keyboard in Figure 2-5.

3.7 SUMMARY

Interest calculations are fundamental to understanding business finance and therefore to business decisions because they deal directly with the time value of money. The remainder of Part 1 deals with the calculation of interest and its bearing on decisions business managers must make in their daily operations. The most common of these interest calculations involve computing the interest for add-on or direct reduction loans and their effective annual interest rate, commonly called *annual percentage rate* (APR). This is an example of precisely where the pocket calculator can daily serve the businessman. The pocket calculator can determine interest, payment schedules, and effective annual interest rate in a simple, straight-forward four-keystroke sequence. This permits quick comparison of alternative types of loans and payment programs, whether to your business by a banking or lending agency or by your business to its creditors. Additionally the pocket calculator frees the businessman and financial analyst from simple and compound interest and discount tables.

CASEBOOK EXAMPLE

Calculate simple interest on 360-day basis.

The Problem

Compute the accrued simple interest on $1000 for 70 days at 9%. Use a 360-day basis.

The Approach

Compute $\text{INTEREST} = (\text{number of days}/360) \times PV \times i/100$.

Typical Keystroke Sequences

Basic Four-Function Algebraic Calculator	Basic Four-Function Reverse-Polish Calculator	HP-70/80/22	Rockwell 204 and NOVUS 6020
(70)	(70)	(70)	(1000)
÷	↑	n	×
(360)	(360)	(1000)	(9)
×	÷	PV	%
(1000)	(1000)	(9)	×
×	×	i	(70)
(9)	(9)	▨	÷
÷	×	INT	(360)
(100)	(100)	17.50	=
=	÷		17.50
17.50	17.50		

KEY

▨ gold key. (HP-22 only; skip for HP-70/80)

( ) data entry.

▢ data output.

CASEBOOK EXAMPLE

Calculate simple interest on 365-day basis.

The Problem

Compute the accrued simple interest on $1000 for 70 days at 9%. Use a 365-day basis.

The Approach

Compute $INT = (\text{number of days}/365) \times PV \times i/100$.

Typical Keystroke Sequences

Basic Four-Function Algebraic Calculator	Basic Four-Function Reverse-Polish Calculator	HP-70/80/22	Rockwell 204 and NOVUS 6020
(70)	(70)	(1000)	(1000)
÷	↑	PV	×
(365)	(365)	(70)	(9)
×	÷	n	%
(1000)	(1000)	(9)	×
		i	70
×	×		
(9)	(9)		÷
÷	×	INT	365
100	(100)	R↓	=
=	÷	x⇄y	
17.26	17.26	17.26	17.26

KEY

gold key. (HP-22 only; skip for HP-70/80)

( ) data entry.

data output.

CASEBOOK EXAMPLE

Calculate the interest of a compounded amount.

The Problem

Calculate the interest earned by $14,000 loaned at 8% for 3 years and compounded monthly.

The Approach

Calculate the difference between $14,000 and the loan's future value.

Typical Keystroke Sequences

HP-22	HP-70/80	Rockwell 204	NOVUS 6020
Annuity SW–End	(14000)	(14000)	(14000)
(14000)	PV	ET	Amt
PV	(8)	PV	(8)
(8)	K	(8)	CHS
	÷	ET	%i
i	i	i/yr	(3)
(3)	(3)	(3)	CHS
	K	×	n
n	×	(12)	FV–Interest
FV	n	=	+
RCL	FV	ET	(14000)
PV	DSP	n	−
−	PV	TA	3783.31
3783.32	−	FV	
	3783.32	−	
		(14000)	
		=	
		3783.27	

KEY

gold key.

(   ) data entry.

☐ data output.

CASEBOOK EXAMPLE

Calculate the exact number of days between two dates.

The Problem

Calculate the exact number of days between September 6 and November 24.

The Approach

Step 1. In the November column find the number that is on a line with 24. We find that November 24 is the 328th day of the year.

Step 2. Find that September 6 is the 249th day of the year.

Step 3. The number of days between these two dates is 79.

Typical Keystroke Sequences

Basic Algebraic Calculator	Basic Reverse-Polish Calculator	HP-80
(328)	(328)	(9.061975)
−	↑	↑
(249)	(249)	(11.241975)
=	−	days
79	79	79

KEY

(   ) data entry.

▭ data output.

CASEBOOK EXAMPLE

Calculate the interest rate per period of a compounded amount.

The Problem

Calculate the annual rate of return required for $5000 to grow to $10,000 in 8 years.

The Approach

Calculate $i = {}^{n}\sqrt{FV/PV} - 1$, where n is the number of compounding periods (8), $FV = \$10,000$, $PV = \$5000$, and i is the annual interest rate.

Typical Keystroke Sequences

Basic Four-Function Algebraic Calculator	Basic Four-Function Reverse-Polish Calculator	HP-70/80/22	Rockwell 204	NOVUS 6020
(10000)	(10000)	(10000)	TA	CE/C
÷	↑	FV	C	CE/C
(5000)	(5000)	(5000)	ET	MR/MC
√	÷	PV	DS	MR/MC
√	(1)	(8)	(9)	(1)
√	↑	n	(10000)	÷
=	(8)	i	÷	(8)
−	÷	9.05077	(5000)	×
(1)	y^x		=	M^+
×	(1)		ET	CE/C
(100)	−		√	(10000)
=			ET	÷
9.05077	(100)		√	(5000)
	×		ET	×
	9.05077		√	MR/MC
			−	Power
			(1)	+
			×	(1)
			(100)	−
			=	×
			9.05076	100
				=
				9.05

KEY
(   ) data entry.

☐ date output.

CASEBOOK EXAMPLE

Calculate the interest rate per period for an ordinary annuity.

The Problem

Calculate the interest rate per year for a loan of $25,000 to be repaid in 40 monthly payments of $742.26.

The Approach

Calculate $i = (PMT/PV)[1 - (1 + i)^{-n}]$; (iteratively), where i is the interest rate per period, PMT is the payment amount, PV is the loan amount, and n is the number of compounding periods.

Typical Keystroke Sequences

HP-70/80/22	NOVUS 6020	Rockwell 204
Annuity SW–End[a]	(25000)	(25000)
(25000)	Amt	ET
PV	(40)	PV
40	n	(40)
n	( ) ←	ET
(742.26)	CHS	n
PMT	%i	( ) ←
i	CHS	ET
(12)	PMT–loan	PMT
×		TA
10.40		PMT

NOVUS 6020: Guess new %i — PMT = 742.26 ? — No → / Yes

Rockwell 204: Guess new i/yr — PMT = 742.26 ? — No → / Yes

(*Continued*)

HP-70/80/22	NOVUS 6020	Rockwell 204
	$i =$ Last guess of $\%i$	$i =$ Last guess of i/yr

[a] HP-22 only.

KEY

( ) data entry.

☐   data output.

◯   mental step by analyst.

CASEBOOK EXAMPLE

Calculate the interest rate per period to achieve a future value for an annuity-due savings program.

The Problem

Calculate the interest rate required to grow $3000 per year payments into $300,000 in 25 years in a "savings type" annuity (annuity due, payment in advance).

The Approach

Calculate i for an ordinary annuity sinking fund where FV = $300,000 + $3000 and $n = 25$ years + 1 year (an interest-rate-equivalent ordinary annuity sinking fund); or calculate $i = (\mathrm{PMT}/\mathrm{FV})[(1 + i)^n - 1](1 + i)$; iteratively, where PMT = $3000, FV = $300,000, and $n = 25$.

Typical Keystroke Sequences

HP-22	HP-70/80	NOVUS 6020	Rockwell 204
Annuity	(3000)	(300000)	(300000)
SW–Begin	PMT	+	+
(3000)	(300000)	(3000)	(3000)
PMT	DSP	+	=
(300000)	PMT	0	ET
FV	+	+	FV
(25)	FV	amt	(25)
n	(25)	(25)	+
i	↑	+	(1)
9.51	(1)	(1)	=
	+	+	ET
	n	n	n
	i	( )	( )
	9.51	$\%i$	ET
		CHS	i
		PMT–Savings	TA
			PMT

Flowchart (NOVUS 6020):

( ) %i, CHS, PMT–Savings → [box] → ⟨ PMT = 3000 ? ⟩

No → (Guess new %i) → back to ( )

Yes → [i = Last Guess of $\%i$]

Flowchart (Rockwell 204):

n ( ) ET i TA PMT → [box] → ⟨ PMT = 3000 ? ⟩

No → (Guess new i) → back to ( )

Yes → [i = Last guess of i]

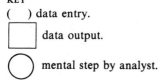

KEY

( ) data entry.

☐ data output.

◯ mental step by analyst.

67

CASEBOOK EXAMPLE

Calculate the interest rate per period of an ordinary annuity sinking fund.

The Problem

Calculate the interest rate required to grow $300,000 (a retirement nest egg) if annual payments of $3000 are made into a sinking fund for 25 years.

The Approach

Calculate $i = (PMT/FV)[(1 + i)^n - 1]$ (iteratively), where $PMT = \$3000$, FV $= \$300,000$, and $n = 25$ years.

Typical Keystroke Sequences

HP-70/80/22	NOVUS 6020	Rockwell 204
Annuity SW-end[a]		
(300000)	(300000)	(300000)
FV	amt	ET
(3000)	(25)	FV
PMT	n	(25)
(25)	( )←	ET
n	%i	n
i	CHS	( )←
10.11	PMT–Savings	ET
		i
		TA
		PMT

(Continued)

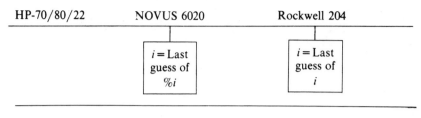

HP-70/80/22   NOVUS 6020   Rockwell 204

[NOVUS 6020] i = Last guess of %i

[Rockwell 204] i = Last guess of i

[a]HP-22 only.

( ) data entry.

☐ data output.

◯ mental step by analyst.

CASEBOOK EXAMPLE

Proceeds of a discounted promissory note.

The Problem—ILPW

Calculate the proceeds of a $3000, 90-day note discounted at 5%.

The Approach

$$\text{discount} = 0.05 \times \$3000 \times \frac{90}{360} = \$37.50$$

$$\text{proceeds} = \$3000 - \$37.50 = \$2962.50$$

Typical Keystroke Sequences

Basic Four-Function Algebraic Calculator	Basic Four-Function Reverse-Polish Calculator	HP-80
(3000)	(3000)	(90)
×	↑	n
(90)	(90)	(5)
÷	×	i
		(*Continued*)

Basic Four-Function Algebraic Calculator	Basic Four-Function Reverse-Polish Calculator	HP-80
(360)	(360)	(3000)
×	÷	FV
(.05)	(.05)	
=		INT
37.50	×	
CHS	37.50	37.50
+	CHS	(3000)
(3000)	↑	x⇄y
=	(3000)	−
2962.50	+	2962.50
	2962.50	

KEY

gold key.

( ) data entry.

☐ data output.

CASEBOOK EXAMPLE

Calculate the proceeds of a discounted interest-bearing promissory note.

The Problem

A note was given on June 12 to Mr. Smith by Mr. Sabin for engineering services. Mr. Smith accepted this note with the understanding that he would collect the $1000, plus interest at 10%, from Mr. Sabin at the end of 3 months. Mr. Smith decides to sell this instrument to his bank on July 15. It is discounted at 6.5%. Calculate the proceeds of the note.

Notice: When a note is discounted, the time is figured in exact days from the date it is "sold" (discounted) up to and including the date of maturity. This period of time is called the term of discount.

The Approach

Face of note	$1000
Interest	$\underline{\quad 25 \quad}$ ($0.1 \times 1000 \times 3/12$)
Maturity value	$1025
Date of maturity	September 12 (3 months from June 12)
Term of discount	59 days (July 15 to September 12)
Rate of discount	6.5%
Discount	$10.92 ($1025 \times 0.065 \times 59/360$)
Proceeds	$1014.08 ($1025 - 10.92$)

Typical Keystroke Sequences

Basic Four-Function Algebraic Calculator	Basic Four-Function Reverse-Polish Calculator
(1000)	(1000)
×	↑
(3)	(3)
÷	×
(12)	(12)
×	÷
(.1)	(.1)
=	×
$\boxed{25}$	$\boxed{25}$
+	(1000)
(1000)	+
=	$\boxed{1025}$
$\boxed{1025}$	STO
STO	↑
	(59)
×	×
(59)	(360)
÷	÷
(360)	(.065)
×	
(.065)	
=	

(*Continued*)

Basic Four-Function Algebraic Calculator	Basic Four-Function Reverse-Polish Calculator
10.92	×
−	10.92
RCL	RCL
=	$x \rightleftarrows y$
CHS	−
1014.08	1014.08

KEY
(   ) data entry.

[   ] data output.

CASEBOOK EXAMPLE

Calculate the proceeds of a non-interest-bearing draft.

The Problem

Calculate the proceeds of a $50,000 draft when a 0.25% collection fee
charged by the bank.

Typical Keystroke Sequences

Basic Four-Function Algebraic Calculator	Basic Four-Function Reverse-Polish Calculator
(50000)	(50000)
×	↑
(.25)	(.25)
÷	×
(100)	(100)
−	÷
	(Continued)

Basic Four-Function Algebraic Calculator	Basic Four-Function Reverse-Polish Calculator
(50000)	125
=	CHS
CHS	(50000)
49875	+
	49875

KEY
(   ) data entry.

☐   data output.

CASEBOOK EXAMPLE

Calculate the proceeds of an interest-bearing draft.

The Problem

Calculate the proceeds of a $50,000, 90-day draft, dated August 1 and bearing an interest rate of 6% per year. The draft is sold to the bank on September 15 at 8.5% and the bank charges a 0.25% collection fee.

The Approach

Face of note	$50,000
Interest (6% of $50,000 for 90 days)	750
Maturity value	$50,750
Maturity date (90 days after August 1)	October 30
Term of discount (September 15 to October 30)	45 days
Discount	$531.83
Collection fee (0.25% of $50,750)	$126.88
Proceeds ($50,750 − $531.83 − $126.88)	$50,091.29

Typical Keystroke Sequences

Basic Four-Function Algebraic Calculator	Basic Four-Function Reverse-Polish Calculator
(90)	(50000)
÷	↑
(360)	↑
×	(90)
(.06)	×
+	(360)
(1)	÷
×	(.06)
(50000)	×
=	
50750	+
×	50750
(45)	↑
÷	↑
(365)	(45)
×	×
(.085)	(365)
=	÷
531.83	(.085)
STO	×
(50750)	531.83
×	STO
(.25)	(50750)
÷	↑
(100)	↑
=	(.25)
126.88	×
+	(100)
RCL	÷
=	126.88
CHS	
+	

(*Continued*)

Basic Four-Function Algebraic Calculator	Basic Four-Function Reverse-Polish Calculator
(50750)	−
=	RCL
50091.29	−
	50091.29

KEY

(   ) data entry.

[   ] data output.

CASEBOOK EXAMPLE

Determine the yield for an annuity due (payments in advance).

The Problem

An $8000 car is leased for 3 years with monthly payments of $144.77 and a salvage value of $3641.33.* Determine the annual yield of this lease.

The Approach

This is an annuity-due problem. Most calculators solve ordinary annuity problems. An ordinary annuity that bears the *same yield* as this annuity-due problem and has the same payment amount, has a total number of pay periods equal to (*a*) the number of payments in the annuity-due less one, and (*b*) a present value that is the initial amount less the first payment.

It follows then that the annual yield is calculated with an *equivalent ordinary annuity* where the total number of pay periods is one less than the total number of periods in the annuity-due, and the payment amount is the same as the annuity-due payment but the present value is reduced by the amount of one payment.

*The present value of the salvage amount is computed first (see Casebook Example, p. 93) and found to be $3057.33, assuming a 6% interest rate.

Typical Keystroke Sequences

HP-22	HP-70/80	NOVUS 6020	Rockwell 204
Annuity			
SW—Begin	CLR	CE/C	TA
(8000)	(8000)	CE/C	CA
↑	↑	MR/MC	(8000)
(3057.33)	(3057.33)	MR/MC	−
−	− ⎫	(8000)	(3057.33)
PV	(164.18) ⎬ *	+	−
(164.18)	PMT ⎭	(3057.33)	(164.18) ⎫ *
PMT	−	−	= ⎭
(3)	PV	(164.18) ⎫ *	ET
▨	(3)	− ⎭	PV
n	K	M⁺	(3)
i	×	(3)	×
(12)	(1) ⎫ *	×	(12)
×	− ⎭	(12)	− ⎫ *
12.74	n	=	1 ⎭
	i	+ ⎫ *	=
	(12)	(1) ⎭	ET
	×	−	n
	12.74	n	( )
		( )	ET
		CHS	i/yr
		%i	AT
		(164.18)	PMT
		amt	
		PV–Loan	
		+	
		MR/MC	
		−	

HP-70/80 column flow: n, i, (12), ×, 12.74

NOVUS 6020 flow: ( ) ← Guess new %i

Rockwell 204 flow: ( ) ← Guess new i/yr

PMT = 164.18 ? No

Yes ↓

Yield = Last guess of i/yr

(Continued)

HP-22   HP-70/80   NOVUS 6020   Rockwell 204

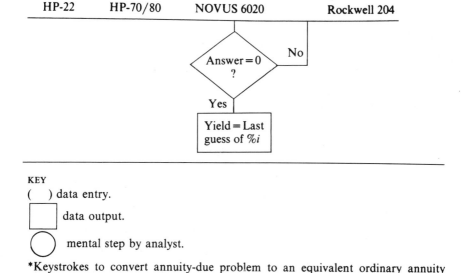

KEY

( ) data entry.

☐ data output.

◯ mental step by analyst.

*Keystrokes to convert annuity-due problem to an equivalent ordinary annuity problem.

▨ gold key.

CASEBOOK EXAMPLE

Calculate the interest rate per period in an annuity-due advance payment program (rents, leases, insurance, etc.).

The Problem

Calculate the interest rate a leasing firm realizes when it leases a $7000 car for 36 months at payments of $150. Assume 32% annual present value depreciation rate.*

*Note that to simplify the problem for this casebook example, the depreciation rate is on the present value. If the future value depreciation rate is used (-27.92%/year for this problem) and a typical cost of capital for leasing firms (6%), the problem would be solved in four steps:

Step 1. Calculate the 3-year depreciated future value of the car (-27.92%/year $= i$).

Step 2. Calculate the present value of the depreciated future value of the car (using 6%/year $= i$).

Step 3. Calculate the depreciation amount (DA).

Step 4. Calculate the interest rate earned on the depreciation amount (IR).

Steps 1 and 2 yield the same as a 32% per year present value depreciation rate.

The Approach

Step 1. Calculate the 3-year depreciated present value of the car (CV).

Step 2. Calculate the depreciation amount (DA).

Step 3. Calculate the interest rate earned on the depreciation amount (IR).

Typical Keystroke Sequences

HP-70/80	NOVUS 6020	Rockwell 204
CLR	CE/C	TA
(7000)	CE/C	CA
PV	MR/MC	
(32)	MR/MC	(7000)
CHS	(32)	ET
i	CHS	PV
(3)	M+	(32)
n	(7000)	ET
FV	×	+/−
CV = 2201.02	MR/MC	ET
CHS	%	i
DSP	+	(3)
PV	×	ET
+	MR/MC	n
DA = 4798.98	%	TA
STO	+	FV
Mᵃ	×	CV = 2201.02
CLR	MR/MC	−
(150)	%	(7000)
PMT	+	=
CHS	CV = 2201.02	ET
Mᵃ	(7000)	+/−
+	−	DA = 4798.98
PV	CHS	−
(36)	DA = 4798.98	(150)
↑	(150)	=
(1)	−	ET
−	MR/MC	PV

(*Continued*)

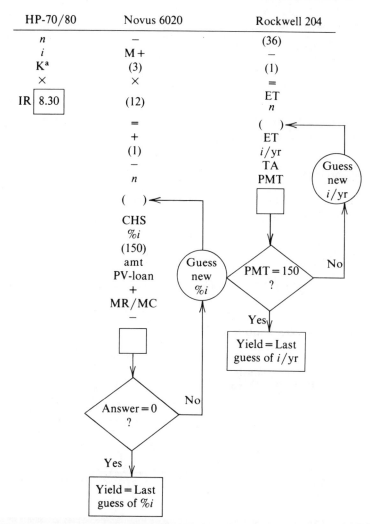

HP-70/80	Novus 6020	Rockwell 204

^aHP-70 only. Use memory with HP-22/80.

CASEBOOK DECISION

Compare two investment alternatives.

The Problem

Your business has $25,000 to invest in one of two bond issue alternatives:

Investment Parameters	Alternative 1	Alternative 2
Present value PV	$25,000	$25,000
Future value FV	$35,000	$50,000
Investment period n	3 years	7 years

Assuming all other factors are the same for both alternatives, decide which alternative is the most profitable.

The Approach

The most profitable alternative is the investment that gives the greatest interest rate per year.

The Method

Compute $i = \sqrt[n]{FV/PV} - 1$ for each alternative—select the alternative with the greatest i.

Typical Keystroke Sequences

Business Reverse-Polish (HP-70/80/22 type)		Business Algebraic (Rockwell-204 type)
Alternative 1	Alternative 2	
		Alternative 1
Annuity SW—End[a]		TA
CLR		CA
(25000)		(25000)
PV		ET
(35000)	(50,000)	PV
FV	FV	(3)
(3)	(7)	ET
n	n	n
i	i	$\langle i \rangle \leftarrow$
11.87	10.41	ET
		i
		TA — Estimate new i
		FV

(Continued)

Business
Algebraic
(Rockwell-204 type)

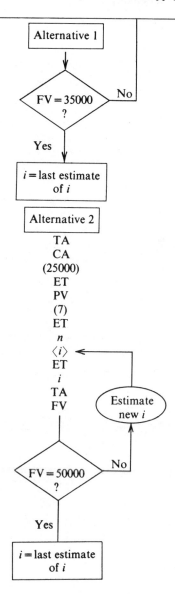

Alternative 1

FV = 35000
?

No

Yes

i = last estimate
of i

Alternative 2

TA
CA
(25000)
ET
PV
(7)
ET
n
$\langle i \rangle$
ET
i
TA
FV

Estimate
new i

FV = 50000
?

No

Yes

i = last estimate
of i

(Continued)

[a]HP = 22 only.

KEY ☐ data output.   ⟨ ⟩ data input.   ◯ mental step by analyst.

Decision

Invest in alternative 1.

CHAPTER 4

CALCULATING PRESENT AND FUTURE VALUES FOR BUSINESS DECISIONS

Comparison of business investment alternatives involves the calculation of present and future values of money. The example given in Chapter 1 ($100,000 invested for 5 years, which generates either a $27,000 per year cash flow for each year, totaling $135,000, or $150,000 at the end of the fifth year) is a case in point. It might seem that the second alternative earns $15,000 more than the first, and thus might be a better investment. This is not the case. The proper way to compare these investment alternatives is on a rate of return basis. To see this, imagine that you take out five separate 10.92% savings accounts and deposit $100,000 into them as follows:

Account 1	$24,341.87
Account 2	21,945.43
Account 3	19,784.91
Account 4	17,837.10
Account 5	16,090.69
Total of All accounts	$100,000.00

The present value of account 1 will grow to a future value of $27,000 at the end of the first year; account 2 will grow to a future value of $27,000 at the end of the second year; the remaining accounts will grow to future values of $27,000 at the end of the third, fourth, and fifth years, respectively. In this sense the first investment alternative with five future value cash flows of $27,000 each has an **equivalent** return of 10.92% on the present value of the money deposited in each account.*

The second alternative, receiving $150,000 at the end of the fifth year, is

---

*The cash flow just discussed **is not** the equivalent of putting $100,000 in a 10.92% rate of return investment and withdrawing $27,000 each year for 5 years.

merely **equivalent** to depositing the entire $100,000 in an 8.45% savings account. Clearly the alternative that is equivalent to the 10.92% annual rate of return is a better investment.

This discussion illustrates that the decisions involving time payments or timed receipt of earnings must be compared on the basis of an equivalent annual rate of return (often called internal rate of return). It also illustrates that a firm grasp of the relationships between present and future values is essential for understanding investment alternatives. This is particularly true when one is trying to evaluate an investment in terms of its **equivalents**. Summarizing then: when investments are analyzed (and present value is known), rate of return is used as the means of comparison.

Rate of return is not the only way to compare investments, to be sure. This is particularly important, however, when comparing alternatives involving long lives. The most commonly used approach to comparing investment alternatives is to compute the **net present value** (NPV) of the alternatives. Net present value is usually computed according to the following procedure (also see Appendix A):

Step 1. Discount the future values of all cash revenues (outputs) generated by an investment to their values in the first year of the investments. Usually the first year is the year the investment is being analyzed, thus is called the present value of the revenues. The annual discount rate is the rate of return *you want to achieve* with the investment.

Step 2. Discount the future values of all cash investments (inputs) required by the investment program to the first year of the program. Usually the first year is the present year and is called the present value of the costs. The annual discount rate is the rate of return *you can get* by lending the cash investments until they are due by the investment program. Usually investment programs require only an "up front" cash payment and then they generate cash returns. In this case the future value of cash investments is a single number that is not discounted.

Step 3. Sum the present values of cash revenues and subtract the present values of all cash investments (costs) to determine the net present value of all cash flows in the investment. If the present value of the discounted revenues exceeds the present value of the discounted costs (investments), the net present value of the investment is positive and the investment rate of return exceeds your desired rate of return—GOOD! If the NPV is negative, the investment rate of return falls short of your desires—BAD!

Government funding decisions for major programs is an interesting and informative example of the use of NPV. The present values of national programs are determined on the basis of *social discount rates* (measures of social value) established by the Office of Management and Budget (OMB) (formerly the Bureau of the Budget). For example, the Defense Department project rate is nominally 10%; Health, Education, and Welfare project discounts are typically 4 to 5%; and certain projects associated with the National Aeronautics and Space Administration are discounted at 10%. To compare one national program with another economists compute the cost of a program in present value dollars and escalate the cost with the inflation schedules provided by OMB. The future value costs are then discounted at their social discount rate and summed to determine the net present value of the agency's program. In this way OMB is able to compare the social worth of national programs from different agencies on a net present value basis and decide which generates the greatest social return. In a similar manner a businessman can compare investment opportunities within his business by establishing "value discount rates" for profit centers within his business.

In business and government alike, it is also important to consider the total program cost in terms of escalated dollars, not just in discounted dollars, because the sum of the escalated dollars for the total life cycle of a program is the amount of *money* (actual cash dollars) that a business (or the nation) must give to the program over its lifetime. Costs in "then-year" dollars are essential for consideration as part of the decision on "new start" programs. A third factor that is increasing in importance is the peak annual funding level associated with an investment program. Here the objective is to escalate the costs computed in present value dollars to future value dollars, and to determine (a) which element of the cash flow is the peak and (b) its amount. Currently OMB is attempting to make most of our major programs satisfy both a peak annual funding limit and a total program cost, a practice familiar to most businessmen.

Similar types of analyses must be conducted to make effective decisions for the smallest of businesses. The issue of peak future value cash flow requirements, present value of investment alternatives, and the inflated/discounted present value of investment program *life-cycle costs* associated with, for example, a product development program are all financial analyses that are required to support business decisions. Such calculations are simple and extremely fast on the pocket calculator. This is particularly important and useful for managers newly appointed to their positions. A recent appointee can learn the financial base of operations of even a fairly large business within a short period of time by having the finance manager present the financial operations in a form that can be set up on a business pocket calculator.

4.1   PRESENT AND FUTURE VALUES DEFINED

Present value and future value are names given to a number of different terms used in financial analysis. Depending on the financial discipline, **present value** can mean:

- The principal–in an interest calculation.
- The beginning bank account balance–in a small business, rate-of-return calculation.
- The original amount–in certain draft and note calculations.
- The selling price–in a real estate mortgage.
- The initial balance–in an annuity calculation.

Similarly, future value can mean:

- The principal plus interest–in a loan calculation.
- The final balance–in a business rate-of-return calculation.
- The face value of a note–when computing discounts.
- The worth of a compound amount.
- The worth of a lump-sum investment.
- The worth of a sinking fund.

Thus present value and future value can have many different meanings for a financial analyst. From the calculator's viewpoint, however, they have very definite meanings specified by the equations solved in the calculator. Fortunately the same equations are used in the same way by the different financial disciplines. These equations make clear that no matter what specific meaning is given to present value and future value, the general definitions are:

present value = the value of money, or its equivalent, at the present time or at a time that is the beginning of a time-value-of-money calculation

future value = the value of money, or its equivalent, at some time in the future. The future value of money is usually associated with the value of money at the end of a time-value-of-money calculation

4.2   PRESENT VALUE IN SIMPLE INTEREST CALCULATIONS

If we rewrite the simple interest formula in terms of the present value, the interest can be written as

$$\text{INT} = \frac{n}{360} \times i \times \text{PV} \quad \text{(ordinary simple interest)}$$

where

$$INT = \text{simple interest}$$

$$n = \text{number of periods}$$

$$i = \text{interest } rate \text{ per period}$$

$$PV = \text{present value}$$

Then the present value can be solved for in the following manner:

$$PV = \frac{INT \times 360}{ni}$$

This formula is used in simple interest calculations in the keystroke sequences shown in the casebook examples for this chapter.

The future value in interest calculations is related to present value according to the formula

$$FV = PV + INT$$

4.3　FUTURE VALUE AND DISCOUNTED NOTES

By definition, a discounted note is based on a percentage of the future value of the note. The relationship between the note discount and the future value is given by

$$\text{discount} = FV \times i \times \frac{n}{360} = D$$

Remember that the future value is the face value of a note and may involve a future value computed on the basis of simple or compound interest.

A useful and easy calculation is to compute the yield on a discounted note, trade acceptance, bill of exchange, or other form of draft. This calculation is based on the formula

$$\text{yield} = FV - D = FV\left(1 - \frac{i \times n}{360}\right)$$

The beginning financial analyst should remember that interest for notes and discounted notes for small amounts and/or short periods of time is usually simple or accrued, and compound interest is seldom involved. However when interest is compounded, the relationships between the future value and present value of the compounded amount must be used to calculate the future value (FV) in the yield equation. Fortunately most of these relationships are built into the business pocket calculator.

4.4 PRESENT AND FUTURE VALUE CALCULATIONS IN COMPOUND INTEREST CALCULATIONS

The simplest relationship that can be developed for compound calculations is

$$FV = PV(1+i)^n$$

Although it is not necessary to understand the compound interest formula to use the pocket calculator, it is worthwhile to examine this one formula because it shows the basis for the growth factor

$$(1+i)^n$$

which is encountered frequently in financial formulas.

First, note that over *one compounding period* the simple interest on a present value (principal) is given by

$$INT_1 = PV_1 \times i$$

The future value for the first compounding period is

$$FV_1 = PV_1 + INT_1$$
$$FV_1 = PV_1(1+i)$$

This future value is then set equal to the present value for the next step. Said mathematically:

$$PV_2 = FV_1$$

It follows then that for the second compounding period the equation

$$FV_2 = PV_2(1+i)$$

computes the future value of the principal and compounded interest. But since

$$PV_2 = PV_1(1+i)$$

it follows that

$$FV_2 = PV_1(1+i)(1+i)$$

or, in simplest terms

$$FV_2 = PV_1(1+i)^2$$

We can expect then that

$$FV_3 \quad = \quad PV_1(1+i)^3$$

$$\vdots \qquad \qquad \vdots$$

$$FV_n \quad = \quad PV_1(1+i)^n$$

4.5 ANNUITIES

Strictly speaking, annuities are cash flows made on a yearly basis. In usual financial parlance, an annuity is a series of cash flows made at equal intervals that may be less than, equal to, or greater than a year. The interval length is called the period of the annuity or the annuity period. An example of an annuity would be a contract to provide retirement income such as established in trust funds or retirement programs. There are two classes of annuities:

- An annuity "certain," which is characterized by the continuance of payments for a specified number of periods. Calculations are based on the assumption that each payment is certain and will be made when due.
- A "contingent" annuity, in which each payment depends on the continuance of some prespecified condition, such as the life of the annuity recipient.

The annuity certain can be considered from two viewpoints: (1) the perpetuity annuity, in which a regular series of payments is made unendingly, and (2) the ordinary annuity that terminates at a predefined number of annuity periods.

Contingent annuities are used in insurance and pension plans and are based on a risk-sharing principle. In these two cases the price of an annuity that pays a given sum for life is based on the life expectancy of the annuity recipient at the time the annuity begins. The concept of insurance is made feasible because the recipient joins with a large number of other people of about the same age in establishing a fund, calculated on the basis of mortality tables, that will be sufficient to pay each person the life income agreed upon. Since some will live longer than others and will receive more payments, they will contribute more to the fund, whereas others will not live long enough to receive all the contributions they have made. This risk-sharing principle makes it possible to purchase an insurance annuity that guarantees much higher payments than could be obtained if the same amount of money were invested at interest. The obvious disadvantage is that when an annuity recipient dies, nothing is left for his heirs.

The types of annuities considered in this book are limited to certain annuities, and of these only ordinary annuities and annuities due are discussed. Since the perpetuity is a special type of ordinary annuity, it too is covered.

4.6 ORDINARY ANNUITY PRESENT AND FUTURE VALUE CALCULATIONS

Annuities are programs under which regular payments are made, usually into a fund to "sink" a debt, such as a bond debt, or to retire a loan (direct reduction of an amortized loan). Sinking funds have a future value that is built on the basis of payments made at regular intervals. The formula for the future value (FV) of a regular equal-payment annuity is

$$FV = PMT \frac{(1+i)^n - 1}{i}$$

where i is the interest rate per compounding period, n is the number of periods, and PMT is the payment amount or annuity amount. This calculation computes the future value of a sinking fund or ordinary annuity. This formula is implemented in the HP-22, HP-70, the HP-80, and the Rockwell-204, and a few other business pocket calculators. It is easy to implement, even on simple calculators that do not have the exponentiation key. The keystroke sequences for calculating the future value of an annuity such as discussed here are seen in Table 4-1.

The direct reduction loan annuity formula involves the present value of the annuity principal required to make a series of amortized payments (PMT) where the annuity principal is operating at an annual interest rate (i) and the payments are made over (n) periods. The formula for the present value required for such an annuity is

$$PV = PMT \frac{1 + (1+i)^{-n}}{i}$$

This formula also appears complicated but is deceptively easy to implement on either a calculator with exponentiation or a simple four-function calculator. As you might expact, these financial functions are built into the business pocket calculators. Keystroke sequences for calculating annuity payments are shown in Table 4-2.

Table 4-1 Typical Keystroke Sequences for Calculating the Future Value of an Ordinary Annuity

Basic Four-Function Algebraic Calculator	Algebraic Business Calculator	Reverse-Polish Business Calculator
$(i)^a$	(i)	(i)
+	ET	i
(1)	i	(n)
=	(n)	n
×	ET	(PMT)
=	n	PMT
=		$\boxed{FV}$
= $\Big\}$ $(n-1)$ times^b	(PMT)	
.		
.	ET	
.	PMT	
=	TA	
−		
(1)	$\boxed{FV}$	
÷		
$(i)^a$		
×		
(PMT)		
=		
$\boxed{FV}$		

^{a}In decimal flow
^{b}Assumes chain multiply.
KEY
( ) data entry.
$\boxed{}$ data output.

Table 4-2 Typical Keystroke Sequences for Calculating the Present Value of Ordinary Annuities

Basic Four-Function Algebraic Calculator	Algebraic Business Calculator	Reverse-Polish Business Calculator
$(i)^a$	(i)	(i)
+	ET	i
(1)	i	(n)
×	(n)	n

(Continued)

91

Table 4-2 (*Continued*)

Basic Four-Function Algebraic Calculator	Algebraic Business Calculator	Reverse-Polish Business Calculator
= ⎫	ET	(PMT)
= ⎪	n	PMT
= ⎬ $(n-1)$ times ^{b}	(PMT)	
. ⎪	ET	PV
. ⎪	PMT	
= ⎭	TA	
$1/x^c$		
CHS	PV	
+		
(1)		
÷		
$(i)^a$		
×		
(PMT)		
=		
PV		

^{a} In decimal flow.
^{b}Assumes chain multiply.
^{c} $\left.\begin{array}{l} \div \\ = \\ = \end{array}\right\}$ $1/x$ on some calculators

KEY
( ) data entry.
□ data output.

4.7 ANNUITIES DUE

Two other types of calculations that appear in the casebook examples for this chapter are those for annuities due. Annuities due are usually associated with savings, rents, leases, and so on. In an annuity due the first payment is made on the first day of the loan period. By contrast, in ordinary annuities the first payment is made at the end of the first period.*
The formula for the present value of an annuity due is

$$PV = PMT \frac{1 + (1+i)^{-n}}{i} (1+i)$$

*See Appendix A.

The future value calculation is

$$FV = PMT \frac{(1+i)^n - 1}{i} (1+i)$$

These formulas are used for calculating, for example, the monthly deposit (to be made at the beginning of each period) that is required to amass a given sum when the number of periods and the interest rate per period are known. This is to be compared with an ordinary annuity calculation, which determines the periodic payment to be made into a sinking fund (FV known) or to retire an amortized loan (PV known) and when the number of periods and the interest rate per period are known and the payment is made at the end of the period.

4.8 SUMMARY

Investment alternatives require a means for common comparison. One of the most frequently used approaches is to consider investment alternatives at the same time. Either the future value or the present value can be used.

The evaluation of many business decisions reduces to understanding of the relationships between interest, number of pay periods, present value, future value, and payment amount. Whereas the financial analyst usually derives the cash flow formulas and makes algebraic comparisons to determine the optimum business operation, it is now possible for relatively inexperienced financial analysts to do this numerically with a pocket calculator in a very short time. The significance of this is that any businessman should be able to find the time to become even more intimately acquainted with financial concepts underlying his business and, if the author's experience is any basis, a surprising number of unexpected findings may be uncovered.

CASEBOOK EXAMPLE

Calculate the present value (PV) of a compounded amount.

The Problem

Compute the amount that should be invested to accrue $25,000 at 7.25% in 5 years.

The Approach

Calculate $PV = FV/(1+i)^n$, where i is a decimal (0.0725), FV is \$25,000, and n is 5.

Typical Keystroke Sequences

Basic Algebraic Calculator	Basic Reverse-Polish Calculator	HP-70/80/22	NOVUS 6020	Rockwell 204
CL	CL	CLR	CE/C	TA
(1)	(1)	(7.25)	CE/C	CA
+	↑	i	(7.25)	(7.25)
(.0725)	(.0725)	(25000)	%i	ET
=	+	FV	(25000)	i
y^x	(5)	(5)	amt	(25000)
(5)	y^x	n	(5)	ET
=	(1)	PV	n	FV
$1/x$	$x \rightleftarrows y$	17617.87	CHS	(5)
×	÷		PV—Interest	ET
(25000)	(25000)		17,617.88	n
=	×			TA
17617.87	17617.87			PV
				17617,87

KEY
( ) data entry.
☐ data output.

CASEBOOK EXAMPLE

Calculate the future value (FV) of a compounded amount.

The Problem

Calculate the future value of \$3600 for 4 years at 8% if interest is compounded semiannually.

The Approach

Compute $FV = PV(1 + i/2)^8$, where 8 is the number of compounding periods, $i/2$ is the semiannual interest rate, and PV is $3600.

Typical Keystroke Sequences

Basic Algebraic Calculator	Basic Reverse-Polish Calculator	HP-70/80/22	NOVUS 6020	Rockwell 204
(8)	(8)	(8)	(8)	(8)
÷	↑	↑	÷	÷
(100)	(100)	(2)	(2)	(2)
÷	÷	÷	=	=
(2)	(2)	i	%i	ET
+	÷	(8)	(8)	i
(1)	(1)	n	n	(8)
=	+	(3600)	(3600)	ET
y^x	(8)	PV	amt	n
(8)	y^x	FV	FV–interest	(3600)
=	(3600)	$\boxed{4926.85}$	$\boxed{4926.85}$	ET
×	×			PV
(3600)	$\boxed{4926.85}$			TA
=				FV
$\boxed{4926.85}$				$\boxed{4926.85}$

KEY
( ) data entry.

$\boxed{}$ data output.

CASEBOOK EXAMPLE

Calculate the future value (FV) of an ordinary annuity sinking fund.

The Problem

Calculate the future value of $100 per month (paid at the end of each month from the start of the program) paid into an 8% investment for 10 years.

The Approach

Calculate $FV = PMT \dfrac{(1+i)^n - 1}{i}$ where $PMT = \$100$, n is 120 months, and $i = 8/(100 \times 12)$.

Typical Keystroke Sequences

Basic Algebraic Calculator	Basic Reverse-Polish Calculator	HP-70/80/22	NOVUS 6020	Rockwell 204
(8)	(8)	(8)	(8)	(8)
÷	↑	↑	CHS	ET
(100)	(100)	(12)	%i	i/yr
÷	÷	÷	(10)	(10)
(12)	(12)	i	CHS	×
STO	÷	(120)	n	(12)
+	STO	n	(100)	=
(1)	(1)	(100)	amt	ET
=	+	PMT	FV—Savings	n
y^x	(120)	FV	⌐18294.61⌐	(100)
(120)	y^x	⌐18294.60⌐		ET
=	↑			PMT
−	(1)			TA
(1)	−			FV
÷	RCL			⌐18294.50⌐
RCL	÷			
×	(100)			
100	×			
=	⌐18294.60⌐			
⌐18294.60⌐				

KEY

(   ) data entry.

 data output.

CASEBOOK EXAMPLE

Calculate the future value of an annuity-due savings program.

The Problem*

Calculate the future value of a savings account where $365 per month is paid into the 7.25% account for 20 years.

The Approach

Calculate $FV = PMT\dfrac{(1+i)^n - n}{i}(1+i)$, where $PMT = 365$, $i = 7.25/(100 \times 12)$, and $n = 240$.

Typical Keystroke Sequences

Basic Algebraic Calculator	Basic Reverse-Polish Calculator	HP-22	HP-70/80	NOVUS 6020	Rockwell 204
(7.25)	(7.25)	Annuity SW–Begin	(7.25)	(7.25)	(7.25)
÷	↑	(7.25)	K	CHS	ET
(100)	(100)	▨	÷	%i	i/yr
÷	÷	i	i	(365)	(365)
(12)	(12)	(365)	(365)	amt	ET
+	÷	PMT	PMT	20	PMT
(1)	(1)	(20)	(240)	CHS	(240)
STO	+	▨	n	n	ET
y^x	STO	n	FV	FV—Savings	n
(240)	↑	FV	(1)	M+	TA
=	(240)	197200.23	DSP	(7.25)	FV
−	y^x		i	÷	(7.25)
(1)	(1)		(100)	(100)	÷
÷	−		÷	÷	

(Continued)

*This problem illustrates that typical calculators sometimes give different answers to the same problem. Correct answer is $197,200.2524.

Basic Algebraic Calculator	Basic Reverse-Polish Calculator	HP-22	HP-70/80	NOVUS 6020	Rockwell 204
(7.25)	RCL		+	(12)	(100)
×	(1)		×	×	÷
(100)	−		197200.25	MR/MC	(12)
×	÷			=	+
(12)	RCL			M+	(1)
×	×			MR/MC	×
RCL	(365)			197200.56	ET
×	×				ET
(365)	197200.24				FV
=					=
197200.27					197198.40

KEY

( ) data entry.

▨ gold key.

☐ data output.

CASEBOOK EXAMPLE

Convert a monthly annuity-due payment to an annual annuity-due payment that has the same yield.

The Problem

Calculate the single annual payment that provides a 10% yield and is equivalent to $350 per month one-year rental.

The Approach

Hold the present value of the annuity-due the same for both payment schedules. Calculate $PV = PMT \dfrac{1 + (1+i)^{-n}}{i}(1+i)$ where $PMT = 350$, $n = 12$, and $i = 10/(100 \times 12)$. Then calculate PMT with PV = results of first calculation, $n = 1$, and $i = 10/100$.

Typical Keystroke Sequences

HP-22	HP-70/80	NOVUS 6020	Rockwell 204
Annuity SW—Begin	(10)	(10)	(10)
(10)	K	÷	ET
▨ (gold key)	÷	(100)	i/yr
i	i	÷	(12)
(1)	(12)	(12)	ET
▨ (gold key)	n	×	n
n	(350)	+	(350)
(350)	PMT	(1)	ET
PMT	PV	+	PMT
PV	(1)	M+	TA
4014.25	DSP	(350)	PV
	i	amt	(10)
	(100)	(10)	÷
	÷	CHS	(100)
	+	%i	÷
	×	(12)	(12)
	4014.25	n	+
		PV-Loan	(1)
		×	×
		MR/MC	ET
		=	ET
		÷	PV
		(1.1)	=
		=	4014.25
		amt	
		(1)	
		n	
		(10)	
		%i	
		CHS	
		PMT—Loan	
		4014.25	

KEY
( ) data entry.

☐ data output.

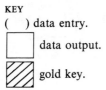 gold key.

99

CASEBOOK DECISION

Calculate periodic payments or lump-sum payment.

The Problem

Examination of your life insurance program reveals that you have two options for life insurance settlement. Your beneficiary can receive either $400 per month for 20 years or a lump sum of $58,149.06. If you invest the lump sum you can realize 5.5% per year. Select one of the two alternative payback insurance payment programs.

The Approach

Calculate the net present value of the annuity and compare it with the lump sum payment. Discount the annuity at 5.5% as a means of comparing it with the lump sum investment yield.

Typical Keystroke Sequences

HP-70/80/22*	NOVUS 6020	Rockwell 204
CLR	CE/C	TA
(5.5)	CE/C	CA
↑	(5.5)	(5.5)
(12) $\}b$	CHS^b	ET
÷	%i	i/yr
i	(400)	(400)
(400)	amt	ET
PMT	(20)	PMT
(20)	CHS^b	(20)
↑	n	× $\}b$
(12) $\}b$	PV—Loan	(12)
×		
	58149.09	=
n		ET
PV		n
58149.06		TA
		PV
		58149.24

(*Continued*)

*HP-22 only: annuity switch to "end."

[a] Exact answer is $58,149.05710; differences due to rounding off.

[b] Conversion to monthly periods.

KEY

(   ) data entry.

data output.

The Decision

Both alternatives have the same net present value. The decision must be based on other factors, such as the current rate of return that can be achieved on the lump sum payment compared with the insurance rate of return. Generally the rate of return established by an insurance company will be more stable but lower than the rate that can be obtained by managing your own annuity program.

CHAPTER 5

PAYMENTS AND NUMBER OF PERIODS IN BUSINESS DECISIONS

Chapter 4 addressed the problem of comparing a program of investment return paid periodically with a return paid only once (say at the end of the investment period). We found that multiple payoffs are a *special case* of a single payoff. The principles that apply to the latter also apply to the former. Since it is important not to confuse the present value and future value analysis methods discussed previously with those presented in this chapter, let us quickly review the present value techniques discussed before.

When comparing purchase alternatives that require payoff in, say, 5 years and 3 years, the present value comparison method is to discount the 5-year and 3-year future values to their present values and select the program that has the least present value. For the first alternative this means working backward from the future value at 5 years to the present value; in the second case we work backward from the future value at 3 years to the present value. In this way the payoff comparison is made in present value dollars. Obviously the same principle applies to a distributed cash flow, regardless of whether the amount of the payment is the same, whether payments are at the beginning or end of a pay period, and whether payment intervals are the same. No matter how the payoff is made, future value alternatives can be compared in a straightforward way on the basis of the present value of the total of all cash flows.

A different type of problem arises when the present value of goods or services and the desired rate of return are known and you wish to offer an attractive **payment program** to your buyer. A related problem is to determine a payment program in a sinking fund that will permit the procurement of a capital asset. Here the future value is established, the rate of return is determined, and a payment program is selected that fits the ability of the business to pay.

This chapter then is concerned with computing combinations of payment periods and payment amounts that achieve desired rates of return or satisfy known future and/or present values. In a credit economy, payment programs (for both income and outgo) are fundamental tradeoffs in a business system to determine *what can be afforded*. Because time and money are directly related, the business manager's decisions often involve tradeoffs between the number and amount of payments in a cash flow situation (independent of whether future value or present value is fixed and desired rate of return is specified). The casebook examples in this chapter are based on the material covered in Chapters 1 to 3. A few sections are devoted here to terminology and to problems that involve payments and number of pay periods. Those already familiar with the financial terminology of payment programs may proceed directly to the casebook examples.

5.1 TYPES OF PAYMENT PROGRAMS

The business decisions related to payments usually fall into two categories: choosing a payment program for goods or services you wish to procure or selecting a payment program to offer to someone who wishes to procure your goods or services.

When you are the offerer, you must determine a set of payment alternatives that you would find acceptable after establishing a desired rate of return.* The present value is the price of your goods or services, and the future value is the amount you wish to receive considering that the income is produced over a period of time.

In the reverse of this situation, someone is providing payment alternatives (future values) to you and you must select that which is most favorable for your particular circumstances. In this case the present value is the present price of the offerer's goods or services. This is a present value problem, and payments are one of the parameters established by (*a*) the offerer's desired rate of return and (*b*) the number of periods over which he will allow the price of the goods or services to be procured.

---

*On a short-term payment program the rate of return might be less than on a long-term program because of the risk associated with long-term economic forecasting.

A third alternative, seldom pursued* in business transactions, is worth considering for every decision involving significant financial consequences when you are the buyer in a payment program. This approach consists of identifying a payment program that favors your business and making a counteroffer.

5.2 CALCULATING PAYMENTS, NUMBER OF PAY PERIODS, AND NUMBER OF COMPOUNDING PERIODS

The preceding chapters covered three of the five important parameters in financial analysis for business decisions. This covers the last two—payments and number of pay periods. The equations used to compute the number of time periods and payments are identical to the equations discussed in Chapters 3 and 4, but here the payments or number of periods are computed in terms of the other parameters.† For example, when considering simple interest the equation for computing the number of periods is

$$n = \frac{\text{INT}}{\text{PV} \times i}$$

For compound interest calculations the number of conversion periods is given by

$$n = \frac{\log \dfrac{\text{FV}}{\text{PV}}}{\log(1 + i)}$$

For ordinary annuities and annuities due, respectively, the number of pay periods is given by

$$n = \frac{\log\left(\dfrac{i \times \text{FV}}{\text{PMT}} + 1\right)}{\log(1 + i)} = \frac{\log\left[\left(\dfrac{i \times \text{PV}}{\text{PMT}} - 1\right)^{-1}\right]}{\log(1 + i)}$$

In a similar way, the number of payments associated with ordinary annuities and annuities due can be computed according to the relation-

---

*Generally a seller offers a payment program and a buyer accepts it or not—it's as simple as that.

†The time period calculations associated with discounting are not discussed here for the obvious reason that notes and drafts are discounted by a bank on the basis of the time over which the note is discounted (or the discount period), which is not typically a parameter that is computed.

ships

$$PMT = \frac{i \times PV}{1 + (1+i)^{-n}} = \frac{i \times FV}{(1+i)^n - 1} \qquad \text{(ordinary annuity)}$$

$$PMT = \frac{i \times PV}{\left[1 + (1+i)^{-n}\right](1+i)} = \frac{i \times FV}{\left[(1+i)^n - 1\right](1+i)} \qquad \text{(annuity due)}$$

Like other financial functions, these can be solved on the business pocket calculator by a keystroke sequence with as few as four keystrokes. Interestingly, only a few more keystrokes are required to solve the equations on the four-function calculator.

The calculation of the number of conversion periods usually produces a number that *is not* an integer (whole number). For example, when computing the number of conversion periods to accumulate $10,000 in a sinking fund that earns interest at a rate of 10% per year with annual payments into the fund of $1000, the pocket calculator solves the equation

$$n = \frac{\log_{10}\left(\dfrac{0.1 \times 10,000}{1000} + 1\right)}{\log_{10}(1 + 0.1)}$$

and gives the result

$$n = 7.27$$

Obviously the equation computes fractional parts of a sinking fund conversion period even though the offerer does not. No resolution of this particular problem is possible using either a table or a calculator. How then does one interpret or use 7.27 years in a program of annual conversions? One views the calculation as a means of getting in the neighborhood of a whole number of conversion periods. Here a 10% per year, $1000 per year sinking fund will generate $9487.17 over a 7-year period, or it will produce $11,435.89 over an 8-year period. Thus solving for the number of conversion periods based on the $10,000 goal identifies the interval that is bounded by two whole numbers that are viable conversion periods. Iterating the payments, interest rate, or both, will permit the finding of a near-integer value of the number of periods if desired.

5.3 THE NATURE OF TIME AND MONEY CALCULATIONS

The discussions of interest, present value, future value, number of pay periods, and payment in this and the preceding chapters deal specifically with various types of financial transactions and analyses. The casebook examples demonstrate the management decision process and the manner in which financial analysis supports business decisions. It is important now to consider the more general nature of time and money calculations. The organization of Chapters 3 to 5 in terms of calculating n, i, PMT, PV, and FV is not accidental. In fact, these are keys that appear on the keyboards of most of the commonly used business calculators. This is significant in and of itself in that the following general statement applies: virtually all the financial calculations of interest to the business manager are combinations of only five parameters. These parameters are:

1. The number of conversion periods.
2. The interest rate per period.
3. The payment per period.
4. The present value of the money in the calculation.
5. The future value of the money in the calculation.

Thus with these five keys and the financial functions that relate them, the business manager can analyze almost all financial aspects of many business decisions.

Although some financial analysts are aware of this fact, most are accustomed to manipulating these relationships only *in their specific disciplines*. Less common is the analyst who can manipulate these factors in many financial disciplines. In fact, it is unusual to find an interdisciplinary analyst who knows that a number of financial disciplines that appear to be quite different are based on the same financial concept and use identical mathematics.

A specific example illustrates this point. It was reported to me by A. J. Laymon of the Hewlett-Packard Corporation that an HP-70 calculator was returned to their Marketing Department, accompanied by a letter stating that the equations used by the device were wrong. The writer of the letter offered a set of corrected equations, but on examination it was found that the "correct" equations were identical to the Hewlett-Packard equations, only the symbols for the variables were different. Unthinkable? Perhaps not—the author has found no common symbolism or equation format in any of the more sophisticated business mathematics or finance books. If anything, the symbolism appears to be quite confusing, especially when an analyst models the dynamics of a fiscal process using differential equations.

Discussions of annuities provide another illustration of the confusion due to ambiguous terminology that can arise in financial analysis. Some annuities are assumed to be paid at the end of an interest-bearing period and others are assumed to be paid at the beginning. For example, rent, leases, and insurance payments are all calculated on the assumption that the payment is made at the beginning of the interest-bearing period. The payments required for a direct reduction loan and ordinary sinking fund are computed on the assumption that the payments are made at the end of the interest-bearing period. This is the difference between an ordinary annuity and an annuity due. The payments are made in two different ways for different purposes, however both carry the same common name— annuity. The equations for computing the payments for these annuities are

$$\text{PMT} = \frac{i \times \text{FV}}{(1+i)^n - 1} \qquad \text{ordinary annuity}$$

$$\text{PMT} = \frac{i \times \text{FV}}{\left[(i+1)^n - 1\right](1+i)} \qquad \text{annuity due}$$

Although the equations look quite different and the words used in each financial discipline are not the same (e.g., rent, pension, payment, loan payment, insurance premium, installment), in fact the results differ only slightly. It is not surprising to find that a banker, accustomed to using the ordinary annuity calculations when handling mortgages and consumer finance loans, compares the results of one of the business pocket calculators with what he finds in his interest tables and is quite satisfied with the results, whereas an insurance underwriter or real estate leasing agent compares the payment calculation results from a business pocket calculator with his annuity (due) calculating tables and finds them somewhat different. This has actually happened. The Hewlett-Packard Corporation has received letters stating that the HP-70 "annuity" calculation is wrong, even though the HP-70 Handbook makes clear the distinction between annuities due and ordinary annuities. Of course the difference is easily handled with only a few keystrokes on any of the business calculators. The point is that in financial analysis certain specific words have many meanings, mathematically speaking, while many different words have only one meaning from a mathematical viewpoint. The word *annuity* is an example of the former and the words *principal, mortgage, price,* and *initial balance,* are examples of the latter, since these are all the present value in an annuity formula.

What can be said precisely is that there are only five parameters in most business-related financial calculations. The business manager who understands this and knows the interrelationships between the five variables is armed with the tools to work in *many* financial disciplines. Thus the manager can require an insurance analyst to put the insurance require- ments analysis in a form that he, the manager, can easily understand, and with just a few more keystrokes he can duplicate and check the annuity calculations of the insurance analyst. In a similar manner, the businessman has the ability to do check-and-balance in all financial dealings with bankers, buyers, finance companies, stock brokers, and others. In a word, these five parameters are the keys to financial analysis. Coincidentally they are the keys on the keyboard of the business pocket calculators. All that remains is to understand the financial functions that interrelate the param- eters. Table 2-5 shows all the twelve financial functions that can be computed on the pocket calculator. These twelve comprise all the calcula- tions that are necessary for a business manager to conduct financial analyses required to support almost any business decision.

Reflect for a moment that there are only five parameters interrelated by twelve functions that are required to perform virtually all financial calcula- tions in making effective business decisions. The businessman and finan- cial analyst involved in interdisciplinary financial analyses might want to memorize these twelve formulas and analyze them to determine their sensitivities (their derivatives) and in general the details of their manipula- tion. The businessman who owns a business pocket calculator has these twelve functions electronically implemented in his pocket calculator; thus he need not memorize the formulas—he can experiment with his calculator to learn these relationships empirically, all without actually knowing the formulas but only understanding how they apply.

Taking the time to experiment with these financial functions on a pocket calculator should prove to be of immeasurable value. You will probably find that certain results are counterintuitive until you have thought your way through the twelve basic financial problems. This is a small price to pay to become a fairly effective interdisciplinary financial analyst. A few weeks devoted to study in the evenings of these financial problems as related to your business can pay off by increasing the rate of return of your business as you learn more about its cash flow. You will have armed yourself with the fundamental tools of the financial analyst for making clear the basic financial concepts underlying business. The author is convinced that the business analyst who masters these twelve formulas (not necessarily algebraically or mathematically, but rather by being able to use a calculator correctly in performing financial calculations) can set very high standards in his business by requiring his associates to justify ex- penditures and investments on the basis of return to the business. Those who comprehend these relationships can very quickly recognize someone who does not. If one of your employees lacks such understanding, some training may be in order.

It is the author's observation that those who understand these formulas generally find innovative and interesting ways to link them together to invent new business systems with profitable cash flow.

5.4   BUSINESS SYSTEMS AS A LINKAGE OF THE TWELVE FINANCIAL FUNCTIONS

All business systems have a cash flow; a part of it results in profit and the other part goes into business operations. In the simplest case, one can compare the bank account for business operating capital at the beginning and end of each year to determine the annual rate of growth of the business. Another part of the cash flow may result in a pension plan for employees, thus ending in annuities. Another part of the cash flow may be in payments made on capital investments, another form of annuity. Most businesses also lease equipment, thereby involving yet another form of annuity. The inputs to the business system can usually be considered as annuities paid directly to the business; and the business pays off annuities. In this sense, all businesses are cash flows linked through one or more of the sets of twelve equations. Sophisticated businesses are linked in a very complicated manner.

CASEBOOK EXAMPLE

Calculate the payments of an ordinary annuity direct reduction loan.

The Problem

Calculate the payment amount on a $25,000 loan to be repaid in 36 monthly installments at an annual interest rate of 11%.

The Approach

Calculate $PMT = (i \times PV)/[1 - (1 + i)^{-n}]$, where i is the interest rate per period in decimal ($11/12 = 0.92$), PV is the present value of the loan ($25,000), and n is the number of compounding periods (36).

Typical Keystroke Sequences

Basic Algebraic Calculator	Basic Reverse-Polish Calculator	HP-70/80/22	NOVUS 6020	Rockwell 204
(11)	(11)	Annuity	(25000)	(25000)
÷	↑	SW—End[a]	amt	ET
(1200)	(1200)	(25000)	(36)	PV
STO	÷	PV	n	(36)
+	STO	(36)	(11)	ET
(1)	↑	n	CHS	n
=	(1)	(11)	%i	(11)
y^x	+	↑	CHS	ET
(36)	(36)	(12)	PMT—Loan	i/yr
CHS	CHS	÷	818.47	TA
=	y^x	i		PMT
CHS	CHS	PMT		818.47
+	(1)	818.47		
(1)	+			
÷	RCL			
(25000)	↑			
÷	(25000)			
RCL	×			
=	$x \rightleftarrows y$			
1/x	÷			
818.47	818.47			

[a]HP-22 only.

KEY

( ) data entry.

☐ data output.

CASEBOOK EXAMPLE

Calculate the payments to an ordinary annuity sinking fund.

The Problem

Calculate the annual payment amount needed to accrue $300,000 in 20 years at 8.25% per year.

The Approach

Calculate $PMT = \dfrac{FV \times i}{(1+i)^n - 1}$ where $FV = \$300{,}000$, $n = 20$, and $i = 8.25/100$.

Typical Keystroke Sequences

Basic Algebraic Calculator	Basic Reverse-Polish Calculator	HP-70/80/22	NOVUS 6020	Rockwell 204
(8.25)	(8.25)	Annuity	(300000)	(300000)
÷	↑	SW—End[a]	amt	ET
(100)	(100)	(300000)	(20)	FV
STO	÷	FV	n	(20)
+	STO	(20)	(8.25)	ET
(1)	↑	n	%i	n
=	(1)	(8.25)	CHS	(8.25)
y^x	+	i	PMT—Savings	ET
(20)	(20)	PMT	6376.31	i
=	y^x	6376.31		TA
−	(1)			PMT
(1)	−			6376.31
÷	RCL			
RCL	÷			
=	(300000)			
÷	$x \rightleftarrows y$			
(300000)	÷			
$1/x$	6376.31			
6376.31				

[a] HP-22 only.

KEY
(   ) data entry.
☐ data output.

CASEBOOK EXAMPLE

Calculate the number of periods to compound to an amount.

The Problem

Calculate the number of compounding periods needed to increase $25,000 to $35,000 at 9% per year, compounded quarterly.

The Approach

Calculate $n = \dfrac{\log \dfrac{FV}{PV}}{\log(1+i)}$ where $FV = \$35,000$, $PV = \$25,000$, and i is a decimal $9/(4 \times 100)$.

Typical Keystroke Sequences

Basic Algebraic Calculator	Basic Reverse-Polish Calculator	HP-70/80/22	NOVUS 6020	Rockwell 204*
(35000)	(35000)	(35000)	(9)	(9)
÷	↑	FV	÷	÷
(25000)	(25000)	(25000)	(4)	(4)
=	÷	PV	=	=
log	log	(9)	%i	ET
STO	(9)	↑	(25000)	i
(9)	↑	(4)	amt	(25000)
÷	(4)	÷	( ) ◄	ET
(400)	÷	i	n	PV
+	(100)	n	FV—Interest ⟨Guess New n⟩	( ) ◄
(1)	÷	$\boxed{15.12}$		ET
=	(1)			n
log	+		No	TA
÷	log		⟨FV = 35000 ?⟩	FV ⟨Guess new n⟩
RCL	÷			

(*Continued*)

*A decimal number cannot be entered into n. The decimal point is ignored and only the whole number is entered. Thus, this problem can only be approximated, i.e., calculated to whole years unless n is entered as months and i is adjusted accordingly.

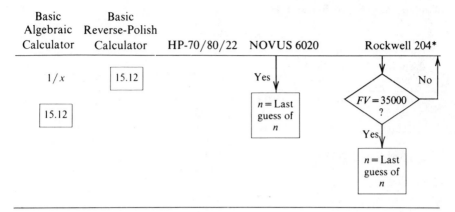

KEY

(   ) data entry.

▢   data output.

◯   mental step by analyst.

CASEBOOK EXAMPLE

Calculate the number of periods to attain a future value in an ordinary annuity sinking fund.

The Problem

Calculate the number of periods needed to increase an annuity of $3000 per year to $300,000 at 8% if the interest is compounded monthly.

The Approach

Calculate $n = \dfrac{\log\left(1 + \dfrac{FV \times i}{PMT}\right)}{\log(1 + i)}$ where $FV = \$300,000$, $PMT = \$3000$, $i = 8/(100 \times 12)$, and n is in months.

Typical Keystroke Sequences

Basic Algebraic Calculator	Basic Reverse-Polish Calculator	HP-70/80/22	NOVUS 6020	Rockwell 204*
(8)	(300000)	(300000)	(8)	(8)
+	↑	FV	CHS	ET
(1200)	(8)	(8)	%i	i/yr
+	↑	↑	(3000)	(3000)
(1)	(1200)	(12)	+	+
=	+	+	(12)	(12)
log	×	i	=	=
STO	(3000)	(3000)	amt	ET
(8)	↑	↑	( ) ←	PMT
+	(12)	12	n	( ) ←
(1200)	+	+	FV—Savings Guess new n	ET
×	+	PMT		n
(300000)	(1)	n	[330.68] No	TA
+	+		FV = 300000 ?	FV Guess[a] new n
(3000)	log		Yes	
×	(8)		n = Last guess of n	No
(12)	↑			FV = 300000 ?
+	(1200)			Yes
(1)	+			n = Last guess of n
log	(1)			
+	+			
RCL	log			
=	+			
[330.68]	[330.68]			

[a] Integers only.

KEY

( ) data entry.

☐ data output.

◯ mental step by analyst.

(Continued)

*A decimal number cannot be entered into n. The decimal point is ignored and only the whole number is entered. Thus, this problem can only be approximated, i.e., calculated to whole years unless n is entered as months and i is adjusted accordingly.

CASEBOOK EXAMPLE

Calculate the number of periods to amortize a loan with an ordinary annuity.

The Problem

Calculate the number of installments needed to pay off an equipment purchase involving a $25,000 loan at 8.25% and payments of a maximum of $3000 per month. Calculate the final payment.

The Approach

Calculate the number of installments. Convert the fraction of the last installment into a final payment that retains the 8.25% annual interest rate by calculating the balance due at the end of the last integer payment period and then determining the payment that yields 8.25% for the fractional payment period that is left.

Typical Keystroke Sequences

$3000 Payment Approach		Alternative Payment Approach	
HP-22	HP-70/80/	HP-70/80/22	Rockwell 204
(8.25)	(8.25)	(8.25)	(25000)
▨	↑	↑	ET
i	(12)	(12)	PV
(3000)	÷	÷	(8.25)
PMT	i	STO	ET
(25000)	(25000)	K	i/yr
PV	PV	i	(3000)
(8)	(3000)	(25000)	ET
STO	PMT	PV	PMT
9	n	(3000)	TA
▨	8.61	PMT	n
BAL	CLR	n	9
1823.04	(3000)	DSP	(25000)
STO	PMT	0	ET
1	(8.25)	9	PV
RCL	↑	(9)	TA
i	(12)	STO	PMT
		M	
		CLR	

HP-22 annotations: Means 8 payments of $3000 and final payment less than $3000

HP-70/80/22 annotations: 9 Installments will result in payments of less than $3000

(*Continued*)

HP-22	HP-70/80	HP-70/80/22	Rockwell 204
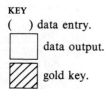	÷	M	2874.13
RESET	i	n	TA
i	(8)	K	
(1)	n	i	i
n	PV	(25000)	
RCL	CHS	PV	867.23
1	(25000)		ET
PV	+	PMT	ET
PMT	STO	DSP	PV
1835.57 } Final Payment	M 8 } Payments	2 2874.14	.1
	CLR	(2874.14)	+
	M	STO	ET
	PV	M	ET
	(9)	CLR	PMT
	˙n	M	=
	(8.25)	PMT	2874.23
	↑	K	
	(12)	i	
	÷	(9)	
	i	n	
	FV	PV	
		(25000.00)	
	1835.57 Overpayment if 9 payments of 2874.14 were made }	−	
		.03	
		CHS	
		DSP	
		PMT	
		+	
	Adjusted final payment }	2874.11	

KEY

(   ) data entry.

☐ data output.

▨ gold key.

CASEBOOK EXAMPLE

Calculate the number of periods in an annuity-due (advance payment) program (rents, leases, insurance, etc.).

The Problem

Calculate the number of payments in a custom lease program under which a $22,000 fleet of cars is being leased at 11% per year and monthly payments of $900.

The Approach

Calculate $n = \dfrac{\log(1+i) - \log\left[1 + i\left(1 - \dfrac{PV}{PMT}\right)\right]}{\log(1+i)}$ where $PV = \$22{,}000$, $i = 11/(100 \times 12)$, and $PMT = \$900$.

Typical Keystroke Sequences

Basic Algebraic Calculator	Basic Reverse-Polish Calculator	HP-22	HP-70/80	Rockwell 204
(11)	(11)	Annuity	(11)	(11)
÷	↑	SW—Begin	K	ET
(1200)	(1200)	(11)	÷	i/yr
+	÷	▨	i	(22000)
(1)	STO	i	(22000)	ET
=	(22000)	(900)	PV	PV
log	↑	PMT	(900)	(900)
STO	(900)	(22000)	DSP	ET
(22000)	÷	PV	i	PMT
÷	CHS	n	%	TA
(900)	(1)	27.52	+	n
CHS	+		PMT	28ᵃ
+	RCL		n	(22000)
(1)	×		27.52	ET
×	(1)			PT
				TA

(Continued)

Basic Algebraic Calculator	Basic Reverse-Polish Calculator	HP-22	HP-70/80	Rockwell 204	
(11)	+			PMT	
÷	log				27 Payments
(1200)	CHS			894.44	of
+	RCL				894.44
(1)				TA	
=	(1)			*i*	
log	+				Total
CHS	log			3044.08	interest
+	STO			ET	paid
RCL	+			ET	
÷	RCL			PV	Overpayment
RCL	÷				if
				−19	28 payments
=	27.52			+	of 894.44
				ET	
27.52				ET	
				PMT	
				=	
				894.24	Final payment

*Works in integer number of pay periods.

KEY

(   ) data entry.

☐   data output.

▨   gold key.

CASEBOOK EXAMPLE

Calculate an amortization schedule for a compounded amount.

The Problem

Calculate an amortization schedule for a $1000 loan to be repaid in one year in six installments at 9% per year.

The Approach

Calculate the amount of payments. Then compute the amount paid to interest; the difference between payment and interest is used to reduce the balance of the loan. The new balance is calculated and the process is iterated.

Typical Keystroke Sequences

HP-70/80/22

Annuity SW-End[a]

(1000)
PV
(9)
←
(12)
÷
(2)
×
i
(6)
n
PMT
[175.53]
STO[b]
M
DSP
i
←
←
(1000)

} Bimonthly payment

2nd Interest portion }
x⇄y
%
[12.59]
M[b]
x⇄y
–

2nd Principal portion }
162.93
–

2nd Remaining balance }
[676.54]
x⇄y
%
10.15
M[b]
x⇄y
–

3rd IP }
10.15
M[b]
x⇄y
–

4th RB }
–
[343.31]
x⇄y
%

IP }
[5.15]
M[b]
x⇄y

PP }
[170.38]

RB }
[172.93]
x⇄y
%

IP }
[2.59]
M[b]

Rockwell 204

(1000)
ET
PV
(6)
ET
n
(9)
+
(6)
=
ET
i
TA
PMT
[175.53]   } Bimonthly payment
(1)
ET
n
TA
i

ET
ET
PV
[676.54]   } 2nd RB
TA
i
[10.15]   } 3rd IP
ET
ET
PV
[511.16]   } 3rd RB
TA
i
[7.67]   } 4th IP
ET
ET

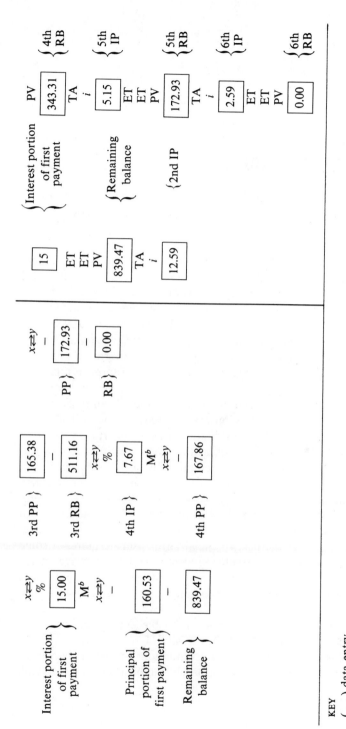

KEY

( ) data entry.

⬚ data output.

[a]HP-22 only.

[b]$STO = STO_1$ and $M = RCL_1$ for HP-70 and HP-22, respectively.

CHAPTER 6

CONSUMER FINANCE

This chapter deals with the time and money aspects of short-term financing. Short-term financing usually has a maximum period of 5 years and can have as short a period as 30 days. The sources of short-term capital include banks and lending agencies to be sure, but they also include the owners of goods, services, or real property purchased. Additionally, understanding short-term financing is important for the business manager because such financing is almost always involved in short-term investments. For example, in many small businesses certain reserve funds lie relatively idle for short periods of time. A certain percentage of these funds may be used by management for short-term employee loans* and short-term financing of ventures undertaken by businesses associated with one's own. If your business requires contingency funds, the loan instruments can be sold to your bank or other buyers and, at the most, your business suffers the loss associated with the buyer's discount. Obviously such short-term loans should be set up to recover the loan cost plus the discount you may incur in selling the notes.

If you or your business hold credit cards and have charge accounts, an understanding of consumer finance will enable you to select the accounts and credit cards that offer the best financial terms. Furthermore, at some time you may require short-term financing from a bank or loan agency for a household or automobile purchase or an investment opportunity. It is important to be able to determine which organization will give you the best deal.

Finally, short-term financing is important to the entrepreneurial businessman. Every finance organization has a rate of return that is usually unknown to the customer. When setting up situations of fast movement of goods, services, and money, you can purposely establish terms for buying

*Such agreements usually involve paycheck deduction payback.

products and services that are in your favor. For *deals* that are sufficiently different from the typical financing problems, a businessman can usually find someone who is interested enough in unusual ventures to be willing to consider the deal. In virtually every organization the author has worked with, there is a manager at some level who enjoys "wheeling and dealing" with his money supply. He is the fellow who likes to "set up a deal" and make it work. Knowing short-term financial analysis allows you to set up your offer, analyze a counteroffer, and negotiate a final offer. In these situations both parties benefit, although your counterpart may accept a deal for something less than his "unpublished" yield. If the amount of the short-term money is fairly sizable, the time spent in working your own deal can save you enough money to be worth the time spent.

A particular example makes this clear. A small engineering firm wants to conduct spectrum analysis of seismic wave forms used in oil exploration. After negotiations, an oil exploration company agrees to give the firm a contract to do the analysis. The spectrum analyzer the engineering firm wishes to buy costs $25,000. You, as president of the firm, decide to buy on time. Usually you would face two choices: (1) borrow money from the bank and buy the analyzer outright, and (2) lease the analyzer.

Still another, more sporting choice is to obtain financing with a venture capitalist associate and offer your terms, pointing out the rate of return for his firm in terms that will state the case most attractively. In certain situations it is possible to set your own terms that are (*a*) acceptable to him, (*b*) advantageous to you, and (*c*) capable of establishing a little more financial leverage than you might have had, had you merely accepted the standard terms offered to you.

The author uses this approach on corporate start-up financing and has always found a better deal than was being typically offered to others.

It should be apparent now that consumer finance and short-term financial analyses are important and should not be overlooked by any business manager or, for that matter, any individual who handles his own personal finances.

This chapter is also important for the businessman directly involved in short-term finance, particularly those who offer consumer credit or short-term financing to their customers. Federal regulations require that the interest rate for every loan be presented as an annual percentage rate (APR) computed according to a prescribed formula set by the U.S. Federal Reserve, namely, *Regulation Z dealing with the Truth-in-Lending Law*. The objective of course is to provide a uniform measure of the cost of borrowed money. The keystrokes for computing APR on a pocket calculator are given in this chapter. Also discussed is the relationship between

APR and other means of presenting short-term loans in an attractive manner. Finally, for the consumer loan specialist, keystroke sequences are given that permit quick calculations of interest, payments for direct reduction loans, and loans in which interest is paid on the unpaid balance.

6.1   INSTALLMENT LOANS

Installment loans are usually characterized in one of three ways:

- Add-on interest loans.
- Loans in which interest is computed on the unpaid balance.
- Amortized loans.

Add-on interest loans are periodic equal amount payment instruments characterized by payments computed by adding the interest (computed on the basis of a specified period of time and interest rate) to the principal and dividing that total by the number of pay periods in which the borrower agrees to pay off the loan to the lender. For example, the payments on a principal of $1000, borrowed at 10% per year *add-on* for one year and repaid in twelve equal installments would be computed as:

Principal	$1000
"Add-on" interest	100 (10% of $1000)
Loan amount	$1100
Payment	$1100/12 = $91.67

Note that $91.67 is actually $91.666666... rounded. The result is that the last payment will be 4 cents too much. The loan would specify that the note on the last payment was to be only $91.63.

Another type of loan that is characterized by unequal payments is the interest on the unpaid balance loan. Equal amounts are paid against the principal of the loan, and the interest is computed on the unpaid balance. The payment is the sum of the payment on the balance plus the interest. In this case the amount of the payments varies but the amount paid on the principal remains the same from payment to payment. For example, if an installment loan of $200 is made on the basis of five payments and 1% interest on the unpaid balance, the loan schedule appearing in Table 6-1 would be applicable.

A third type of installment loan is the amortized direct reduction loan. Here all payments are the same, but the interest is paid first on each installment and the principal is reduced with whatever remains after the interest payment. For example, a $194.14 direct reduction loan, based on 1% per payment period and five payments, requires a $40 payment per period to repay the loan. The payment schedule for this loan is given in Table 6-2. Usually add-on interest loans are repaid according to an amortized payment schedule in which the interest rate per period is the APR. Obviously loans such as those in Tables 6-1 and 6-2 can be set up and worked on the pocket calculator in fairly short order. The casebook examples furnish additional material for study.

Table 6-1   Payment Schedule for a Loan on which Interest Is Based on the Unpaid Balance

Payment Number	Balance	Payment Against Balance	Payment Against Interest	Total Payment
1	$200	$ 40	$4.00	$44.00
2	160	40	3.20	43.20
3	120	40	2.40	42.40
4	80	40	1.60	41.60
5	40	40	.80	40.80
Total		$200	$12.00	$212.00

Table 6-2   Payment Schedule for a Direct Reduction Loan

Payment Number	Balance	Payment Against Balance	Payment Against Interest	Total Payment
1	$194.14	$ 38.06	$1.94	$ 40
2	156.08	38.44	1.56	40
3	117.64	38.82	1.18	40
4	78.82	39.22	.78	40
5	39.60	39.60	.40	40
Total		$194.14	$5.86	$200

6.2   COMPARISON OF LOAN ALTERNATIVES

Consider the problem of buying a Corvette. The dealer's price is $11000. If you make a $3000 down payment, the principal of a loan to purchase the car is $8000. If the dealer's lending agency is willing to allow 7% per year on a 3-year add-on loan to be paid in 36 installments, the add-on interest is

21% of the $8000, which is $1680. This brings the total note to $9680. When $9680 is divided by the number of payments (36), we find that each monthly payment is $268.89.

Now suppose you borrow the money from a wealthy friend who allows you to amortize the loan over the 36 months but asks for 12% interest. If you were not familiar with installment loan financing, the finding that the friend's 12% amortized loan costs less than the 7% add-on loan offered by the car dealer, would be almost counterintuitive. More specifically, it will cost $265.71 per payment to amortize the individual's loan, compared with the $268.89 for the add-on loan. Even more surprising, 12.83% of the unpaid balance is the interest paid on the dealer's loan, **not** 7%. The point is, when offered loan options one must have a common way to compare them, since the stated interest rates mean different things on different types of loans. For the financial analyst to understand the difference, he needs only be told how the interest is calculated in each loan situation.

Interest for the add-on loan is computed directly by multiplying the total number of years times the interest per year and multiplying this product by the principal; that amount is added to the amount required by the borrower, and we arrive at the face value of the note. The equation is

$$INT = i \times PV \times n$$

where INT is the interest, i is the interest rate per installment period, n is the number of installments, and PV is the loan principal.

The computation of interest on a percentage of the unpaid balance of a loan is also straightforward. Here the interest is based only on the remaining balance at the beginning of each pay period. Obviously the interest is applied to a declining balance. The average balance on which the interest operates is the sum of the balance on the first payment period and the last payment period divided by 2. Thus the interest is equal to the average balance times the interest rate per period times the number of periods over which the loan is given. Here the average balance is computed with the formula

$$AVG\ BAL = \frac{BAL_1 + BAL_{last}}{2}$$

Then the interest is computed with the formula

$$INT = i \times n \times AVG\ BAL = i \times n \times \frac{BAL_1 + BAL_{last}}{2}$$

which can be roughly estimated with the formula

$$INT \approx i \times n \times \frac{P}{2}$$

where P is the loan principal. Note however that when interest is paid on the unpaid balance, the payment *per period* varies. This is because under the terms and conditions of such loans, a fixed installment will be paid against the principal, the interest is computed separately, and the payment is the sum of the installment and the interest for that period.

The "average balance" method of computing interest can be used to estimate the cost of an amortized direct reduction (ordinary annuity) loan. The results will be *less* than the *true* cost of such a loan. For typical automobile loans the error is on the order of 4 to 5%. For appliance-type loans the error is on the order of 2 to 3% and for typical real estate mortgage loans the error is on the order of 20 to 30%.

The idea of the "average balance" loan principal is important because it shows "mathematically" that the *effective principal* of an amortized direct reduction loan is only half that of an add-on interest loan. This is why the add-on interest rate generates about twice as much interest as an amortized interest rate (for the same effective principal).

Ultimately, then, how does one compare the interest rates of any two loans? The answer is straightforward and is established by the truth-in-lending laws. The interest rate for any loan must be specified in terms of the annual percentage interest rate computed as though the loan were an annual payment direct reduction loan. The simplest calculation involves knowing only the present value of the loan, the payment amount, and the number of payments to be made. Then the interest rate is computed with the keystroke sequences shown in Table 6-3.

Table 6-3 Typical Keystroke Sequences for Computing Annual Percentage Interest Rate

Algebraic Business Calculator	Reverse-Polish Business Calculator
(PV)	(PV)
ET	PV
PV	(PMT)
(n)	PMT
ET	(n)
n	n

(*Continued*)

Table 6-3 (*Continued*)

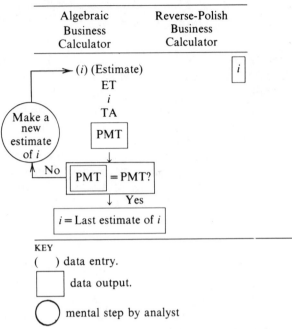

Algebraic Business Calculator	Reverse-Polish Business Calculator

KEY

(   ) data entry.

☐   data output.

◯   mental step by analyst

6.3   PAYMENT PLANS

Payment plans offered by retailers are money loans but are associated only with installment payments for the purchase of goods. Generally goods can be bought outright at the sale price or they can be purchased for an amount *down* and a certain amount per month. Obviously the latter alternative is equivalent to a loan except that the terms are different. When goods are purchased on installment plans, the seller includes a *carrying charge* or *credit charge*. This is added to the purchase price of the article, and regular payments are made until the item is paid for. One kind of carrying charge is the *fixed sum* (or *flat sum*), which is a specified amount to be added to the cost of the goods at the time of purchase. This is equivalent to add-on interest from the standpoint of the cash transaction. The other type of installment purchase simply charges interest on the unpaid balance of the account. This is identical to the loan carrying interest on the unpaid balance. The only difference between a money loan and an installment purchase plan is that you can add regularly to your charge account without going through the formality of separate loan proceedings.

6.4 TRUE INTEREST RATES

Prior to the Truth in Lending Law, financing agencies and lending institutions sought to find a method or technique for computing a *"true"* interest rate. A number of methods were experimented with, but finally the Federal Reserve Board and certain consumer advocate organizations settled on the "constant-ratio" method for computing interest rates. The equation for this method is

$$EIR = \frac{2 \times m \times INT}{PV(n+1)}$$

where EIR is the effective interest rate, m is the number of installments per year, INT is the interest to be paid for the money borrowed, PV is the present value of the loan principal, and n is the number of payments.

If we rewrite this equation as

$$INT = \frac{P}{2} \times EIR \times \frac{n+1}{m}$$

it is easy to recognize the similarity between the EIR in the constant-ratio formula and i in the average-balance formula. In this sense the agreement was near the APR calculations required today but only for small installment loans.

These "true-interest" formulas were once widely used. Notes on the true-interest rate or average-balance rate are sometimes encountered, reflecting interest rates on credit paper written prior to the Truth in Lending Law. These formulas, which can be used to unravel the earlier quotations of "true" interest, are presented here more for the sake of completeness than utility.

6.5 REBATES AND THE RULE OF 78

A rebate is an allowance, deduction, or refund of part of the price paid for goods or services. The rule of 78 is a technique for amortizing a consumer finance charge using the sum-of-the-months' digits method. The rule of 78 method is common for computing interest rebates on consumer finance loans that are paid in full before the end of the loan period.

In the sum-of-the-months' digits method of amortization, the amount reduced each period is obtained by multiplying the amount being amortized by a fraction determined as follows:

Count the number of amortization periods remaining before the loan is paid in full—call this number A.

Example: remaining payments $3, 4, 5 \rightarrow A = 3 + 4 + 5 = 12$.

Count the total number of amortization periods—call this number B.

Example: all payments $1, 2, 3, 4, 5 \rightarrow B = 1 + 2 + 3 + 4 + 5 = 15$.

The amortization fraction is the ratio A / B.

Example: $12 / 15 = 0.8$.

More generally, if the total finance charge is FC, the interest charged in the kth month of an n-month amortization period is given by the formula*

$$\mathrm{INT}_k = \frac{2(n - k + 1)}{n(n + 1)} \, \mathrm{FC}$$

and the rebate is computed on an "average interest" basis. That is,

$$\mathrm{REBATE} = \frac{\mathrm{INT}_k}{2} \times (n - k)$$

An example of a rebate using the rule of 78 clarifies the method. If \$1045.94 is the finance charge on a 36-month installment payment program for a Cadillac and the loan is paid off on the eighth installment, the rabate is

$$\mathrm{REBATE} = \frac{(36 - 8) \times (36 - 8 + 1)}{36(36 + 1)} \, \$1045.94 = \$637.62$$

CASEBOOK EXAMPLE

Calculate ordinary, commercial, and accurate simple interest.

The Problem

Calculate the (*a*) *ordinary*, (*b*) *commercial*, and (*c*) *accurate* interest on \$500 at 6% for a loan dated July 6 and due September 6 of the same year.

---

*In the general formula for sum-of-the-months' digits amortization fraction, k is the current installment number, n is the total number of installments, and FC is the total finance charge.

The Approach

(*a*) Ordinary interest: $PV = 500$, $i = 6/(100 \times 360)$, approximate number of days $= 60 = n$, and $INT = PV \times i \times n$.

(*b*) Commercial interest: $PV = 500$, $i = 6/(100 \times 365)$, exact days $= 62 = n$, and $INT = PV \times i \times n$.

(*c*) Accurate interest: $PV = 500$, $i = 6/(100 \times 365)$, exact days $= 62 = n$, and $INT = PV \times i \times n$.

Typical Keystroke Sequences

	Basic Four-Function Algebraic Calculator			Basic Four-Function Reverse-Polish Calculator		
(*a*)	(*b*)	(*c*)	(*a*)	(*b*)	(*c*)
(60)	(62)	(62)	(60)	(62)	(62)
×	×	×	↑	↑	↑
(6)	(6)	(6)	(6)	(6)	(6)
÷	÷	÷	×	×	×
(36000)	(36500)	(36500)	(36000)	(36500)	(36500)
×	×	×	÷	÷	÷
(500)	(500)	(500)	(500)	(500)	(500)
=	=	=	×	×	×
5.00	5.10	5.10	5.00	5.10	5.10

KEY
( ) data entry.
☐ data output.

CASEBOOK EXAMPLE

Calculate the APR (annual percentage rate) for an ordinary direct reduction loan.

The Problem

For a direct reduction loan, calculate the APR. For this example the money borrowed is $2000, the number of payments is 10, and the payment amount is $220 paid monthly.

The Approach

Step 1. Determine the total amount borrowed. This amount should include all fees and charges to be paid by the loan.

Step 2. Determine the number of pay periods.

Step 3. Determine the payment amount.

Step 4. Solve for the interest rate per period using the ordinary annuity formula built into the business pocket calculator.

Typical Keystroke Sequences

HP-70/80/22	NOVUS 6020	Rockwell 204

^{a}HP = 22 only.

( ) data entry.

☐ data output.

◯ mental step by analyst.

CASEBOOK EXAMPLE

Calculate an installment purchase plan

The Problem

For $60 to be paid in six $10 installments plus a charge of 1.5% on the unpaid balance per month, calculate (a) the monthly payment schedule, (b) the total cost on the installment plan, and (c) the difference between the cash and installment price.

The Approach

Prepare an installment purchase plan schedule.

Month	Balance	Installment Payment	Service Charge (1.5%)	Total Payment
1	$60	$10	$0.90	$10.90
2	50	10	0.75	10.75
3	40	10	0.60	10.60
4	30	10	0.45	10.45
5	20	10	0.30	10.30
6	10	10	0.15	10.15
Total	00	$60	$3.15	$63.15

Total cost on the installment plan $= \$63.15$.
Installment charge $=$ installment price $-$ cash price $= \$63.15 - \$60.00 = \$3.15$.

Typical Keystroke Sequences

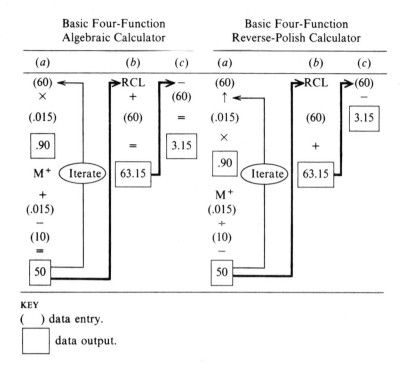

	Basic Four-Function Algebraic Calculator			Basic Four-Function Reverse-Polish Calculator		
(a)	(b)	(c)	(a)	(b)	(c)

(a)	(b)	(c)	(a)	(b)	(c)
(60)	RCL	−	(60)	RCL	(60)
×	+	(60)	↑	(60)	−
(.015)	(60)	=	(.015)	+	3.15
.90	=	3.15	×		
M⁺ (Iterate)	63.15		.90 (Iterate)	63.15	
+			M⁺		
(.015)			(.015)		
−			÷		
(10)			(10)		
=			−		
50			50		

KEY
(   ) data entry.
□   data output.

CASEBOOK EXAMPLE

Calculate the rebate on a prepaid loan using the rule of 78.

The Problem

Calculate the rebate on the finance charge for a prepaid 36-month loan of $5000 at 12% after the thirteenth installment is paid. Use the rule of 78 (sum-of-the-months' digits method) to compute the rebate.

The Approach

Step 1. Calculate the payment amount on the loan.
Step 2. Calculate total of all payments.

Step 3. Calculate the difference between the total (step 2 result) and the loan principal to compute the finance charge (FC).

Step 4. Calculate the finance charge rebate using the rule of 78:

$$\text{REBATE}_k = \frac{(n-k+1)(n-k)}{(n+1)(n)} \text{ FC}$$

where $n = 36$ and $k = 14$ (thirteenth month already paid).

Typical Keystroke Sequences

HP-70/80/22	NOVUS 6020	Rockwell 204
(5000)	(5000)	(5000)
PV	amt	ET
(36)	(36)	PV
n	n	(36)
(1)	(12)	ET
i	CHS	n
PMT	%i	(12)
x	CHS	ET
(36)	PMT-Loan	i/yr
×	×	TA
DSP	(36)	PMT
PV	=	×
−	+	(36)
FC = 978.58	(5000)	
↑	−	ET
(36)	M+	ET
↑	CE/C	PV
(14)	(36)	×
−	+	(22)
STO}$_a$	(14)	×
M ∫	−	(23)
↑	22	÷
(1)	×	(36)
+	(23)	÷
M^a	÷	(37)
×	(36)	=
×		

(Continued)

HP-70/80/22	NOVUS 6020	Rockwell 204
(36)	÷	371.74
÷	(37)	
(36)	×	
↑	MR/MC	
(1)	=	
+	371.72	
÷		
371.74		

[a]$\underset{M}{STO} = \underset{1}{STO}$ and $M = \underset{1}{RCL}$ for HP-70 and HP-22, respectively.

KEY

(   ) data entry.

☐   data output.

CHAPTER 7

MERCHANDISING CALCULATIONS

Although merchandising is not the principal means of developing revenues for all businesses, in the majority of enterprises certain products are bought from wholesalers and sold at retail with the merchant taking a profit. This is sufficient reason to review the basic mathematics of merchandising.

Four conceptually simple aspects are always computed in the buying and selling of merchandise. These are markup, markdown, discounts, and profit and loss.

7.1 MARKUP

Merchandising is the business of buying goods at one price and selling them at another to make a profit. First, the definition of a few terms is in order. The difference between cost and selling price of the merchandise is the *gross profit* or *markup*. The *net price* is the price of the merchandise. *Total cost* is the cost of the merchandise plus the expenses associated with handling and transportation from the place of purchase to the place of sale. *The net profit* is the gross profit minus the operating cost. The sales are the revenues. The revenues must be sufficient to pay all operating expenses with an amount remaining, called a net profit. Markup then is defined to be

$$\text{markup} = \text{selling price} - \text{cost price}$$

Markup is usually quoted as a percentage of either the selling price or the cost price. Unfortunately there is no standard among merchants for describing percentage markup. The method used depends on a number of factors, including the method of keeping track of inventory, the type of merchandise, the accounting system, and the historical precedents set by previous businessmen. Generally manufacturers, wholesalers, and small retail stores use a cost-price basis for markup, as

$$\text{percentage markup} = \frac{\text{markup}}{\text{cost price}}$$

Large retail stores, on the other hand, use selling price as a markup basis, as

$$\text{percentage markup} = \frac{\text{markup}}{\text{selling price}}$$

7.2 MARKDOWN

Markdown, a price reduction that is computed on the selling price, is defined as

$$\text{markdown} = \text{original selling price} - \text{actual selling price}$$

Markdown quoted as a percentage of the original selling price is given by

$$\text{percentage markdown} = \frac{\text{markdown amount}}{\text{original selling price}}$$

Markdowns are straightforward calculations on pocket calculators with percent keys. The general procedure is seen in Table 7-1. The casebook examples at the end of this chapter illustrate the keystroke sequences for computing all the markup and markdown problems encountered in typical merchandising.

7.3 CASH AND TRADE DISCOUNTS

Reductions in cost price are often allowed to encourage prompt payment of invoices or bills of goods. These incentives are called cash discounts and are offered only by merchants and businessmen involved in the buying and selling of goods. The calculation of cash discounts is not difficult. An acquaintance with the terminology of cash and trade discounts is almost as important as the calculations themselves. Cash discounts reflect themselves immediately in savings. Thus it is important for a merchant to capitalize on every opportunity to save money and increase his return on investment.

Table 7-1   Typical Keystroke Sequences for Calculating Markups and Markdowns

Basic Four-Function Calculator	Reverse-Polish Business Calculator (HP-70/80/22 type)
$\left(\begin{array}{c}\text{Selling}\\\text{price}\end{array}\right)$	$\left[\begin{array}{c}\text{Original}\\\text{selling}\\\text{price}\end{array}\right]$
−	$\left.\begin{array}{c}\text{STO}\\ \text{M}\\ \uparrow\end{array}\right\}{}^{a}$
$\left(\begin{array}{c}\text{Cost}\\\text{price}\end{array}\right)$	$\left(\begin{array}{c}\text{Cost}\\\text{price}\end{array}\right)$
=	−
$\boxed{\text{Markup}}$	$\boxed{\text{Markup}}$
÷	M^{a}
$\left(\begin{array}{c}\text{Selling}\\\text{price}\end{array}\right)$	÷
=	$\boxed{\%\ \text{Markup}}$ in decimal
$\boxed{\%\ \text{Markup}}$ in decimal	M^{a}
$\left[\begin{array}{c}\text{Original}\\\text{selling}\\\text{price}\end{array}\right]$	$\uparrow$
−	$\left(\begin{array}{c}\text{Actual}\\\text{price}\end{array}\right)$
$\left(\begin{array}{c}\text{Actual}\\\text{price}\end{array}\right)$	−
=	$\boxed{\text{Markdown}}$
$\boxed{\text{Markdown}}$	M^{a}
÷	÷
$\left[\begin{array}{c}\text{Original}\\\text{selling}\\\text{price}\end{array}\right]$	$\boxed{\%\ \text{Markdown}}$
=	
$\boxed{\%\ \text{Markdown}}$	

[a] $\text{STO}_{\text{M}} = \text{STO}_{1}$ and $\text{M} = \text{RCL}_{1}$ for HP-70 and HP-22, respectively.

KEY

( ) data entry.

$\boxed{}$ data output.

Cash discounts are based on the terms agreed to in the sale of goods. If no terms are indicated on an invoice or bill of sale, it is understood that the bill should be paid on or before 30 days from the date of the invoice or on the first of the next month. Obviously no cash discount is involved.

Generally bills not paid within 30 days of the invoice date are subject to an interest charge. Invoices carrying the term $n/30, n/60, n/90, \cdots$ indicate that they must be paid by 30, 60, or 90 days, respectively, or an interest charge will be made. Here n stands for net. When a bill is described at \$100 $n/30$, it means that \$100 must be paid within 30 days of the invoice date or interest will be charged on \$100. Cash discounts are often allowed if a bill is paid within a certain number of days. For example, a bill marked 3/10, n/60, is read, "The net amount must be paid on or before 60 days–a 3% discount will be allowed if paid within the first 10 days." That is, the net amount must be paid during the period beginning on the eleventh day and ending on the sixtieth day. If the bill is paid on or before the tenth day, the discount is allowed. Occasionally an inducement is specified by 3/10, 2/20, n/30. This means a 3% discount is allowed if the bill is paid on or before the tenth day, and a 2% discount is allowed if the bill is paid on or after eleventh day but on or before the twentieth day; the net must be paid on or after the twenty-first day but on or before the thirtieth day with no discount, but there is no penalty either.

Another standard form of marking invoices and bills is

2%–15th EOM   or   2%–15th prox.

Both mean the same thing; that is, a 2% discount will be allowed if the invoice is paid during the first 15 days of the month next following the date of the invoice. Here both EOM and prox. mean "the end of the month".

Another factor commonly encountered in the terms of a purchase is the postdating of an invoice for goods. Some seasonal procurements made in the winter are actually sold in the summer. Consequently the terms for procurements of this type usually involve postdating. When cash discounts are allowed on invoices that are postdated, the date of the invoice (not the date of the purchase order) is used to determine the discount term.

In other cases goods can be sold at once but the materials that are required to manufacture them may not be immediately available. In this case the terms of the agreement may be based on the date of receipt of goods (ROG), not the date of the invoice nor the date of the purchase order.

Another instance of using the ROG as the determining date involves merchandise transported by slow means from the source to the merchant.

Since merchants do not want to carry the invoice penalties associated with transportation delays, frequently they establish the terms of the agreement based on the ROG date.

Some manufacturers grant extra dating on their invoices, usually symbolized as 3/10-60X, 3/10-60 EX, or 3/10-60 extra. All these indicate that an additional 60 days are added to the basic 10 days over which the 2% discount is allowed, for a total of 70 days from the date of the invoice as the period allowed for the discount. Extra dating is usually associated with seasonal procurements when postdating of an invoice is not desired.

Finally, when partial payments are made against an invoice during a period in which a cash discount is allowed, the discount is allowed only against the amount of the payment made.

7.4   TRADE DISCOUNTS

In the same way that cash discounts are allowed for prompt payment of bills, trade discounts are allowed to induce the procurement of goods. Trade discounts are reductions in the price of an article but are not based on the price of the article (as in markdowns); rather, they are computed from the total amount of the invoice or the catalog or "list" price of the article. They are always expressed as a percentage of the list price or total of the invoice. Trade discounts may consist of a single discount or of a series of discounts called chain discounts. Trade discounts usually refer to the discounts allowed by manufacturers and wholesalers to merchants and are not given by retailers. Trade discounts are allowed for (*a*) those who buy a large quantity of merchandise, (*b*) those who have excellent credit, (*c*) special interest groups such as schools and churches, and (*d*) preferred customers.

Some large wholesalers distribute annual catalogs containing prices and furnish their salesmen with discount sheets. The prices in such low-cost catalogs are moderately elevated, and the discount sheets are used by the salesmen as a means of adjusting prices according to the fluctuations of business.

Again definition of a few terms is in order. When discussing trade discounts, the *catalog price* is called the *list price*. The percentage of reduction in list price is called the *trade discount*. The *net price* is the difference between the catalog price and the amount of the trade discount. That is:

$$\text{net price} = \text{list price} - \text{trade discount amount}$$

Trade discounts are usually quoted as list price less the percentage of discount. For example, if the list price is $100 and the trade discount is 30%, we say $100 less 30%. If a chain discount of 30%, 10%, 5% is allowed, we say $100 less 30%, 10%, 5%. Chain discounts are computed by discounting the original amount or price of the invoice to determine the net amount after the first discount. The second discount is computed on the net amount after the first discount. This in turn allows the determination of the net amount after the second discount. The third discount is applied to the net amount after the second discount to determine the final net amount. The following example illustrates this.

Chain Discount on $100 less 30%, 10%, and 5%

Original amount	$100.00
First discount (30%)	30.00
First discounted amount	$70.00
Second discount (10%)	7.00
Second discounted amount	$63.00
Third discount (5%)	3.15
Third discounted amount	$59.85

Previously, discount tables were used to compute chain discounts for discounting large sales (the losses from errors in hand calculation of chain discounts by unskilled employees led to the use of tables for simple discounting). Now that the pocket calculator is available, however, this is no longer necessary. The pocket calculator can do chain discounts with a few simple keystrokes and with greater accuracy than can be achieved from trade discount tables, as illustrated by Table 7-2.

Table 7-2   Typical Keystroke Sequences for Calculating $100 less 30%, 10%, and 5%

Basic **Algebraic** Four-Function Calculator and Algebraic Business Calculator	Reverse-Polish Business Calculator
(100)	(100)
×	↑
(.7)	(.7)
=	×
[1st discounted amount]	[1st discounted amount]
×	(.9)
(.9)	×
=	[2nd discounted amount]

(*Continued*)

Table 7-2 (*Continued*)

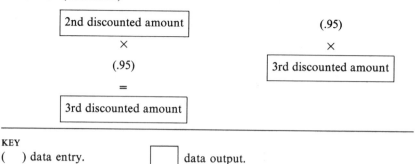

KEY
( ) data entry. ☐ data output.

Occasionally it may be desirable to compute the single discount equivalent of a chain discount, as when comparing a purchase of goods offered on a single discount basis against goods offered on a chain basis. The calculation is straightforward, and Table 7-3 illustrates the method of comparison.

Table 7-3 Typical Keystroke Sequences for Calculating the Single Discount Equivalent of $100 less 30%, 10%, and 5%

Basic Algebraic Four-Function Calculator and Algebraic Business Calculator	Basic Four-Function Calculator and Reverse-Polish Business Calculator
(100)	(100)
×	↑
(.7)	↑
×	(.7)
(.9)	×
×	(.9)
(.95)	×
÷	(.95)
(100)	×
=	−
CHS	
+	40.15
1	
×	
(100)	
=	
40.15	

KEY
( ) data entry. ☐ data output.

7.5   PROFIT AND LOSS

After all the merchandising is done and the trade discounts are taken, the cash discounts are allowed, the markups are made on the goods sold quickly and the markdowns are taken on the goods that sold poorly, the bottom line must be the determination of profit and loss. The objective of the merchant is to buy and sell goods at a profit. The difference between the selling price and the cost price is called the gross profit, which, as mentioned before, is the net profit plus all operating expenses. Thus we can write the profit equations as

$$\text{gross profit} = \text{selling price} - \text{cost price}$$

$$\text{gross profit} = \text{operating expenses} + \text{net profit}$$

Therefore

$$\text{net profit (or loss)} = \text{gross profit} - \text{operating expenses}$$

Thus

$$\text{net profit (or loss)} = \text{selling price} - \text{cost price}$$

$$- \text{operating expenses}$$

It follows that we can compute any one of these four terms if the other three are known. For new businesses, of course, certain terms must be estimated. Operating expenses for some new businesses can be determined on the basis of ratios for a similar business; such figures are readily available from banks or from the federal Small Business Administration.

7.6   MERCHANDISING AND THE TIME VALUE OF MONEY

Perhaps the most significant observation today's merchant can make is that even on very short-term loans and credit, he must carefully consider the time value of money, in view of the inflation rates and cost of capital, cost of goods, reduced money supply, cost of materials, and warehousing delays that can be expected. Heretofore it has been sufficient to determine a maximum operating expense to establish a competitive edge over those who are selling the same merchandise "up the street." A good merchant's business is no longer that simple, and his prices must be based on a pricing structure that takes into account the cost of capital, the inflation rate, and the type of inventory accounting—first-in-first-out (FIFO) or last-in-first-out (LIFO). Generally the result is that prices will be much higher than in the past. If he establishes his prices in this manner and begins losing to his competitor who is underpricing because of slow reaction to the pressures of inflation, he must recognize that only time will tell who is to survive. Either the merchant pricing correctly will find ways to operate on a competitive basis, while taking inflation into account, or he can "wait it out" until the cash flow crunch strikes his competitor. If a merchant finds that he cannot reduce his operating expenses, he runs the risk of losing all his customers before the cash crunch catches up with his competitor (remember, a lot of cash can flow while a business is on the "going-out-of-business" curve). Ultimately it boils down to this: the merchant who survives in this current period of change is the one who (a) most quickly adapts to inflation, (b) establishes wise buying and shrewd pricing practices, and (c) trades short-term losses against long-term survival and return to more stable gains.

It is unfortunate that business mortality is extremely high during this period. Obviously some good businesses fail to survive the transients involved in business readjustment, while some of the less worthy businesses remain in operation. Eventually the changes in the economic system should catch up to all merchants. It seems reasonable to expect that those who learn the manipulations associated with the time value of money will stand an eminently better chance of surviving and growing than those who do not. Because the business pocket calculator is designed with preprogrammed time-value-of-money calculations, it should be an invaluable tool to the modern merchant.

CASEBOOK EXAMPLE

Calculate a retail margin.

The Problem

A product sells for $39.95. It costs $33.00. Determine the margin.

The Approach

A commonly used relation between cost, selling price, and margin is

$$\text{margin} = \frac{\text{sell} - \text{cost}}{\text{cost}} \times 100$$

Use this equation to calculate the margin for this problem.

Typical Keystroke Sequences

Basic Four-Function Algebraic Calculator	Basic Four-Function Reverse-Polish Calculator	Rockwell 204
(39.95)	(39.95)	(39.95)
−	↑	ET
(33.00)	↑	SELL
÷	(33.00)	(33.00)
(39.95)	−	ET
×	$x \rightleftarrows y$	COST
(100)	÷	TA
=	(100)	MARGIN
17.40	×	17.40
	17.40	

KEY
( ) data entry.

⬚ data output.

CASEBOOK EXAMPLE

Calculate cash discount.

The Problem

Mr. Smith received an invoice dated January 10, terms 2/10, n/30, for $130.60 less a trade discount of 10%. He paid this bill on January 20. Calculate the payment amount.

Typical Keystroke Sequences

Basic Four-Function Algebraic Calculator	Basic Four-Function Reverse-Polish Calculator
(130.60)	(130.60)
×	↑
(.98)	↑
×	(.02)
(.90)	×
=	−
115.19	↑
	↑
	(.1)
	×
	−
	115.19

KEY

( ) data entry.

□ data output.

CASEBOOK EXAMPLE

Calculate single trade discount.

The Problem

A television set is listed at $525 less 15%. Calculate the amount of discount and net price.

The Approach

Step 1. $525.00   list or catalog price
Step 2.   78.75   discount ($525 × 0.15)
         $446.25   net price (amount paid)

Typical Keystroke Sequences

Basic Four-Function Algebraic Calculator	Basic Four-Function Reverse-Polish Calculator
(1)	(525.00)
−	↑
(.15)	↑
×	(0.15)
(525.00)	×
=	−
446.25	446.25

KEY
(   ) data entry.
☐ data output.

CASEBOOK EXAMPLE

Calculate a series of trade discounts (chain discounts).

The Problem

The series of discounts 13%, 11%, and 5% is to be deducted from the total of an invoice amounting to $185. Calculate the net price and amount of the discount.

Typical Keystroke Sequences

Basic Four-Function Algebraic Calculator	Basic Four-Function Reverse-Polish Calculator
(1)	(185)
−	↑
(.13)	↑
=	(.13)
STO	×

(Continued)

Basic Four-Function Algebraic Calculator	Basic Four-Function Reverse-Polish Calculator
(1)	−
−	↑
(.11)	↑
=	(.11)
×	×
RCL	−
=	↑
STO	↑
(1)	(.05)
−	×
(.05)	−
=	
×	136.08
RCL	CHS
×	(185)
(185)	+
=	
	48.92
136.08	
CHS	
+	
(185)	
=	
48.92	

KEY
(   ) data entry.

[ ] data output.

CASEBOOK EXAMPLE

Calculate retail profit and loss.

The Problem

Calculate the per-calculator profit or loss of the sales of a calculator under the following conditions: selling price, $99.95; cost price, $48.80; and actual sales costs, $4207 per 100 calculators.

The Approach

Here we use the relation

$$\text{net profit} = \text{selling price} - \text{cost price}$$
$$- \text{operating expenses}$$

Typical Keystroke Sequences

Basic Four-Function Algebraic Calculator	Basic Four-Function Reverse-Polish Calculator
(4207)	(99.95)
÷	↑
100	(48.80)
=	−
+/−	(4207)
+	↑
(99.95)	(100)
−	÷
(48.80)	−
=	9.08
9.08	

KEY

(   ) data entry.

⬚ data output.

CHAPTER 8

REAL ESTATE CALCULATIONS

This chapter dealing with financial analysis and decisions associated with the real estate business covers both commercial and personal home buying calculations. Although this is not a chapter on how to set up a real estate investment, it will be clear after working through the casebook examples that real estate investment alternatives and investment programs are easy to analyze and can be very attractive investments.

A few definitions and real estate investment analysis concepts are in order for those who have turned to this chapter without reading the foregoing material. Throughout this chapter the following definitions will apply:

n = number of periods involved in an investment
i = interest rate per period (usually stated as an annual interest percentage)
PMT = payment at the end of a time period
PV = present value or initial amount, which is the value of money at the beginning of the first period
FV = final amount, which is the value of money at the end of the last period

Interest is compounded at the same time that payments are due.

The interest rate is expressed as a percentage, not as a decimal.

Although many business pocket calculators are designed to solve ordinary annuities (payments made at the end of a period), keystroke sequences have been included for solving annuity-due problems (payments made at the beginning of a period). Annuity-due calculations are important in real estate because rents and leases are annuities due, whereas mortgages are ordinary annuities.

Real estate is treated as a special topic in this book for three reasons.

1. A lot of money can be made or lost on a single deal. Making money requires a clear understanding of both depreciation and cost of capital (interest paid on the money borrowed) if the return is to be properly tax sheltered.

2. The largest single personal investment that most individuals make is in real estate; thus the topic is of significant personal interest.

3. The financial language of real estate investments is quite different from other financial disciplines.

For these reasons the casebook examples and discussion in this chapter present finance in the real estate business in a *learn-by-doing mode* on the pocket calculator.

This chapter covers the three most common problems* in real estate financial analysis: ordinary mortgages, mortgages with balloon payments, and mortgage prices and yields. Additionally, rent and lease calculations are discussed and net present value cash flow analysis is presented in connection with real estate investments. Particular attention is given to appreciation/depreciation calculations and their relationship to taxes, and to equity calculations from the standpoint of investment yield.

8.1 ORDINARY MORTGAGE CONCEPTS

A *mortgage* is the legal instrument for securing money (or money's worth) by making it chargeable to property, real or personal. If the debt is not paid by a time agreed upon by the parties, the creditor may *foreclose*, sell the property, and pay himself from the proceeds of the sale. In the United States a mortgage is usually a formal *deed of conveyance* specifically stating that the mortgage is to be security for a debt.

The history of mortgages is quite fascinating. The development in English common law of the concept of offering the ownership of real estate for money has been turbulent, and the problems associated with mortgages have been resolved only in the last few hundred years by permitting the mortgagor to retain the deed to the land. In earlier times (when the mortgagee held the land as security), if the mortgagor defaulted on the money payment agreement, the mortgagee owned both the land and the money paid to the date of default. This was obviously an inequitable situation if, say, the default occurred on the last payment.

*Appendix D contains the U.S. Department of Housing and Urban Development's guide and new procedures for disclosing settlement costs. The HUD publication is an important guide for circumventing other types of financial problems in real estate.

By the time of the Restoration, the custom of the mortagee's taking possession of the real estate had been almost abandoned; the mortgagee was permitted to claim interest on the loan, and he was given the right to foreclose if the mortgagor defaulted on the loan. Prior to this time and before the usury concept of money allowed interest to be charged on the money itself, the mortgagor usually had to give up title to the land in order to borrow the money. Once the foreclosure clause was allowed, the mortgagee usually preferred to waive his right to possession. By allowing the mortgagor to remain in possession of the real estate, one eliminates the need to account to the mortgagee for the rentals and profits made on the real estate.

Mortgages of real property in the United States have two conceptually different foundations. Some of the states follow what is known as the *title* theory of mortgage. A *title mortgage* retains the form and language of the old English *common-law conveyance* on specified conditions. Among the states that hold to the title approach to mortgages, there is only one consistent factor in the mortgages, namely, the *right* of the mortgagee to possession. Actual possession of the real property almost always remains with the mortgagor. Other states and United States jurisdictions follow the *lien approach* to mortgages. Here the mortgage deed is said to give title to the creditor, but in fact no title passes and, in the absence of agreement to the contrary, the creditor has no right to possession. Instead the creditor secures a *claim* (a *lien*) on the property described in the deed and may sell the property if the mortgagor defaults in his obligation.

Upon default by the mortgagor, the mortgagee may take a number of actions. In almost all states he may proceed as if he were a typical creditor and either (1) ignore the lien and sue the mortgagor directly for the debt, or (2) foreclose on the mortgaged property, in which case he must comply with state law regulating foreclosures.

A few states still permit *strict foreclosure* wherein the entire debt must be paid a day after default or title passes to the mortgagee. The mortgagor is not entitled in this case to any surplus if the property is worth more than the debt. Conversely, however, if the value of the property is less than the debt, the mortgagee may sue for the difference in a separate action.

It is interesting that the most often used method of foreclosure in the United States is a public sale, which is always made under the supervision of a *court of equity*. If the sale exceeds the debt, the mortgagor may get some of his money back. Interestingly, the sale is usually conducted by a sheriff or other officer of the court, and the mortgagee may be (and often is) the purchaser at the sale. If the proceeds of the sale are insufficient to pay the debt, the mortgagee may obtain a judgment for the deficiency.

Another type of mortgage commonly encountered is the *deed of trust*, which is used in about half the states. Here the borrower conveys to a third party the holdings of the property in trust for the holder of a note for money. The third party trustee is a fiduciary to both the debtor and the creditor and is subject to the rules and controls of the state's courts. The trustee is charged to carry out the terms of the mortgage without going into court. If there is a default, the trustee's sale transfers to the purchaser all title that the mortgagor had at the time he executed the deed of trust as security for the loan. Once again, a public sale is the usual means for resolving the default. The difference between this method for handling default and the default under the supervision of a court of equity is that here both the mortgagor and the mortgagee agree on a trustee beforehand.

Chapter 2 discussed discounting on future values of notes and the service charges that banks can add for the handling of negotiable instruments. In the case of a mortgage, a banking institution may increase its yield over and above the yield set by the usury laws of the state by including discounting and service charges. In a sense these are means of circumventing the maximum rate of interest restrictions set by the states.

The most commonly used method for payment on a mortgage is amortization (direct reduction loan). Ordinary mortgages are characterized by repayment of the money borrowed by the mortgagor in equal installments paid at regular intervals. The amount of principal and interest paid varies during the course of the repayment period, since interest accrues on the remaining balance. Thus during the early term of a mortgage most of the payment is applied to the interest, whereas only a small amount of payment goes into reducing the principal. Figure 8-1, which shows the percentage of the payment that goes into the interest as a function of the number of payments for a typical ordinary mortgage, illustrates all the typical problems covered in the casebook examples.

Obviously one of the problems encountered in both personal and business real estate dealings is the determination of the amount of the payment required to fully amortize a mortgage at a given annual interest rate. To perform this calculation the data required are

- The present value of the mortgage.
- The interest being paid on the mortgage.
- The number of periods over which the mortgage is to be fully amortized.

The seller in this case would ask, "What monthly payment is required for me to realize the equivalent of *n* years' growth on my property at today's inflation rate?" For example, a $50,000 home will be worth

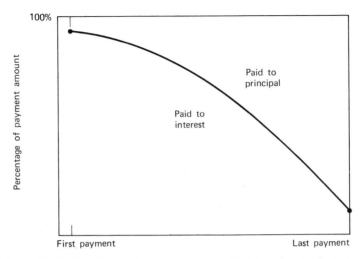

100%

Percentage of payment amount

Paid to
principal

Paid to
interest

First payment   Last payment

Figure 8-1. Distribution of typical mortgage payment to interest and principal over the loan period.

$212,227.84 in 20 years at a 7.25% per year rate of inflation. To at least match the inflation rate and to fully amortize a $50,000 mortgage in 20 years requires monthly payments of $395.19 for a total payoff of $94,845.60. But this is not anywhere near the $212,227.84 *future value* of the home. How does this make sense?

The buyer would ask, "What is my monthly payment if I am to amortize this $50,000 home on a 20-year loan at a 7.25% interest rate?" The answer to this question is also $395.19; which means that the buyer will eventually pay $94,845.60 for a $50,000 home. How does this make sense? The real estate businessman reader may think this example is trivial, yet this is the type of question the author encounters when home-owning clients ask for guidance in understanding a real estate mortgage. The answer, of course, has three parts.

1. If a single payment were made to buy the house at the start of the investment period, the payment would be $50,000.

2. If the single payment were made at the end of the investment period, the amount would be $212,227.84 ($50,000 at today's value grows to $212,227.84 in 20 years at an annual growth rate of 7.25%).

3. When a number of periodic payments of $395.19 are made to retire the debt, and the principal of the loan is continuously reduced, the result is that the $94,845.60 paid is between the $50,000 present value and the $212,227.84 future value of the home.

We examine this type of problem in more detail in the casebook examples at the end of the chapter. It will be clear that the pocket calculator can be used as a convenient tool for teaching buyers as well as salesmen, brokers, appraisers, and other real estate businessmen the principles of real estate finance. In fact, a good business pocket calculator is a relatively inexpensive "teaching machine" to educate people in financial analysis and to develop their confidence in the financial aspects of their particular deal with your business.

8.2   A DETAIL ABOUT CALCULATING THE NUMBER OF PAYMENTS

A calculation that arises in almost all real estate analyses is the determination of the number of payments to fully amortize a mortgage. This calculation has three aspects. The first is the most straightforward; that is, given the mortgage value and the interest rate per year and the payment to be made, determine the number of periods over which the mortgage can be amortized. In the less straightforward case, the investor knows (*a*) the equivalent future value he wishes to realize from his investment in the real property, (*b*) the possible payments, and (*c*) the interest rate per period.

The former problem is that of the buyer and the latter is that of the seller. A related problem calls for the determination of the number of payment periods when (*a*) the present value or mortgage value of the property is known, (*b*) the desired rate of return is given, and (*c*) the equivalent future value that the seller wishes to realize is specified. These problems, discussed in the casebook examples, are similar to the problems covered in Chapter 5. What is important about these problems is that the number of pay periods must be an integer (a whole number). Generally when the number of pay periods is computed with a pocket calculator it is not an integer. When this situation is encountered, the problem is recalculated using the nearest integer to the noninteger number of pay periods. For example, if one calculates the number of payments to amortize a $50,000 mortgage with payments of $500 per month at a 7.25% per year interest rate, it is found that 153.86 payments are required. If 153 payments are used as the number of payments, the amount of each payment becomes $501.70. If 154 payments are used, the payments become $499.72. A third way to resolve this difficulty is to make 153 payments of $500 and a final payment (154th) of $456.89. However the problem is solved, the business pocket calculator is ideal for this type of alternative payment program analysis. One way to win the confidence of potential buyers is to quickly set up alternative payment programs. Also, offering fast, flexible financial analysis service to a buyer will help you better understand his financial position and thereby better evaluate his ability to support the purchase.

8.3   ANNUAL PERCENTAGE RATE CALCULATIONS

Another calculation frequently encountered in real estate analysis is the determination of annual percentage rates on mortgages. Both the mortgagor and the mortgagee must know the annual percentage rate of a given real estate investment to permit comparisons of loans from different financial institutions. As mentioned in the sections on interest in Chapters 2 and 6, the only effective means of comparing investment alternatives is knowing the annual percentage rate of return made (or paid). The lender must know the APR because under current law he is required to state it in the mortgage instrument.

Most mortgages involve four parties: the lender, the mortgagor, the real estate agent, and the real estate broker. To close a deal, each must interact with the others. In all cases each must understand the annual percentage rate on the proposal, particularly when there are fees and points being traded. The most straightforward calculation is associated with the annual percentage rate when there are no fees. In this case it is only necessary to know the mortgage value, the payments, and the number of periods.

From the viewpoint of the mortgagee or lender, the annual rate of return can be computed based on the future value he wishes to achieve, the payments that are being made, and the number of periods involved in the payoff. And finally, as a check and balance, the interest can be related to an equivalent present value invested over a number of periods to achieve the desired future value. All these situations are covered in the casebook examples. Examples of the same calculations are also made when fees are charged by the broker and/or the lender. The significance of the impact of fees on annual percentage rate, payments, the number of periods of the loan, and other factors, is so substantial that casebook examples are given showing a number of payment program alternatives and illustrating the significance of searching for the best possible real estate loan. Perhaps the most important lesson is that at some level in most banks and with many brokers one can *negotiate* fees. Keep in mind that one has not really *negotiated* the best deal until he finds those people and gets the lowest possible fees allowable by law and the policies of the organization.

The key to profitable commercial real estate investments is to shelter the income from taxes. This is usually achieved through

- A minimum cash investment (maximizes interest paid—good for the lender).
- A large investment principal (maximizes depreciation allowed—good for the investor).
- Careful management of the income and property to achieve the maximum allowable earnings and appreciation with a minimum of **actual value depreciation.**

When properly set up, a commercial property's interest and depreciation exceed virtually all the earnings, thus sheltering the actual cash earnings from taxes. The sheltered cash earnings and the difference between the actual depreciation or appreciation and allowed depreciation can result in substantial cash return considering the limited capital investment. In short, the yield can be considerable.

At tax time then, it is necessary to calculate the accumulated interest paid on a note over a specified period of time. Another familiar problem entails determining the remaining principal balance at a given time, or more generally, the entire amortization schedule. This type of calculation is covered in the casebook examples, along with the number of payments required to reach a specified principal balance.

8.4 BALLOON PAYMENTS: WHAT AND WHY

Usually made at the end of the investment period, balloon payments are significantly larger than periodic payments in a regular amortized mortgage payment program. Balloon payments are common in establishing second mortgages on properties held by corporations and also for organizing the procurement of a facility (building) or even a home when it is expected that the balloon payment will be refinanced at the time it becomes due. Balloon payments usually accompany the last periodic payment in a mortgage payoff and generally are specified in one of two ways: (*a*) the borrower or mortgagor specifies the maximum amount of the balloon payment that he wishes to make, or (*b*) the lender specifies the maximum amount of balloon payment that he will allow.

Balloon payments on second mortgages are usually limited to the *forecasted appreciation* of the real property over the number of periods of interest and are *never allowed to exceed what the holder of the second mortgage can get out of the mortgage.* Both situations are considered in the casebook examples. Understanding mortgages with balloon payments is essential to the business manager who ties up investment monies in facilities or mortgages or deeds of trust. By using amortized mortgages with balloon payments, a business can keep its money working for the stockholders.

8.5 INVESTMENTS AND MORTGAGES

Like notes, bonds, and drafts, mortgages are negotiable instruments. As mentioned in Chapter 2, the price paid for a mortgage is based on its future value minus the buyer's discount and fees. Obviously the purchase of mortgages is another opportunity for investment, provided the mortgage can be bought for less than the future value (principal balance) of the mortgage. It is important therefore to be able to determine what price should be paid for a mortgage to ensure that yield objectives are met. Also important is the ability to compute the yield of a mortgage, to permit comparison of mortgage alternatives. Obviously the buying and selling of mortgages can involve complicated calculations.

The casebook examples deal with the expected yield from fully amortized mortgages, the expected yield from mortgages with balloon payments, the price an investor can afford to pay for fully amortized mortgages to achieve a desired yield, and the price an investor can afford to pay for a mortgage with balloon payments to achieve a desired yield. Since in the buying and selling of mortgages the number of periods and the payments are already set by the mortgage, only the price of the mortgage or the desired yield is computed. Of course the future values can be determined for these investments, and that is of interest to the business investor who is concerned with checks and balances. We return to these considerations in the casebook examples.

8.6 CERTAIN APPRECIATION AND DEPRECIATION DETAILS

Problems of appreciation and depreciation of real properties are common in the real estate field. Appreciation is computed on the basis of a compound annual appreciation rate. Compounding is done in a manner identical to the compounding of interest in that the compounding occurs at the end of the periods of the investment. Short-term appreciation can be computed on a linear trend line basis.* Casebook examples of both are given.

*See Chapter 9 for details.

Depreciation, on the other hand, is calculated in a number of different ways and applied only to certain parts of the real estate investment. Thus although the value of a facility on a piece of land depreciates over a period of time, the land value itself may appreciate in an amount that is greater than the depreciation of the facility. In this case there may be an overall appreciation of the real property.

Another difficulty associated with calculating appreciation of land is that whereas the land value appreciates in a compound interest manner, a facility on the land may be depreciated in a number of "allowed" ways. The IRS allows only straight line depreciation over the lifetime of the depreciable facility. Excessive depreciation over and above the straight line depreciation must be computed and accounted for when determining the taxes associated with a real estate transaction.

Chapters 1 and 3 indicated that the future value of a compounded amount is a straightforward calculation. The casebook examples for this chapter are redundant in some respects to those presented earlier, the difference being that this chapter is devoted exclusively to real estate problems. Compounded depreciation of real property can also occur. Here again is a source of confusion. The casebook examples of depreciation clearly distinguish between compounded depreciation, accelerated depreciation, and straight line depreciation, and give instances in which each is applicable.

The government allows a depreciation of the value of an asset over its useful lifetime. There are three commonly accepted methods for computing the depreciation. They are: the straight line method, the sum-of-the-years digits method, and the declining balance method. The two latter methods allow more depreciation to occur early in the life of the asset than the straight line method. Figure 8-2 compares the three methods. To differentiate among the methods, a number of points need to be made regarding the calculation of depreciation by each of the three.

1. In the declining balance method the salvage value is not subtracted from the book value before the decline of the balance is calculated. What is left at the end of the decline is the book value.

2. With straight line depreciation calculations the salvage value is subtracted from the book value before the straight line depreciation is applied. The remaining value that results is the depreciable remaining value. For tax purposes it is necessary to add this depreciable remaining value to the salvage value to determine the actual value of the asset.

3. With the sum-of-the-years' digits method, the salvage value must be subtracted from the book value before the depreciation is calculated. Thus

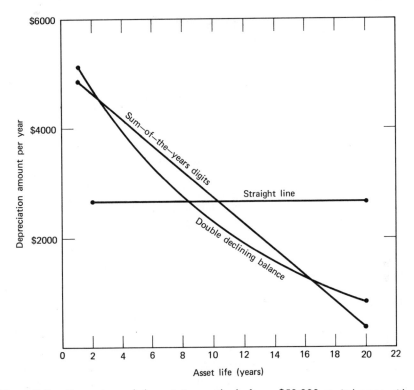

Figure 8-2. Comparison of depreciation methods for a $50,000 capital asset with a 20-year life.

the remaining value is the depreciable value, not the book value. To recover the book value it is necessary to add the salvage value to the remaining depreciable value.

4. Land does not wear out; thus its cost may not be depreciated.
5. In most real property analyses the cost of improvements to land (facilities, fixtures, buildings, etc.) must be considered separately from the cost of the land before calculating the depreciation on the real property.
6. When computing straight line depreciation of real property, the salvage value must be subtracted before the value of the property is depreciated.
7. When computing depreciation based on the sum-of-the-years' digits method, the salvage value must be subtracted from the book value before the method is applied.

8. When computing real property value depreciation using the declining balance method, the salvage value need not be subtracted from the book value but the book value may never fall below the salvage value.

9. If a depreciation schedule other than straight line depreciation is used, the excess depreciation must be calculated at the time of the real property's sale for determination of taxes.

The straight line method of depreciation is an annual depreciation calculated by subtracting from the value of the real property the cost of the land and the salvage value, and dividing that result by the useful life expectancy.

The declining balance method allows accelerated depreciation compared with the straight line method. It is a calculation of a constant percentage of the remaining book value to determine the depreciation amount. The remaining book value then is the previous book value less the depreciation amount.

The sum-of-the-years' digits method is an accelerated form of depreciation based on a common-sense technique for calculating depreciation featuring a "depreciation fraction". The numerator of the depreciation fraction is the sum of the remaining number of years of useful life, and the denominator is the sum of the years of useful life. For example, when calculating a 4-year declining balance depreciation amount, the first year is depreciated by 4 tenths (.4), which is 4 divided by 10 (which is the sum of 4 + 3 + 2 + 1). The second year is depreciated by 3 divided by 10 or 3 tenths, the third year is depreciated by 2 tenths, and the last year by 1 tenth. The total depreciation is, by definition, 10 tenths of the value of the asset (i.e., the full value of the asset).

8.7 CALCULATING RENTS AND LEASES WITH AN ORDINARY ANNUITY CALCULATOR

Rents and leases are characterized as annuities whose payments occur at the beginning of each period. These are termed annuities due. The only difference between ordinary annuities and annuities due is in relation to payments—whether they are "*in advance*" or "*in arrears*." All the techniques and problems previously discussed are applicable to annuity-due calculations. Many pocket calculators are based on ordinary annuity calculations, and the keystroke sequences must be modified to account for this difference. When calculating annual return or yield rate it is necessary to calculate the number of periods for one less than the total number of periods in the ordinary annuity and adjust the present value by subtracting one payment. When calculating the number of periods in an investment, it is necessary to modify the present value or payment amount by the addition of the interest period for one payment. The importance of these slight modifications is made clear in the keystroke sequences that follow for annuity-due calculations.

One pocket calculator that solves *both* ordinary annuity and annuity-due problems is the Hewlett-Packard HP-22. This calculator has a switch with which the user can select the type of annuity problem to be solved. Effectively the switch instructs the HP-22 to modify the calculations as described in the preceding paragraph, then uses the ordinary annuity calculation circuitry to solve the annuity-due problem. This feature is so useful that most business calculators will probably incorporate it eventually. For this book, however, it is instructive to understand the procedure for using an ordinary-annuity calculator to solve annuity-due problems, and the casebook examples are selected to illustrate the procedure. HP-22 keystrokes illustrate the advantage of the annuity-due switch in financial calculator analysis. This feature is one worth shopping for when you buy your next business and financial calculator.

CASEBOOK EXAMPLE

Determine the payment amount for a fully amortized mortgage.

The Problem

Determine the monthly payment to amortize a 25-year, 9.25%, $50,000 home mortgage.

Typical Keystroke Sequences[a]

HP-22	HP-70/80	NOVUS 6020	Rockwell 204
Annuity SW—End	(25)	(25)	(25)
(25)	K	CHS	×
▨	×	n	(12)
n (9.25)	n	(9.25)	=
			(*Continued*)

HP-22	HP-70/180	NOVUS 6020	Rockwell 204
	(9.25)	CHS	ET
i	K	%*i*	*n*
(50000)	÷	(50000)	(9.25)
PV	*i*	amt	ET
PMT	(50000)	CHS	*i*/yr
428.19	PV	PMT—Loan	(50000)
	PMT	428.19	ET
			PV
	428.19		TA
			PMT
			428.19

KEY

( ) data entry.

☐ data output.

▨ gold key.

[a]Virtually all business calculators display numbers rounded to two places past the decimal place. Be advised, however, that an analyst should calculate numbers carrying as many places past the decimal point as the calculator will allow. In this way the calculator retains as much accuracy as the electronics will allow, yet conveniently displays results in dollars and cents format. This technique leads to slight inconsistencies when *inverting* problems to check results. For example, using the *payments displayed* in this problem's answer and the 300-month horizon, the actual present value of the payment stream (the mortgage amount) is $49,999.89, eleven cents different from the $50,000 used to calculate the payment.

CASEBOOK EXAMPLE

Calculate the maximum mortgage an investor can afford: Method 1.

The Problem

A potential home buyer can afford to pay $500 per month as a mortgage payment. Assuming he obtains a 25-year mortgage at 9.25%, calculate the largest mortgage he can afford.

Typical Keystroke Sequences*

HP-22	HP-70/80	NOVUS 6020	Rockwell 204
Annuity SW—End	(500)	(500)	(500)
(500)	PMT	amt	ET
PMT	(25)	(25)	PMT
(25)	K	CHS	(25)
////	×	n	×
n	n	(9.25)	(12)
(9.25)	(9.25)	CHS	=
////	K	%i	ET
i	÷	PV—Loan	n
PV	i	⌐58385.23⌐	(9.25)
⌐58385.17⌐	PV		ET
	⌐58385.17⌐		i/yr
			TA
			PV
			⌐58385.17⌐

KEY
(   ) data entry.

☐   data output.

//// gold key.

*Not all calculators give the same result

CASEBOOK EXAMPLE

Calculate the maximum mortgage an investor can afford: method 2.

The Problem

Calculate the mortgage amount that a home buyer can afford if his gross salary is $25,000 per year, he carries $4000 of long-term debt, and he desires a 30-year mortgage at 9.25%. Assume the buyer must qualify at 4:1.

The Approach

Step 1. Subtract from the gross salary the amount of income needed to retire the long-term debt.

Step 2. Calculate the monthly gross income.

Step 3. Divide the result by 4 and use this as the payment amount.

Step 4. Determine the mortgage amount on the basis of payments, the interest rate, and the number of periods.

Typical Keystroke Sequences*

HP-22	HP-70/80	NOVUS 6020	Rockwell 204
Annuity SW—End	(25000)	(25000)	(25000)
(25000)	↑	+	−
↑	(4000)	(4000)	(4000)
(4000)	−	−	÷
−	(12)	÷	(12)
(12)	÷	(12)	÷
÷	(4)	÷	(4)
(4)	÷	(4)	=
÷	PMT	=	ET
PMT	(9.25)	amt	PMT
(9.25)	K	(9.25)	(9.25)
▨	÷	CHS	ET
i	i	%i	i/yr
(30)	(30)	(30)	(30)
▨	K	CHS	×
n	×	n	(12)
PV	n	PV—Loan	=
53180.15	PV	53180.17	ET
	53180.15		n
			TA
			PV
			53180.32

KEY

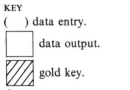

(   ) data entry.

▢   data output.

▨   gold key.

*Not all calculators give the same result

CASEBOOK EXAMPLE

Calculate the last payment in a simple mortgage.

The Problem

Generally the rounding of payment amounts causes the last payment to differ from the regular annuity payments.

To fully amortize a 25-year, $50,000, 8.75% mortgage, the payment is $411.0718133. If this amount is rounded to two places, the payment amount is $411.07. Determine the last payment, assuming the ordinary annuity is paid with the rounded amount.

The Approach

Step 1. Calculate the present value (mortgage value) of 300 payments of $411.07 at 8.75% per year.

Step 2. Subtract the results of step 1 from the desired $50,000 mortgage value.

Step 3. Calculate the future value of the difference calculated in step 2 at the time of the last payment.

Step 4. Add the amount of step 3 to the regular annuity payment to determine the last payment amount.

Typical Keystroke Sequences**

HP-22	HP-70/80	NOVUS 6020	Rockwell 204*
Annuity SW—End	(300)	(300)	(8.75)
(411.07)	n	n	ET
PMT	(411.07)	(8.75)	i/yr.
(8.75)	PMT	CHS	(411.07)
▨	(8.75)	%i	ET
			PMT
i	K	(411.07)	(50000)
(50000)	÷	amt	ET
PV	i	PV—Loan	PV
(300)	PV	−	TA
STO	$\boxed{49999.78}$	(50000)	n
			$\boxed{301}$
9	CHS	+	

(*Continued*)

HP-22	HP-70/80	NOVUS 6020	Rockwell 204
[gold key]	(50000)	amt	ET
			ET
BAL	+	(8.75)	PV
[1.95]	[0.22]	CHS	+
			ET
RCL	STO	%i	ET
PMT	M	(300)	PMT
+	CLR	n	+
[413.02]	M	FV—Interest	=
	PV	+	[412.21]
	(300)	(411.07)	
	n	+	
	(8.75)	[412.66]	
	K		
	÷		
	i		
	FV		
	[1.95]		
	(411.07)		
	+		
	[413.02]		

KEY

(   ) data entry.

[ ] data output.

[gold key] gold key.

*Solves this problem more easily by first determining the number of whole payments and then adjusting the final payment to account for the fractional overpayment required.

**Not all calculators give the same result. The correct answer is $413.02.

CASEBOOK EXAMPLE

Determine payments for a mortgage with a specified balloon payment.

The Problem

Determine the minimum monthly payment required to amortize a $15,000, 9.25%, 14-year mortgage with a balloon payment not to exceed $3000.

The Approach

Step 1.   Determine the present value of the final (balloon) payment.

Step 2.   Subtract the present value of the balloon payment from the mortgage amount. Call this the remaining mortgage amount.

Step 3.   Calculate the periodic payments based on the remaining mortgage amount to be paid in 13 years, 11 months.

Typical Keystroke Sequences

HP-22	HP-70/80	NOVUS 6020	Rockwell 204
Annuity SW—End	(3000)	(3000)	(3000)
(3000)	FV	amt	ET
FV	(9.25)	(9.25)	FV
(9.25)	K	CHS	(9.25)
▨	÷	%i	ET
i	i	(14)	i/yr
(14)	(14)	CHS	(14)
▨	K	n	×
n	×	CHS	(12)
PV	n	PV-Interest	=
STO	PV	M+	ET
1			n
▨	825.78	(9.25)	TA
RESET	CHS	CHS	PV
RCL	(15000)	%i	ET
i	+	(13)	+/−
i	STO	×	+
RCL	M	(12)	(15000)
n	CLR	=	=
(1)	M	+	ET
−	PV	(11)	PV
n	(13)	+	ET
(15000)	K	(0)	ET
RCL	×	+	n
(1)	(11)	n	−
			(Continued)

HP-22	HP-70/ 80	NOVUS 6020	Rockwell 204
−	+	MR/MC	(1)
PV	*n*	−	=
PMT	(9.25)	(15000)	ET
151.20	K	+	*n*
	÷	amt	TA
	i	CHS	PMT
	PMT	PMT-loan	151.20
	151.20	151.20	

KEY

(   ) data entry.

☐ data output.

▨ gold key.

CASEBOOK EXAMPLE

Determine balloon payment amount.

The Problem

Calculate the balloon payment on a $60,000, 9.25%, 25-year mortgage with monthly payments of $500. The balloon payment is made at the end of the twenty-fifth year.

The Approach

Step 1. Calculate the present value of a 9.25%, 25-year, $500 per month payment stream.

Step 2. Subtract the results of step 1 from $60,000.

Step 3. Calculate the future value of the difference calculated in step 2 at the time of the final payment ($n = 300$).

Step 4. **Add the result of step 3 to $500 to calculate the final payment.**

Typical Keystroke Sequences

HP-22	HP-70/80	NOVUS 6020	Rockwell 204
Annuity Sw—End	(9.25)	(9.25)	(9.25)
(9.25)	K	CHS	ET
gold key	÷	%i	i/yr
			(25)
i	i	(25)	×
(25)	(25)	CHS	(12)
			=
gold key	K	n	ET
n	×	(500)	n
(500)	n	amt	(500)
PMT	(500)	PV—Loan	ET
PV	PMT	−	PMT
CHS	PV	(60000)	TA
(60000)	CHS	+	PV
+	(60000)	amt	ET
STO	+	(25)	+/−
1	STO	CHS	+
gold key	M	n	(60000)
			=
RESET	CLR	(9.25)	ET
RCL	M	CHS	PV
i	PV	%i	TA
i	(25)	FV—Interest	FV
RCL	K	+	+
n	×	(500)	(500)
n	n	+	=
RCL	(9.25)	**16664.60**	**16663.34**
1	K		
PV	÷		
FV	i		
RCL	FV		
PMT	(500)		
+	+		
16665.22	**16665.23**		

KEY

( ) data entry.

□ data output.

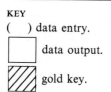 gold key.

CASEBOOK EXAMPLE

Calculate the number of payments required to retire a fully amortized mortgage.

The Problem

A $57,000 mortgage, bearing 9.25%, is to be retired with $468.92 monthly payments. Calculate the number of payments required to pay off the mortgage.

Typical Keystroke Sequences

HP-70/80/22	NOVUS 6020	Rockwell 204
Annuity SW—End[a]	(57000)	(57000)
(57000)	amt	ET
PV	(9.25)	PV
(9.25)	CHS	(9.25)
↑	%i	ET
(12)	( )	i/yr
÷	n	(468.92)
i	CHS	ET
(468.92)	PMT—Loan	PMT
PMT		TA
n		n
360.02		361 Number of payments
		ET
		ET
		PV
		+
		ET
		ET
		PMT
		=
		8.36 Last payment[b]

NOVUS 6020 flowchart: PMT—Loan → [box] → decision ⟨PMT = 468.92⟩; No → Guess new n → back to ( ); Yes → n = Last guess of n

---

[a]HP-22 only.

[b]The Rockwell 204 conveniently automates the "last payment" calculation as shown here.

KEY
( ) data entry.   ☐ data output.

CASEBOOK EXAMPLE

Determine the remaining balance at the end of a specified time on a mortgage.

The Problem

Determine the remaining balance after 7 years of payments on a 9%, 30-year, $50,000 mortgage. The monthly payment is $402.31.

The Approach

Step 1. Calculate the exact number of payments to fully amortize the loan.

Step 2. Calculate the number of *the last* payment.

Step 3. Calculate the present value of a payment stream of 18 years (25 years − 7 years) of $402.31 payments at 9% per year. The present value of this payment stream is the remaining balance of the mortgage.

Typical Keystroke Sequences

HP-22	HP-70/80	NOVUS 6020	Rockwell 204
Annuity SW—End	(50000)	(402.31)	(402.31)
(9)	PV	amt	ET
▨	(402.31)	(9)	PMT
i	PMT	CHS	(9)
(50000)	(9)	%*i*	ET
PV	K	(30)	*i*/yr
(402.31)	÷	+	(30)
PMT	*i*	(7)	−
(7)	*n*	−	(7)
↑	(84)	CHS	×
(12)	−	*n*	(12)
×	STO	PV—Loan	=
STO	M		ET
9	CLR	46820.08	*n*
▨	M		TA
BAL	*n*		PV

(*Continued*)

HP-22	HP-70/80	NOVUS 6020	Rockwell 204

| 46820.38 | (402.31) | | 46820.13 |

PMT
(9)
K
÷
i
PV

| 46820.38 |

KEY

( ) data entry.

☐ data output.

▨ gold key.

CASEBOOK EXAMPLE

Determine the interest paid during a specified period and the remaining balance at the end of that period for a real estate investment.

The Problem

For income tax purposes it is required that an investor know how much interest he has paid on a mortgage during the previous year. Assume that the monthly payments are $300 and the mortgage bears 9.25% for 30 years. Also assume that the payments made during the preceding year were numbers 20 through 31.

The Approach

Step 1. Calculate the remaining balance at the beginning of the period following payment 19.

Step 2. Calculate the remaining balance after payment 31.

Step 3. Calculate the amount of principal paid during the previous year by subtracting the balance at the beginning of the time frame from the balance at the end of the time frame.

Step 4. Calculate the total amount paid during the year.

Step 5. Subtract the principal amount paid during the year from the total amount paid to determine the accumulated interest during the year.

Typical Keystroke Sequences

HP-22	HP-70/80	NOVUS 6020	Rockwell 204
Annuity SW—End	(300)	(9.25)	(300)
(300)	PMT	CHS	ET
PMT	(9.25)	%i	PMT
(9.25)	K		(9.25)
▨		(30)	ET
	÷	×	i/yr
i	i	(12)	(30)
(30)	(30)		×
▨	K	=	(12)
n	×	+	=
PV	(19)	(19)	ET
STO	−	−	n
1	n		TA
▨		n	PV
	PV	(300)	36466.51
		amt	(19)
RESET	36081.15	PV—Loan	ET
RCL	STO	M+	n
			TA
i	M	(30)	i
i	DSP	×	(12)
RCL	n	(12)	ET
PMT	(19)	=	n
PMT	+	+	TA
RCL	(31)	(31)	i
1	−	−	3326.10
PV	n	n	
(20)	PV	(300)	
STO	35807.24	amt	
8	CHS	(9.25)	
(31)	M+	CHS	
STO	DSP	%i	
9	PMT	PV—Loan	

(*Continued*)

HP-22	HP-70/80	NOVUS 6020	Rockwell 204

	K	CHS
ACC	×	M+
3326.09	M	(300)
	−	×
	3326.09	(12)
		=
		+
		MR/MC
		−
		3326.06

KEY
( ) data entry.

☐ data output.

▨ gold key.

CASEBOOK EXAMPLE

Calculate annual percentage rate when fees are involved.

The Problem

The truth-in-lending laws (Regulation Z) require that the annual percentage rate associated with a mortgage be specified. The calculation is straightforward when fees are not involved, but it is slightly more complex when fees must be included. Calculate the annual percentage rate for (*a*) mortgages with fees that are expressed as a percentage of the mortgage amount—called points, (*b*) mortgages when the fees are given as a flat charge, and (*c*) mortgages when fees are presented as points plus a flat charge.

Calculate the APR for a $50,000 mortgage for 25 years at 9.25%, where the mortgage bears additional fees of 3 points and $200.

The Approach

Step 1. Calculate the mortgage payments based on a $50,000 present value, 9.25% interest rate, and 25 years.

Step 2. Deduct the fees from the $50,000—called the adjusted mortgage value.

Step 3. Recalculate the interest rate per year based on the payments from step 1, the adjusted mortgage value and the 25-year investment horizon.

Typical Keystroke Sequences

HP-22	HP-70/80	NOVUS 6020	Rockwell 204
Annuity SW—End	(25)	(25)	(25)
(50000)	K	CHS	×
PV	×	n	(12)
(9.25)	n	(50000)	=
▨	(50000)	amt	ET
i	PV	(9.25)	n
(25)	(9.25)	CHS	(50000)
▨	K	%i	ET
n	÷	CHS	PV
PMT	i	PMT—Loan	(9.25)
428.19	PMT	M+	ET
STO	428.19	(50000)	i/yr
1	STO	×	TA
▨	M	(3)	PMT
RESET	DSP	%	428.19 = x
RCL	PV	−	(50000)
n	(3)	(200)	×
n	%	−	(3)
RCL	−	amt	%
1	(200)	(25)	ET
PMT	−	CHS	+/−
RCL	STO	n	−
PV	K	( )◄	(200)
(.97)	CLR	CHS	+
×	K	%i	(50000)
(200)	PV	CHS	=
−	M	PMT—Loan / Guess	ET
		+ \ new %i	PV
		MR/MC	( )◄
		−	ET
			i/yr

(*Continued*)

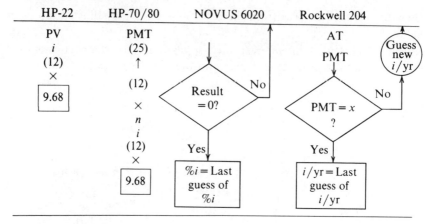

KEY
(   ) data entry.

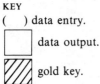 data output.

gold key.

CASEBOOK EXAMPLE

Calculate the compounded appreciation: land.

The Problem

Calculate the value at the end of two years of an acre of land that is presently priced at $4000 and is expected to appreciate at the compounded rate of 7% per year.

Typical Keystroke Sequences

HP-70/80/22	NOVUS 6020	Rockwell 204
Annuity Switch-End[a]	(7)	(7)
(7)	%i	ET
i	(4000)	i
(4000)	amt	(4000)

(Continued)

HP-70/80/22	NOVUS 6020	Rockwell 204
PV	(2)	ET
(2)	n	PV
n	FV—Interest	(2)
FV		ET
	4579.60	
4579.60		n
		TA
		FV
		4579.60

KEY
( ) data entry.
⬚ data output.

[a] HP-22 only

CASEBOOK EXAMPLE

Calculate the compounded appreciation rate of property.

The Problem

Property bought 5 years ago for $55,000 is currently selling for $95,000. Determine the compounded appreciation rate.

Typical Keystroke Sequences

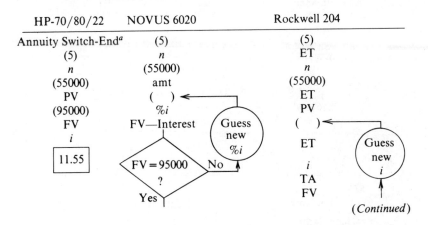

HP-70/80/22	NOVUS 6020	Rockwell 204
Annuity Switch-End[a]	(5)	(5)
(5)	n	ET
n	(55000)	n
(55000)	amt	(55000)
PV	( )	ET
(95000)	%i	PV
FV	FV—Interest	( )
i		ET
11.55		i
		TA
		FV

(*Continued*)

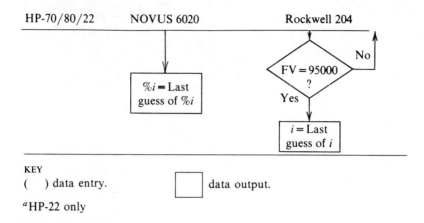

KEY
(   ) data entry.   ☐ data output.

*ᵃ*HP-22 only

CASEBOOK EXAMPLE

Calculate the compounded appreciation: house.

The Problem

What will be the future value of a house currently worth $50,000 if the annual rate of appreciation is 7.25% and the expected date of sale is in 7 years.

Typical Keystroke Sequences

HP-70/80/22	NOVUS 6020	Rockwell 204
Annuity Switch-End*ᵃ*	(50000)	(50000)
(50000)	amt	ET
PV	(7.25)	PV
(7.25)	%i	(7.25)
i	(7)	ET
(7)	n	i
n	FV—Interest	(7)
FV		ET
	81611.44	n
81611.45		TA
		FV
		81611.47

KEY
(   ) data entry.   ☐ data output.

*ᵃ*HP-22 only

CASEBOOK EXAMPLE

Determine the price to pay for a discounted mortgage to achieve a desired yield.

The Problem

Determine the discount price to pay on 25-year, $30,000 fully amortized mortgage at 7.5%, with monthly payments of $221.70, if you wish to realize a 12% yield on the mortgage instrument.

The Approach

Simply calculate the net present value of the $221.70 monthly cash flow for the 300 months, assuming a 12% yield.

Typical Keystroke Sequences

HP-22	HP-70/80	NOVUS 6020	Rockwell 204
Annuity Switch-End[a]	(221.70)	(221.70)	(221.70)
(221.70)	PMT	amt	ET
PMT	(25)	(25)	PMT
(25)	K	CHS	(25)
▨	×	n	×
n	n	(12)	(12)
(12)	(12)	CHS	=
▨	K	%i	ET
i	÷	PV—Loan	n
PV	i		(12)
⟨21049.65⟩		⟨21049.65⟩	ET
	PV		i/yr
			TA
	⟨21049.65⟩		PV
			⟨21049.65⟩

KEY
( ) data entry.

▭ data output.

▨ gold key.

[a] HP-22 only

CASEBOOK EXAMPLE

Determine the price of a mortgage instrument with a balloon payment.

The Problem

Calculate the price to be paid for a $10,000, 9.25%, 9-year mortgage, with periodic payments of $124.82 and a final balloon payment of $2000; the desired yield is 12%.

The Approach

Step 1. Compute the present value of the $2000 balloon payment at a 12% yield.

Step 2. Compute the present value of the $124.82 annuity for the 9-year less one month period at a 12% yield.

Step 3. Sum the results of steps 1 and 2 to determine the discounted price for the mortgage instrument to achieve the 12% yield.

Typical Keystroke Sequences

HP-22	HP-70/80	NOVUS 6020	Rockwell 204
Annuity Switch-End[a]	(2000)	(2000)	(2000)
(2000)	FV	amt	
FV	(9)	(12)	ET
(9)	K	CHS	FV
▨	×	%i	(12)
n	n	(9)	ET
(12)	(12)	CHS	i/yr
▨	K	n	(9)
i	÷	CHS	×
PV	i	PV—Interest	(12)
STO	PV		=
1		682.84	ET
	682.84	M+	n
▨	STO	(12)	TA
RESET	M	CHS	PV
(124.82)	CLR	%i	
PMT			

(*Continued*)

HP-22	HP-70/80	NOVUS 6020	Rockwell 204
RCL	(124.82)	(9)	
i	PMT	×	682.84
i	(9)	(12)	(124.82)
RCL	K	=	ET
n	×	+	PMT
(1)	−	1	ET
−	(1)	−	ET
n	n	n	n
PV	(12)	(124.82)	−
RCL	K	amt	(1)
1	÷		=
+	i	PV—Loan	ET
8890.60	PV	8177.75	n
			TA
	8177.75	M+	PV
	M+	MR/MC	8177.75
	8860.60	8860.59	+
			(682.84)
			=

KEY

(   ) data entry.

☐   data output.   ▨ gold key.

^{a}HP-22 only

CASEBOOK EXAMPLE

Straight line depreciation of real estate.

The Problem

Using the straight-line depreciation method, calculate the annual depreciation allowance for the first 2 years of a $125,000 building to be depreciated over 30 years with a $10,000 salvage value.

The Approach

Step 1. Calculate the *depreciable amount* = initial value plus improvement costs minus salvage value.

Step 2. Divide by the depreciation period (useful life). The result is the *annual depreciation allowance*.

Step 3. Multiply the depreciation allowance by the number of years depreciated and subtract from the depreciable amount to determine the *remaining depreciable value*.

Typical Keystroke Sequences

HP-22	HP-70/80	NOVUS 6020	Rockwell 204
(125000)	(125000)	(125000)	(125000)
↑	↑	+	−
(10000)	(10000)	(10000)	(10000)
−	−	−	÷
STO	STO	÷	(30)
1	K	(30)	=
(30)	↑	=	ET
÷	(30)	M+	i
STO	÷	(125000)	(125000)
2	STO	+	−
RCL	M	(10000)	(10000)
1	K	−	−
RCL	M	MR/MC	ET
2	−	−	ET
−	111166.67		i
111166.67		111166.67	
RCL	M	MR/MC	=
2	−	−	111166.67
	107333.33		−
	:	107333.34	ET
−	:		ET
		:	i
107333.33		:	=
:			107333.34
:			:
			:

KEY

(   ) data entry.

☐   data output.

CASEBOOK EXAMPLE

Sum-of-the-years' digits method of depreciation of real estate.

The Problem

Using the sum-of-the-years' digits formula, calculate the annual depreciation allowance for the first 2 years of a $125,000 building to be depreciated over 30 years with a $10,000 salvage value.

The Approach

Step 1. Determine the depreciable amount – improvement costs plus original cost minus salvage value.

Step 2. Calculate the depreciation factor $= [2(L-P+1)]/[L(L+1)]$, where $L=30$ and $P=$ year of depreciation.

Step 3. Compute the annual depreciation allowance, which is the depreciation factor times the depreciation amount.

Step 4. Determine the remaining depreciable amount.

Step 5. Iterate steps 3 and 4 for the number of years of the depreciable life.

Typical Keystroke Sequences

HP-70/80/22	NOVUS 6020	Rockwell 204
(125000)	(125000)	(30)
↑	+	+
(10000)	(10000)	(1)
−	−	=
STO $\Big\}^a$ K	(30)	ET
(30)	n	PMT
↑	SOD	−
(31)	7419.35	(1)
×	EX	×
STO $\Big\}^a$ M	SOD	(2)
(30)	7172.04	÷

(Continued)

HP-70/80/22	NOVUS 6020	Rockwell 204
↑		(30)
		÷
(1)		ET
−		ET
(1)		PMT
+		×
(2)		(115000)
×		=
M^a		
÷		7419.35
K^a		
		ET
×		ET
		PMT
7419.35		−
(30)		(2)
↑		×
(2)		(2)
−		÷
(1)		(30)
+		÷
(2)		ET
×		ET
M^a		PMT
÷		×
K^a		(115000)
		=
×		
		7172.04
7172.04		

^{a} $\underset{K}{STO} = \underset{1}{STO}$ and $\underset{M}{STO} = \underset{2}{STO}$ and $M = \underset{2}{RCL}$ and $K = \underset{1}{RCL}$
for HP-70 and HP-22, respectively.

KEY

( ) data entry.

[ ] data output.

CASEBOOK EXAMPLE

A discussion of equity investment analysis on the HP-80 calculator*

*By permission from the Hewlett-Packard Corporation. Discussion drawn from the HP-80 Real Estate Applications Manual.

Equity investment analysis is a method of evaluating income producing real estate investment alternatives on a *pretax* basis. Two key factors in this type of analysis are the anticipated income stream that the property will provide and the property's projected resale value at the end of the investment horizon. Based on this and the current price of the property, an equity yield rate can be found giving an indication of the profitability of the investment.

One of the basic equations used in real estate equity analysis relates the income stream, sales price, projected appreciation or depreciation, and amount of mortgage as follows:

$$R = Y - MC \frac{-\text{apprec.}}{+\text{deprec.}} \frac{1}{S_n} = \frac{\text{NOI}}{\text{price}}$$

where

R = reversion

Y = equity yield rate

M = mortgage

C = mortgage coefficient (imbedded in calculation)

$1/S_n$ = sinking fund factor for depreciation or appreciation

NOI = net operating income

Without using any tables the HP-80 enables the user to evaluate his potential investment to determine whether it meets his objectives. Solutions for equity yield rate and equity investment value are included in the sections that follow.

A brief explanation of terms frequently used in real estate analysis is given here in order to aid in understanding the problems and results more fully.

Annual net cash flow is the annual net operating income minus the annual debt service (i.e., annual mortgage payments).

Reversion is the future sales price minus the mortgage balance at the end of the projection period.

Equity yield rate is that annual rate at which the present value of the net annual cash flows plus the present value of the equity reversion equals the equity investment value.

Equity investment value is the equity in the property at the beginning of the projection period.

Overall capitalization rate is the net operating income divided by the selling price.

Equity Yield Rate

Given the projection period in years, reversion amount, annual net cash flow, and equity investment value, the equity yield rate can be calculated as follows:

1. Calculate and enter reversion; press $\boxed{\text{SAVE}\uparrow}$ 100 $\boxed{\div}$ $\boxed{\text{STO}}$.

2. Enter number of years projection; press
    $\boxed{\text{SAVE}\uparrow}$ 2 $\boxed{\div}$ 365 $\boxed{\times}$ $\boxed{n}$.

3. Enter net annual cash flow; press $\boxed{\text{RCL}}$ $\boxed{\div}$ 2 $\boxed{\times}$ $\boxed{\text{PMT}}$.

4. Enter equity investment value, press $\boxed{\text{RCL}}$ $\boxed{\div}$ $\boxed{\text{PV}}$.

5. Press 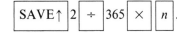 $\overset{\text{YTM}}{\boxed{}}$ i 2 $\boxed{\div}$ to obtain equity yield rate.

The Problem

An apartment complex is listed for $1,960,500 and has an annual net operating income of $166,315.40. The prospective buyer is considering a down payment of $572,500 and will finance the remaining $1,388,000 for 29 years at 8%. If the property appreciates a total of 20% over the next 10 years, what would the equity yield rate be?

The Approach

Using calculations from other sections it is found that the monthly mortgage payments are $10,270.45 and therefore the annual net cash flow is $43,070 (NOI − debt service = net cash flow). The remaining mortgage balance at the end of 10 years will be $1,201,922.57. To calculate the reversion at the end of the tenth year, find the future sales price and subtract the remaining balance.

Typical Keystroke Sequence

Enter	See Displayed	
1960500 $\boxed{\text{SAVE}\uparrow}$ 20 $\boxed{\%}$ $\boxed{+}$	2352600.00	Future sales price reversion

(*Continued*)

Enter	See Displayed

$$1201922.57 \boxed{-} \qquad\qquad 1150677.43$$

To find equity yield rate:

1. $1150677.43 \boxed{\text{SAVE}\uparrow}$

   $100 \boxed{\div} \boxed{\text{STO}} \qquad\qquad 11506.77$

2. $10 \boxed{\text{SAVE}\uparrow} 2 \boxed{\div} 365$

   $\boxed{\times}\boxed{n} \qquad\qquad 1825.00$

3. $43070 \boxed{\text{RCL}} \boxed{\div} 2 \boxed{\times} \boxed{\text{PMT}} \qquad 7.49$

4. $572500 \boxed{\text{RCL}} \boxed{\div} \boxed{\text{PV}} \qquad 49.75$

5. $\boxed{\text{YTM}} \boxed{i} 2 \boxed{\div} \qquad\qquad 13.00 \qquad\qquad$ Equity yield rate

Equity Investment Value and Present Value

Given the desired equity yield rate, projection period, annual net cash flow, and the reversion, the HP-80 can solve for the equity investment value and present value of the investment (current sales price).

Information is entered as follows:

1. Enter projection period in years; press $\boxed{n}$. Enter equity yield rate in percent; press $\boxed{i}$. Enter the reversion, press $\boxed{\text{FV}}\boxed{\text{PV}}\boxed{\text{STO}}$ to find the present value of the reversion.

2. Enter the projection period in years; press $\boxed{n}$. Enter the equity yield rate in percent; press $\boxed{i}$. Enter the annual net cash flow press $\boxed{\text{PMT}}\boxed{\text{PV}}$ to obtain the present value of the net cash flows.

3. Press $\boxed{\text{RCL}}\boxed{+}$ for the equity investment value.

4. Enter mortgage amount, press $\boxed{+}$ to obtain current sales price or present value.

The Problem

An investor has some money he wants to invest in real estate. One of his alternatives is a warehouse, currently leased for 10 years, which generates $26,460 annually before debt service (NOI). Because the warehouse is located in a growth area, he estimates the property should sell for $420,000 at the end of 10 years. He can obtain an 8.5%, 20-year mortgage for $240,000 which would have monthly payments of $2,082.78. If his desired yield is 11% over 10 years, what would his equity investment value be and how much could he pay for the property (what is the current sales price)?

Typical Keystroke Sequence

	Enter	See Displayed	
	Calculate reversion		
	8.5 SAVE↑ 12 ÷ i	0.71	Periodic interest rate
	2082.78 STO PMT	2082.78	
	240000 PV n	240.00	Exact number of payments to amortize loan
	120 − n	120.00	
	8.5 SAVE↑ 12 ÷ i	0.71	
	RCL PMT PV	167984.38	Remaining loan balance after 10 years
	CHS 420000 + STO	252015.62	Reversion value
1.	10 n 11 i RCL FV		
	PV STO	88755.99	Present value of reversion
2.	10 n 11 i 2082.78		
	SAVE↑ 12 × CHS	− 24993.36	Annual debt service
	26460 + PMT PV	8637.38	Present value of net cash flows
3.	RCL +	97393.37	Equity investment value
4.	240000 +	337393.37	Current sales price

CASEBOOK EXAMPLE

Worksheets for real estate calculations on the HP-70.

Many users who frequently do the same types of calculations may find it convenient to draw up forms containing the actual keystrokes necessary to obtain the required answers. In this way, consistency is guaranteed no matter who does the actual computation. Example worksheets for the HP-70 are shown below.

Purchaser _____ Seller _____
Address _____ Address _____
_____
Phone: Office _____ Res. _____ Phone: Office _____ Res.. _____

Property _____ Selling Office _____ Phone _____
Address _____ Salesman _____ Phone _____
A.P.N. _____ Previous Taxes _____ Assessments _____
Date of sale _____ Date of application _____ Estimated closing date _____
Loan type _____ Loan placed with _____
Appraised at $ _____ Origination fee _____ Loan points _____
Interest rate _____ %   Number of years _____ Selling price $ _____

[ENTER↑] [ENTER↑] Percent loan _____ [%] = Loan amt. $ _____ [STO] [M] [−]

Down payment $ _____ [R↓] = SALE PRICE

FIXED CLOSING COSTS
Standard Title Policy and Escrow Fees

_____ [−] [ENTER↑] [ENTER↑] _____ [×] _____ [+] $ _____ [x ≷ y]
(base)   (rate)   (base amount.)

ATA Title policy and inspection

_____ [×] _____ [+] $ _____ [+]
(rate)   (base amount)

Credit report fee $ _____ [+]

California tax service $ _____ [+]

Drawing and recording $ _____ [+]

Continued

Appraisal report $_____ +

Termite report $_____ +

Photos, inspections, mileage $_____ +

Drawing loan documents $_____ +

Septic tank and water inspection $_____ +

M   Origination fee, ____ Pts % | x ≷ y | R↓ $_____ +

Other $_____ +

EST. TOTAL FIXED COSTS $_____

Purchaser's Income Qualifications

Annual base income $_____ ENTER↑

Overtime _____ ENTER↑ .5 × $_____ +

Spouse annual income $_____ +

Stock/bond dividends $_____ +

Rents/leases $_____ +

Other $_____ +

GROSS ANNUAL INCOME $_____ 12 + ENTER↑ ENTER↑

Loans $_____ ENTER↑

Charge accounts $_____ +

                                                $_____ +

Other $_____ + 12 +

Monthly installment payments $_____ +

                                                $_____ +

Continued

AVERAGE MONTHLY DEBT	$ _____ **–**
Adjusted monthly income	$ _____ ( ) **+**
EST. MAXIMUM MONTHLY PAYMENT	$ _____

MONTHLY PAYMENT

Mortgage payment (prin + int)

___ **n** — **i** — **M** — **PV** — **PMT** ___ $ _____

(periods) (int/pd)

FHA/MGIC Insurance/month $ _____ **+**

Home and fire insurance/month $ _____ **+**

Taxes/month $ _____ **+**

EST. TOTAL MONTHLY PAYMENT $ _____

Another area where a worksheet is helpful is income property analysis. The following outline covers most basic considerations used in such analyses. It is not intended to be the definite analysis worksheet but rather to be used as a guide in making your own form for analyzing properties.

Property Description

Location _____

Type of property _____

Market value _____ Land _____

Improvements _____

Personal property _____

Total _____

Financing

Existing

First mortgage $ _____ at _____ %

     for _____ years.

     Monthly payment $ _____

Second mortgage $ _____ at _____ %

     for _____ years.

     Monthly payment $ _____

Potential

$ _____ at _____

     for _____ years.

     Monthly payment $ _____

$ _____ at _____ %

     for _____ years.

     Monthly payment $ _____

Income	
Gross scheduled income	_____
less vacancy and credit losses	_____ −
equals Gross operating income	_____
less Operating expenses	_____ −
less Taxes	_____ −
less Insurance, etc.	_____ −
equals Net operating income	_____
less Interest	_____ −
less Depreciation	_____ −
equals Taxable income (Loss)	_____
Income tax (Savings)	_____
Net operating income	_____
less Annual debt service	_____ −
equals Gross spendable income	_____
less Income tax	_____ −
less Capital improvements	_____ −
equals Net spendable income	_____
plus principal payment	_____ +
equals Net equity income	_____

PART 2

BUSINESS SYSTEMS ANALYSIS ON THE POCKET CALCULATOR

CHAPTER 9

BUSINESS STATISTICS

The pocket calculator is ideal for the statistical analysis of business because the keystroke sequences are easy and straightforward, requiring little or nothing in the way of special techniques. More important is the correct use of statistics in business decisions and business systems analysis, and therefore this chapter deals with concepts, definitions, and uses of business statistics.

It is tempting to jump into advanced applications of statistics, but the level of detail has been purposely restricted to the elementary concepts of probability, sampling, and estimation. The use of statistics for business decision making, as discussed in Chapters 2 and 10, is put on somewhat firmer ground in this chapter. Finally, because many businessmen must employ control techniques to monitor processes characterized by an increasing degree of automation, the topic of confidence intervals is touched on lightly.

Consider the set of all people in the United States of America—a population of approximately 212 million, each individual having certain characteristics. Within this population there are groups of people sharing the same characteristics. There is a group that is male, a group that is female, a group that is white, a group that is black, a group whose height is greater than 5 feet, and many other groups. Thus in the same way that individuals are characterized by individual traits, groups are characterized by group traits. Statistics is the mathematical discipline for quantifying group characteristics. Specifically, 50% of the population in 1950 was female, 10% was black, and the median age of all Americans was 30.2 years. Statistics is the field of mathematics for analyzing the properties of groups.

The three most fundamental concepts associated with any group are its frequency distribution, its measure of central tendency, and its measure of variability. Frequency distributions in their simplest form are the number of people of a population that are in a given group. For example, if we break down the heights of adult human beings into ten groups, such as the number whose height is between 0 and 1 foot, the number whose height is between 1 and 2 feet, the number between 2 and 3 feet, the number between 3 and 4 feet, the number between 4 and 5 feet, and so on, to the number whose height is between 9 and 10 feet, we can form a table for an array of numbers (Table 9-1), which when plotted graphically appears as shown in Figure 9-1. Figure 9-1 is an example of a frequency distribution.

It is apparent from Figure 9-1 that there are very few adults taller than 7 feet. It is also apparent that most adults are members of the group whose height is between 5 and 6 feet. This is an indication of the *central tendency* of all these groups. It is also apparent that there is a spread or *variance* about the central tendency of plus or minus a foot. One can then specify

Table 9-1   Height of American Adults

Height Group (feet)	Percent of American Adults (%)	Cumulative Percentage (%)
0–1	0	0
1–2	0	0
2–3	0	0
3–4	0	0
4–5	4	4
5–6	89	93
6–7	7	100
7–8	0	100
8–9	0	100
9–10	0	100

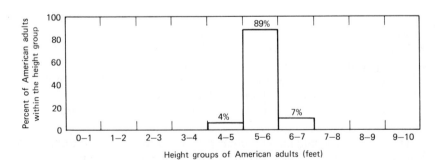

Figure 9-1.   Frequency distribution of American adult height.

this distribution of heights among the adults in the United States by stating that the *average* height is between 5 and 6 feet, plus or minus one foot.

We have seen that groups are characterized less by the individual characteristics of the individual members of the group than by the fact that there is a group within a *population* that satisfies some criterion. Thus it is possible to count the number of people in such groups and form a frequency distribution.

We have seen that a frequency distribution can be characterized by the measures of central tendency or the tendency to bunch up and *center* on some number. Furthermore we have seen that it is possible to judge from a frequency distribution the measures of variance of distribution about the central tendency. The remainder of this chapter deals with the mathematical techniques for computing measures of central tendency and variance and how they are used both for large and small populations and *samples* of these populations to forecast markets, determine trends, test hypotheses, control quality, and formulate decision problems to improve business decision making.

Since human intuition is a form of implicit statistical analysis, the real question confronting a businessman is, "Why should I study statistics and learn to use it in my business?" The answer is found in some of the recent research conducted by business and systems analysts which indicates that human beings tend to throw away some 50 to 80% of the information available to them by failing to use correct statistical analysis techniques.[*] This is an exciting finding, since it shows that the businessman who is comfortable with statistics will have a competitive edge over one who is not. The author's personal experience is a case in point. Before he began using statistical decision-making tools, one venture was going out of business. The author learned the techniques of statistically estimating costs and revenues, whereupon the reason the business was in trouble became apparent, and it was a simple matter to turn it around to produce a sturdy 28% annual rate of return. The gist of the idea of statistical business analysis hinges on statistically estimating revenues and costs because

$$\text{profit} = \text{revenues} - \text{costs}$$

If you were told that the *most likely* revenues of a small business were $500,000 and the *most likely* costs were $300,000, should you expect the

[*]L. D. Phillips and W. Edwards, "Conservatism in a Simple Probability Inference Task," *Journal of Experimental Psychology*, **72** (1966), 346–354.

W. Edwards, "Conservatism in Human Information Processing." B. Kleinmuntz (Ed.), *Formal Representation of Human Judgment*, Wiley, 1968, pp. 17–52.

Ralph F. Miles Jr., *Systems Concepts*, Wiley, 1973, pp. 90–94.

venture to return a profit? The answer is **No!** Surprised? What you were not told is that the revenues and costs are statistically distributed as shown in Figure 9-2, which reveals that although the most likely profit is estimated to be +$200,000, the **expected** profit is −$30,000.* The message is clear—to understand a business, it is important to be able to describe its cash flow on a statistical basis, enabling yourself to visualize financial risks.

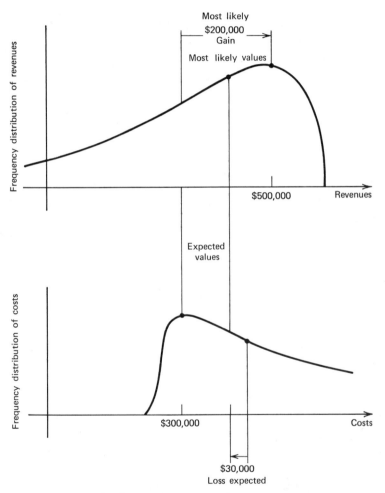

Figure 9-2. Frequency distribution of revenues and costs.

*The most likely value of a revenue or cost distribution is the amount at which the distribution reaches its peak. The amount which divides the area under the frequency distribution curve into two equal parts is the expected value of the revenues or costs.

9.1   CONSTRUCTING FREQUENCY DISTRIBUTIONS

Consider the set of 20 numbers of Table 9-2. Now consider the following set of five groups:

Group	Definition
1	Numbers between 4 and 5
2	Numbers between 5 and 6
3	Numbers between 6 and 7
4	Numbers between 7 and 8
5	Numbers between 8 and 9

Table 9-2   A Set of 20 Numbers

4.53	5.81	8.22	6.19	5.17	6.88	7.35
6.73	5.05	7.52	5.96	6.64	7.96	
7.91	6.27	6.54	8.06	6.82	6.73	7.31

To make a histogram, one counts the number of numbers that reside in the group. A graph can be constructed as in Figure 9-3. Since the total number in all groups is 20, the percentage of the total *population* can be computed by taking the ratio of the number in each group to the population size. The

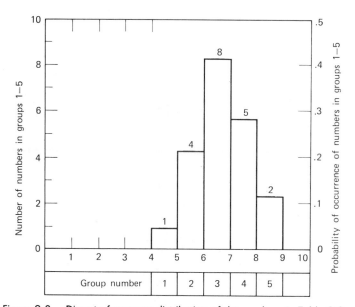

Figure 9-3.   Discrete frequency distribution of the numbers in Table 9-2.

standard form for the frequency distribution is a plot of this percentage as a function of the group size, also as shown in Figure 9-3. Frequency distributions are either continuous or discrete. The frequency distribution in Figure 9-3 is discrete. A continuous frequency distribution is sketched in Figure 9-4. Discrete and continuous distributions differ in that the latter has (mathematically speaking) an infinite number of population members. Another way to think of this is to realize that what causes the quantization and jumpiness of the discrete distribution is that the smallest change from step to step is a jump in each group of one number of the total population. If the population is of size N, the probability changes for that group by $1/N$. The jumpiness is from step to step in a discrete distribution and is a minimum of $1/N$ in size. As N gets large the jump size gets small, and the distribution goes from a grainy stairstep appearing function to a continuous smooth curve.

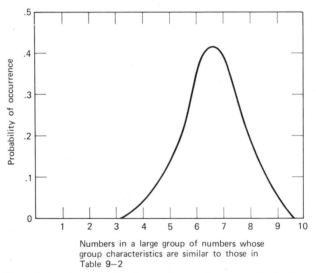

Numbers in a large group of numbers whose group characteristics are similar to those in Table 9–2

Figure 9-4.   An example of a continuous frequency distribution.

9.2   MEASURES OF CENTRAL TENDENCY

As indicated previously, a measure of central tendency is a number (technically called a *statistic*) that can be computed from a population of numbers and typifies or is the *average* of the characteristics of the group. There are three useful and usual measures of central tendency: the mean, the median, and the mode.

The mean value is computed by adding all the numbers in a group of numbers and dividing by the number of numbers in the group. The mean of a day's sales is computed by adding the value of all the sales and dividing by the total number of sales. For example:

Sales
—————
$100
130
260
195   number of   average $= \dfrac{\$1546}{7} = \$220.86$ per sale
352   sales $= 7$
97
412
—————
$1546 = total sales

This is one of the statistics that even the simplest four-function pocket calculator is ideally suited to compute.

The median is the middle value in a set of measurements. In this example the median is the middle value of the set of sales. To find the median, arrange the sales in an array with the largest sale at the top and the smallest sale at the bottom. Then simply find the middle number in the array to determine the median of the distribution. In this case the median is 195 as

$$
\begin{array}{l}
\text{Ordered array} \\
\text{of sales—largest} \\
\text{to the smallest}
\end{array}
\left\{
\begin{array}{l}
412 \\
352 \\
260 \\
195 \leftarrow \text{Median} \\
130 \\
100 \\
97
\end{array}
\right.
$$

The mode (most likely value) of a *population* of numbers is the number that occurs at the peak of the distribution. The mode of a *distribution* is the number that occurs most often in a group of numbers. In a bar graph situation it is the tallest bar in the graph. Another way to determine the mode of a distribution is to form the array just discussed for finding the median and identify the number that occurs most often. The mode of the discrete frequency distribution shown in Figure 9-3 is group 3—the numbers between 6 and 7.

In a sense these measures of central tendency are the values that *typify* a frequency distribution. This means that a single number can replace the group of data "on the average." Of particular importance throughout this chapter is the concept of the mean. A formula that we use to symbolize computing the mean is

$$\mu = \bar{X} = \frac{\sum\limits_{j=1}^{N} X_j}{N} = \frac{\sum X}{N}$$

where $\bar{X}$ is the mean, X represents each of the individual observations, N is the number of observations, and Σ indicates the operation of summing all the values of X.

9.3 MEASURES OF DISPERSION

This section is devoted to the quantification or measurement of the dispersion associated with a data population. One obvious measure of this dispersion is the range of the frequency distribution. The range is measured by taking the difference between the largest and smallest values in the population. Of more immediate interest, however, is the dispersion about the mean (the dispersion about the central tendency). The most common measure of the dispersion about the mean is called the standard deviation. The standard deviation is computed in a five-step procedure.

Step 1. Compute the mean.

Step 2. Compute the difference between each of the data in the population and the mean. This is a measure of the distance of the *datum* from the mean value of the population.

Step 3. Compute the square of each of the differences computed in step 2 and sum all these values.

Step 4. Divide the sum computed in the last part of step 3 by the number of data in the population.

Step 5. Compute the square root of the results of step 4. This procedure generates the standard deviation of the data about the mean. An example of this calculation appears in Table 9-3. The formula that symbolizes the calculation of standard deviation is

$$\sigma = \sqrt{\frac{\Sigma(x - \mu)^2}{N}}$$

Table 9-3   Calculating the Standard Deviation for the Set of Numbers: 1, 2, 3

Step 1.	$\dfrac{1+2+3}{3}=2$	Mean
Step 2.	$(1-2)=-1$ $(2-2)=0$ $(3-2)=1$	Calculate the difference between each of the data in the population and the mean.
Step 3.	$(-1)^2=1$ $(0)^2=0$ $(1)^2=\dfrac{1}{2}$	Calculate the square of each of the differences from step 2.
Total		
Steps 4 and 5.	$\sqrt{\tfrac{2}{3}}=0.81649697.$	

9.4   SAMPLES

Consider now a very large population such as that of the United States. How can one make reasonable estimations of the group characteristics of this population? For example, if a businessman wants to market a new product, such as a new type of pocket calculator, how can he make judgments about the marketplace without actually selling pocket calculators all over the United States? The answer is, of course, that predictions are made about the population on the basis of small samples. This is a key word—**sample**—since it has a specific meaning in statistics. A sample is not one thing, as ordinary usage usually implies. A statistical sample is a group of data selected from a population whose statistical characteristics are expected to hold for the entire population. Once again, a sample and a population are both groups of data. The population is a large group; the sample is a small group. The sample is a small subset of the population. If a sample of a population is based on random tests of the population, we would expect the statistics of the sample to match the statistics of the population. It is important to recognize, however, that the sample of the population **is not** the population. There is always some measure of uncertainty in attributing the statistics of the sample to the statistics of the population. Thus in sampling we need to establish a *confidence level* in the statistics of the sample. Stated slightly differently, we want to quantify the confidence we have in computing the statistics of the population based on only a small sample of that whole population. Our objective in this section is to illuminate the process of making predictions about populations based on (smaller) samples of the populations. Also we discuss the confidence with which predictions about the samples can be made based on information about the overall populations.

9.5 DEFINITIONS

A **population** is all events or observations or measurements of a particular type.

A **sample** is a smaller number of events or observations or measurements from a population taken in a way that allows every possible event or observation an equal chance of occurring. Our objective is to use statistics to make statements about (*a*) what a sample is probably like (on the basis of information about the population) and (*b*) what the population is probably like based on information taken from a sample.

A **parameter** is a number used to characterize a population frequency distribution. Said in another way, a number used to characterize a population is called a parameter. A number used to characterize a sample distribution is called a **statistic**. In our example of the population of the United States, the mean height of all the country's inhabitants is called a parameter. However the mean height of the inhabitants of Miles City, Montana, is called a statistic. Our problem is, given the measurement of the average height of people in Miles City, Montana, what can be said about the average height of all the people in the United States? Similarly, given the average height of all the people in the United States, what can be said about the people in Miles City, Montana? In other words, how can we reason back and forth from population to sample and from sample to population? Said slightly differently, how can we reason from statistics to parameters and from parameters to statistics?

To better understand this question, conduct the following experiment. Let us determine the proportion of times that a flipped coin will come up heads. Flip the coin twice and note how often it comes up heads. The results of these two tosses constitute the sample of which the results of all possible tosses constitute the population.

Based on the experiment, we can now compute the proportion of times the coin came up heads with the formula

$$p = \frac{\text{number of heads}}{\text{total number of tosses}}$$

$$= \begin{cases} p = 1 & \text{if the coin came up heads twice} \\ p = .5 & \text{if the coin came up heads once} \\ p = 0 & \text{if the coin came up tails both times} \end{cases}$$

The value of p is the *statistic*. It describes the statistical characteristics of the sample. It is generally accepted that the *parameter* describing the population of all possible coin flips is $P = .5$. It is obvious that there is a difference between P and p. The question, of course, given any one of three values of p, is what is the confidence that the value selected is representative of P? It is most important to note that $p = 1$ can occur only one way and $p = 0$ can occur only one way, but there are two ways for $p = .5$ to occur. On the basis of this information we can draw a frequency distribution for the statistic associated with a sample and make a judgment on the confidence associated with saying $P = .5$ based on our 2 coin tosses. Since 2 of the possible 4 outcomes of the 2 tosses won't agree with saying $P = .5$, you might think that $P = .5 \pm .25$ based on viewing the distribution possible outcomes assuming $P = .5$. In general, sample statistics have distributions in the same way that any group of data can have distributions and can be used to judge the confidence in an estimate.

Another obvious question is, "What is the relationship between the distribution of the sample and the distribution of the population?" The answer is straightforward. If $\mu_{\bar{X}}$ is the mean of the sample and $\sigma_{\bar{X}}$ is the standard deviation of the mean of the sample, while μ is the mean of the population and σ is the standard deviation of the population, the statistics and the parameters are related according to the equations

$$\mu_{\bar{X}} = \mu$$

$$\sigma_{\bar{X}} = \frac{\sigma}{\sqrt{n}}$$

These equations hold when the sample size is 30 or greater. When the sample size has n observations and the population has a finite size, say N_p, the relationships take the form

$$\mu_{\bar{X}} = \mu$$

$$\sigma_{\bar{X}} = \frac{\sigma}{\sqrt{N}} \left(\frac{N_p - N}{N_p - 1} \right)^{1/2}$$

We have not yet seen how to compute either the mean or the standard deviation of a population having an extremely large number of samples. This requires the population to be described by a *statistical distribution*. The distributions characterize specific types of *random processes*. Mathematicians have derived these distributions, and when statistical information is quoted, a statement is also made about the type of distribution the data apply to.

The most commonly encountered *random variables* can usually be described by one of three well-known mathematical distributions: the binomial distribution, the Gaussian distribution, and the Poisson distribution. The coin-flipping problem is characterized by a *binomial distribution*.

9.6 THE BINOMIAL DISTRIBUTION

Suppose the results of an event are binary; that is, only two possible outcomes can occur, and one of them has a certain probability of occurring—call it p—and the other occurs with the probability $q = 1 - p$. Such a problem is characterized by the binomial distribution when the number of experiments, measurements, or observations is very large. For example, if a coin is weighted to ensure that the probability of its landing heads up occurs 75% of the time, the probability of its landing tails up is obviously .25 (or $1 - .75$). When only a small number of coin tosses is made (say 100 or less),

$$Np = \text{expected number of heads in } N \text{ coin tosses}$$

and N is the number of trials. In this case $N = 100$ and $p = 75$. The standard deviation σ is estimated by

$$\sqrt{Npq} = \text{standard deviation of heads occurring in } N \text{ coin tosses}$$

Here

$$p = .75$$
$$\therefore q = (1 - .75) = .25$$

Thus we can *ESTIMATE* the expected number of heads that will result from 100 coin tosses as

$$u = 75 = 100 \times .75$$
$$\sigma = 4.33 = \sqrt{100 \times 0.25 \times 0.75}$$

Thus speaking roughly,

$$\text{the number of heads} \cong 75 \pm 4$$

Said slightly differently, if you have a 75% probability of selling a product, you have a 25% probability of not selling it. If 100 customers come into your store, the probable number of sales you will make is 75 and the standard deviation in the number of sales is 4.33.

Suppose the number of customers is only 10; then we have

1. The mean number of sales is expected to be

$$7.5 = 10 \times .75 = Np = \mu$$

2. The variance in the number of sales is expected to be

$$1.37 = \sqrt{10 \times .75 \times .25} = \sqrt{Npq} = \sigma$$

3. Thus, again roughly, number of sales $\cong 7 \pm 1$

There is an important lesson to be learned here: note that a variance of 4 sales out of 75 expected sales is only 5% of expected sales, whereas a variance in one out of 7 expected sales is 14% of the expected sales. The message is clear: the business risk (σ) declines as the number of potential customers goes up. We can write the risk-to-return ratio as follows:

$$\frac{\sigma}{\mu} = \frac{\sqrt{Npq}}{Np} = \frac{\sqrt{q}}{\sqrt{Np}}$$

Thus, no matter what the business p and q are, to halve your risk you must quadruple your potential customers. From this analysis it's easy to see why advertising is so important to business. Whether it is location and window display area or a massive direct-mail campaign, you can't overlook the value of advertising to broaden your business base so as to reduce your business risk.

9.7 THE GAUSSIAN DISTRIBUTION

A more familiar distribution, the Gaussian distribution, is very important because mathematicians have shown that the sum of a great number of non-Gaussian distributions approaches a Gaussian distribution. Again, when summing together a number of random variables whose distribution is non-Gaussian, the distribution of the sum is Gaussian. We find this useful later in discussing estimates of business risk analysis, testing hypotheses, and estimating expected returns on investments.

The Gaussian distribution is characterized by the mean and standard deviation of the "bell-shaped" curve, which is well known to most businessmen. Keep in mind that the binomial and Gaussian distributions are merely extensions of the frequency concept just discussed for populations of data events, observations, or measurements. It is very important for the business manager to recognize that the concepts of statistics are extremely simple and their extension to probability distributions is straightforward. A difference between the analysis of small populations and large populations is that the quantization or graininess in the distribution curve is less for populations with large numbers. In fact, as the number of observations becomes unbounded (a more exact definition of infinity), the distribution tends to become a smooth curve.

9.8 THE POISSON DISTRIBUTION

Another type of distribution commonly encountered in business systems analysis is the Poisson distribution. The Poisson distribution can never be less than zero and, like the binomial distribution, it is characterized by one number. The single number for the binomial distribution is the probability of success (or the probability of failure) of an experiment that can have only a binary result. The single number that characterizes the Poisson distribution is the mean of the distribution. An example of a Poisson-distributed random process is the amount of cash in a cash register after many transactions at the end of a business day. If this variable is monitored over a period of, say, 1,000 days (and all other things are equal), the average balance will be found to be λ and the standard deviation will be found to be $\sqrt{\lambda}$ when the money is expressed in dollars and the number of dollars is greater than 100. Thus just as one can say for the binomial distribution that after a large number of trials the expected value of N trials is $\mu = Np$ and the variance is $\sigma = \sqrt{Npq}$, the mean for a Poisson distribution can be said to be given by

$$\mu = \lambda$$

and the standard deviation by

$$\sigma = \sqrt{\lambda}$$

9.9 USING THE BINOMIAL PROBABILITY DISTRIBUTION

The coin-sampling problem demonstrated that when $P = .5$ the frequency distribution for a small sample of the coin tosses (two in our case) can be determined through a simple counting procedure. It is possible to develop sampling distributions for p for other values of P. In fact most books on statistics contain entire tables of frequency distributions (or binomial probabilities). These sampling distributions are listed in a table of binomial probabilities. To use such a table you must know the sample size and P. The sample size is usually denoted by N. An example of such a table appears in Appendix B. What is shown in the table, then, is the probability of occurrence of X, where X is the number of successful events. For $P = .5$ and $N = 2$, the probability that no heads were achieved (zero successes) is .25 as discussed before. Also, the probability that at least one head would be achieved in the two trials is .5 and that both trials would result in heads is .25, all as seen before, using your judgment from viewing the distribution of the possible outcomes of the two tosses.

A very important point needs to be made: the binomial probability table is only useful for analyzing binary statistical situations in which the number of data in the population is larger than the sample size by a factor of 25. That is, if you choose a sample of 5 to estimate the parameters of the population, the population must include at least 125 elements.

9.10 USING THE NORMAL OR GAUSSIAN DISTRIBUTION

The Gaussian or normal distribution is one of those most often used in statistics and business decisions analysis. This distribution is characterized as being the sampling distribution when the number of measurements in the sample is very large. When working with the normal distribution, two sets of means and standard deviations must be considered:

1. The population mean and the standard deviation which are the two parameters in the Gaussian distribution that are used to compute the Gaussian distribution tables.

2. The sample mean and the standard deviation, where the number of numbers in the sample is finite and the sampling distribution of the mean has a mean value and a standard deviation.

Our task is to make clear the distinction between these two sets of means and standard deviations.

As mentioned previously, the mean (μ) and the standard deviation (σ) of the population are the two parameters used in the Gaussian distribution formula to compute the Gaussian distribution tables. The *sample mean and standard deviation* are computed by

$$\overline{X} = \frac{\sum\limits_{N}^{N} X}{N}, \qquad S = \frac{\sum\limits^{N} (x - \overline{x})^2}{N - 1}$$

Here the sample mean and standard deviation apply to a single sample of a large population. A number of samples of the population can be taken, in this case a number of means can be computed, and this mean has a mean value denoted by $\mu_{\overline{X}}$ and the standard deviation of the means is given by σ_X. We call this the sampling distribution of the means of a number of samples of the population. This is not as confusing as it sounds. First, the mean μ and the standard deviation σ are associated with the population that has a large number of members (e.g., the population of the United States). If you take a sample of 10,000 people in Miles City, Montana, you can compute a mean $\overline{X}$ and a standard deviation S for any group characteristic you wish to test. You can also sample Houston, Texas, St. Louis, Missouri, Seattle, Washington, and Washington D.C., and you will probably get five different $\overline{X}$s and Ss. Thus one can draw a frequency distribution for $\overline{X}$. This frequency distribution also has a measure of central tendency called $\mu_{\overline{X}}$. Since the sample means have a distribution, they also have a standard deviation. This is the parameter $\sigma_{\overline{X}}$. The relationship between the mean and the standard deviation of the sampling distribution of the means is given by

$$\mu_{\overline{X}} = \mu = \overline{X}$$

$$\sigma_{\overline{X}} = \frac{\sigma}{\sqrt{N}} \cong \frac{S}{\sqrt{N}}$$

These are the equations that were previously shown to be the relationships that permitted us to sample a population.

Chapter 10 discusses the central limit theorem, a powerful theorem in statistics, that states that the sampling distribution of $\overline{X}$ tends to be Gaussian. In fact if the sample size becomes greater than 30, the sampling distribution is almost exactly a Gaussian distribution.

For a number of samples greater than 30, the shape of the sampling distribution is, for all practical purposes, that of the Gaussian distribution. It is characteristic of the Gaussian distribution that 68.2% of the observations always lie between $\mu_{\overline{X}}$ and $\mu_{\overline{X}} \pm \sigma_{\overline{X}}$, 95.4% of the observations lie between $\mu_{\overline{X}}$ and $\mu_{\overline{X}} + 2\sigma_{\overline{X}}$, 99% of the observations lie between $\mu_{\overline{X}}$ and $\mu_{\overline{X}} \pm 3\sigma_{\overline{X}}$, and so on. It is very important to remember that no matter what the shape of the frequency distribution of the population being sampled, the distribution of the means of a number of different samples of the population is Gaussian. It should be clear now that if we want to know the region within which the mean lies 99% of the time, it is only necessary to compute $\mu_{\overline{X}} \pm 3\sigma_{\overline{X}}$. Said another way, given any estimate of μ based on a sample of the population, we can compute the "Z" score of that particular estimate of the mean by taking the difference between $\overline{X}$ and the mean and dividing by the standard deviation. The Z score is the number of standard deviations away from the mean a particular sample mean is located. Tables of the Gaussian distribution curves are usually prepared to give the probability that a single measurement lies in the interval zero to Z. Clearly, one minus that probability is the probability that a number of the distribution selected at random will lie outside the interval zero to Z. These tables are called one-sided Gaussian probability distributions or one-sided normal distributions. Often the tables are given as areas under the normal curve. The table of areas under the normal curve provides the probability of a sample mean between μ and $\mu \pm Z$. A Gaussian distribution table is included in appendix C for convenience.

9.11 PROBABILITY TREES

Perhaps one of the most important tools a business manager can acquire is the use of probability trees. A tree of probabilities is a way of visualizing probabilities associated with any multistage binary process. This is important because management decisions involve taking or not taking an action, a binary process. Thus one can make a *tree* of decisions and their consequences and the probabilities of the occurrence of the consequences. Probability trees can be used for estimating the overall consequences of any decisions.

All trees have nodes and branches. The nodes represent either decisions or consequences. The branches indicate conditions resulting from the decisions. The ultimate consequences of a set of decisions are indicated by the outcomes at the end of the tree. The modern concept of effective decision making is to break down the decision problem into stages of decisions and consequences, then build the probability trees that compute the probable consequences associated with all possible decisions resulting in some course of action. An example of a probability tree for decision making was shown in Figure 2-1.

An example of a simpler two-stage binary random process that we have already examined is the tree associated with two flips of a coin. Two possible results can occur: on the first flip the result can be heads or tails, and heads or tails can result on the second flip of the coin. Although it is not the intention of most business managers to model business decisions by coin flipping (even though occasionally it may appear to the members of the board that the president operates in this way), the example serves to illustrate that the probability of the outcome of the first coin toss is 50%, and this can be illustrated by putting the percentage on the branch (Figure 9-5). Similarly, the next stage of the two-stage coin toss can be quantified

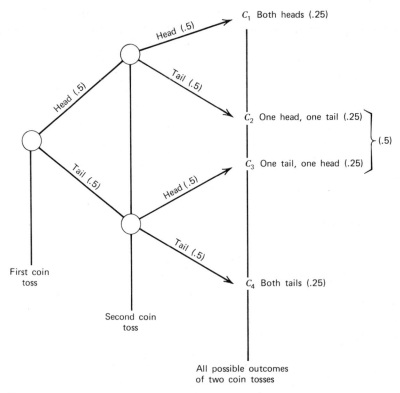

Figure 9-5.   Probability tree of outcomes for two coin tosses.

by putting the probability on the branches of the second stage of the decision-making process. There are then four possible outcomes.

1.   Both coins are heads, as in node C_1.
2.   One coin is a head and the other is a tail, as in node C_2.
3.   One coin is a tail and the next coin is a head, as in node C_3.
4.   Both coins are tails, as in node C_4.

The probabilities of the eventual outcomes are merely the respective products of the probabilities along each of the branches, also as shown in Figure 9-5.

Building probability trees is useful for determining the probable outcomes of decisions when one includes the value of a branch as well as the probability of traversing the branch. The product of the two is the expected value of that branch. Probability trees based on expected value are particularly useful for examining alternative bid decisions on proposals when the resources are finite.

The value of probability trees is that they help the business manager quantify the results he can expect by the consequences of choosing an option on the basis of his best guess of the probabilities of what will happen.

The source of this technique for assisting businessmen in making decisions has been hard to identify. However it is used by students at the Harvard Business School and the Sloan School of Management in case history investigations of business corporations. The ultimate success of this decision-making technique is in selecting the criteria by which a decision is made. It is less crucial that any one criterion can be used to make a decision than that in the process of quantifying the problem and making the probability tree, one comes to understand better the decision to be made and its consequences. It is also important that the process ensures consistency in evaluation or scoring of any given option, where consistency indicates (a) that the proper values of the contracts are considered, (b) that the proper values of the return on investment are used, and (c) that the sum of the probabilities of win is 1.

Obviously the technique can be extended to business alternatives that have many decision stages and numerous outcomes. A common technique in distinguishing between a binary decision (i.e., the decision to bid or not to bid; to invest or not to invest) and between the three or four consequences of those decisions is to symbolize the decisions under your control as square nodes and to symbolize the consequences that are beyond your control as round nodes, as in the example of Figure 2-1. The same process is used for computing expected values of each branch of the tree, such as

- An **expected** return on an investment.
- Probable **expected** earnings.
- **Expected** profit.
- **Expected** loss.

That is, the value (e.g., investment, earnings, profit, loss) of the branch and the probability of traversing the branch are multiplied together and summed along the nodes when expected results are computed; or if the probabilities of traversing a sequence of paths are computed alone, the probabilities are multiplied together.

9.12 ESTIMATING TECHNIQUES

We have discussed the question of estimating the statistics of a sample when given the parameters of a distribution. Now we want to estimate the parameters of a population when the statistics of a sample are given. Said another way, we are concerned with estimating μ, σ, and P, given $\overline{X}$, S, and p. The formulas for estimating the parameters of a distribution are straightforward:

$$\mu = \overline{X} = \frac{\sum\limits_{}^{N} X}{N}$$

We estimate the standard deviation of the population with the formula

$$S = \frac{\sqrt{\Sigma(X - \overline{X})^2}}{n - 1}$$

It follows then that the estimate of P is made with the statistic p. Thus we can summarize in the following manner:

1. The statistic used to estimate P is p.
2. The statistic used to estimate σ is S.
3. The statistic used to estimate μ is $\overline{X}$.

The most important matter then is to determine the confidence we have in the estimate of μ. Obviously confidence varies as a function of the number of samples taken. As before, we must find the standard deviation of the estimate of μ, which by definition is the standard deviation of $\overline{X}$, which is given by

$$\sigma_{\overline{X}} = \frac{\sigma}{\sqrt{N}}$$

where σ is estimated with S. What conclusions does this allow? The answer: the estimate of μ based on n samples will be within $\sigma_{\overline{X}}$ of the real μ approximately 68% of the time; it will be within $2\sigma_{\overline{X}}$ approximately 95% of the time; and it will be within $3\sigma_{\overline{X}}$ 99% of the time. Said another way, the estimate of the mean of the population lies in the interval $\overline{X} \pm 1\sigma$ 68% of the time, $\overline{X} \pm 2\sigma$ 95% of the time, and $\overline{X} \pm 3\sigma$ 99% of the time. A third way of thinking of this involves the realization that there is a 99% confidence that the mean lies between $\overline{X} \pm 3\sigma_{\overline{X}}$.

9.13 CONFIDENCE INTERVAL

A common technique in business is to establish control charts for expenditures, products developed, quality control, and other variables. A control chart is merely a measurement of a parameter to be tracked as a function of time or the number of items produced; the mean of a small number of samples is taken, compared with the mean based on a large test sample, and plotted on a control chart. In the control chart in Figure 9-6, we see the sample mean and the allowed variance associated with a machine designed to cut a one-yard strip of material used in clothing manufacture. The objective is to ensure that the machine does not go out of adjustment and produce 10,000 oversized pieces of material (a costly error). The approach is to take a sample of 1000 cuttings and compute a mean and the 3σ variance when the machine is being carefully monitored for proper operation. For the remainder of the manufacturing period the objective is to set the machine to allow the (highly paid) operator to spend time adjusting other manufacturing machines. To ensure that the machine is operating satisfactorily, he draws nine samples every hour, computes the mean, and plots it on the control chart, where the limits are set by $\mu_{\overline{X}} \pm 3\sigma_{\overline{X}}$ and $\sigma_{\overline{X}}$ is computed based on nine samples and the standard deviation measured from the 1000-sample test run. Explicitly the formulas used to compute the limit are

$$\text{upper limit} \quad = 3\sigma_{\overline{X}} = \frac{3\sigma}{\sqrt{9}} = \frac{3\sigma}{3} = \sigma$$

$$\text{lower limit} \quad = -3\sigma_{\overline{X}} = \frac{3\sigma}{\sqrt{9}} = \frac{-3\sigma}{3} = -\sigma$$

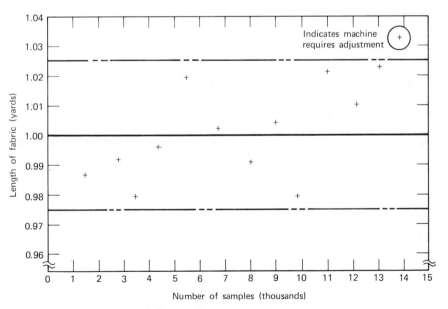

Figure 9-6. Typical control chart used to monitor a fabric cutter.

Clearly when the samples' mean exceeds the $3\sigma_{\overline{X}}$ limit, it is time to readjust the machine. Of course $2\sigma_{\overline{X}}$ could be used to set the limit. If a $1\sigma_{\overline{X}}$ or a $2\sigma_{\overline{X}}$ limit is used, the machine must be adjusted more frequently because there is a higher probability that the sample mean will lie outside the $1\sigma_{\overline{X}}$ or $2\sigma_{\overline{X}}$ limits. Of course a common-sense approach to this situation is as follows: set the limits at $1\sigma_{\overline{X}}$, thus ensuring that approximately 68% of the time the sample mean will lie within the limit; have the machine adjusted more frequently during the fully automatic operation, and as confidence is gained that the deviation occurring is the normal deviation associated with sampling and is not due to the machine's going out of tolerance, the limits can be expanded to $2\sigma_{\overline{X}}$, then finally to $3\sigma_{\overline{X}}$ after some reasonable experience is gained in the fully automatic operation of the machine.

9.14   STATISTICAL FORECASTING TECHNIQUES

Forecasting the profits from a business venture, the growth or decline of sales, or the growth or decline of a market, is difficult at best, and individuals who have a stake in the outcome of the forecast tend to be subjective. One of the business manager's more demanding tasks is to retain objectivity in business decisions based on forecasts of growth or decline. An approach the author has used to guard against subjectivity is to cross-check "judgment" forecasts using statistical forecasting techniques whose mathematical nature retains at least an element of objectivity. *Curve fitting* techniques are based on mathematical criteria that rise above the details of the forecast to be made or the consequences of the outcome of the forecast. "Least squares" forecasting is an example.

Least squares is a technique of *fitting* a given type of curve through a set of scattered points on a graph in such a way that the standard deviation of the data from the curve is a minimum. When the graph abscissa is time, the ordinate is said to vary with time. A *forecast* is an estimate of the value of the ordinate given a value of the abscissa that is beyond the range of the data.

Once a statistical *curve fit* to the data is done, the curve is used to forecast future outcomes and compare them with the more subjective *manual* forecasts. If enough difference exists, of course, the people involved will need to get together and iron out the differences. In a sense, then, statistical curve fitting becomes a *check and balance* on the manually prepared forecasts. When a little common sense is exercised in preparing the statistical forecasting, the two approaches tend to track each other fairly well—more is said on this later.

Linear Regression

Linear regression is a name given to fitting a straight line that passes through a set of data relating two business variables. Examples of pairs of business variables appear in Table 9-4. The straight line establishes a *trend* between the two variables, thus is often called a trend line. Usually one of the variables is time, and trend lines refer to the trend of the business over a period of time. The intervals between the time periods are usually fixed, but this need not be the case. In fact, to fit a curve to a set of data points requires no restriction on the intervals between the variables. Equal intervals are used primarily because data on business are gathered monthly or annually, and virtually all the business data are "equal interval" data by the very nature of the generation of the data.

A number of business pocket calculators have linear regression calculation capability built into them, and they work in a quite simple and very useful way. The objective is to fit a line (the equation for a line is $y = A + Bx$) through a set of data pairs (y and x). The problem is to

Table 9-4 Pairs of Business Variables

(a) 2 Million Dollars per Year Business		(b) Wholesale Price Index, Seasonally Adjusted (1967 = 100)	
Year	Profit	Month	Index
1970	$ − 90,000	1974	
1971	10,000	January	145
1972	14,000	February	147
1973	96,000	March	150
1974	196,000	April	152
1975	312,000	May	153
		June	154
		July	156
		August	163
		September	166
		October	168
		November	171
		December	172
		1975	
		January	171
		February	170
		March	169
		April	169
		May	171
		June	171
		July	173

determine A and B from the set of ys and xs input into the calculator. When the user inputs

$$y_1 \quad \text{and} \quad x_1$$
$$y_2 \quad \text{and} \quad x_2$$
$$y_3 \quad \text{and} \quad x_3$$
$$\vdots \qquad\qquad \vdots$$
$$y_n \qquad\qquad x_n$$

the calculator's job is to automatically compute A and B so that the line

$$y = A + Bx$$

best* passes through the point pairs (y_i, x_i). The calculator calculates A with the equation

$$A = \frac{\Sigma y \Sigma x^2 - \Sigma x \Sigma xy}{n \Sigma x^2 - (\Sigma x)^2}$$

and B with the equation

$$B = \frac{n \Sigma xy - \Sigma x \Sigma y}{n \Sigma x^2 - (\Sigma x)^2}$$

The point is this—the calculator is automatically doing a lot of work that you would otherwise have to do manually. To calculate A and B by hand for only ten pairs of three-digit ys and xs would involve

$$K = 6N + 14$$

where $N =$ number of point-pairs times number of digits and $K =$ number of keystrokes. For this case $K = 196$. In addition, you must keep track of where you are in the algebra of the problem!

On reflection, it is hardly surprising that statistical forecasting is not used by many business executives—too hard to do manually, even using a basic four-function pocket calculator. The calculators that have the job *preprogrammed* now make it convenient for even the busy executive to run a statistical curve fit, with the data input being the only required keystrokes.

Now consider the data in Table 9-4a. If we plot the data as shown in

---

*Best in the sense of minimizing the sum of the square of the variance of each y_i from $y = A + Bx$ at x_i over the range of i from zero to n.

Figure 9-7, a straight line appears that can probably be fit through the data points, thus can be used to predict the company's profits in the near future.

On the HP-22 (a typical business pocket calculator), the keystrokes for finding the straight line profit = $A + B \times$ (number of years since 1970) are as follows:

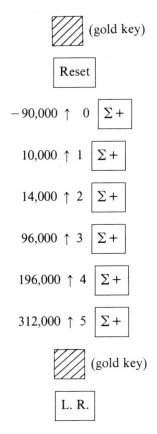

That's all!

To estimate the profits in 1978, you need only key in 8 (years from 1970) and stroke the gold key, followed by the $\hat{y}$ key, to find that the estimated earnings are $506,095.24. Amazing, the computational power of these little low-cost machines. But it gets better.

Clearly straight line forecasting is useful for short-range consideration. What about long-range forecasts or forecasts of exponential growth or

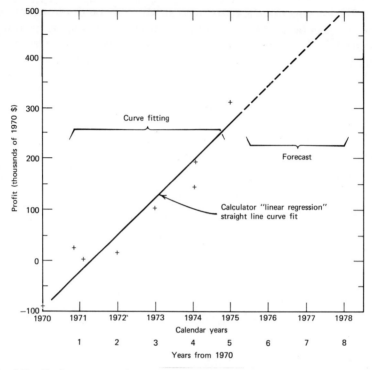

Figure 9-7. Profit per year of a growing 2 million dollar business; plus sign indicates actual data "point pairs."

decline? In these cases it would be better to try to fit the exponential curve

$$y = be^{mx}$$

to the data, not $y = A + Bx$. Well, notice that taking the logarithm of the exponential equation yields

$$\ln(y) = \ln(b) + (mx)\ln(e)$$

Since $\ln(e) = 1$, we see that

$$\ln(y) = \ln(b) + mx$$

If we let $\ln(b) = A$ and $B = m$, we can rewrite this equation in the form

$$\ln(y) = A + Bx$$

which is the same form as the straight line equation. Thus if we input the variables $\ln(y)$ and x instead of y and x, we can calculate a straight line curve fit through $\ln(y)$. Then in the last step, calculate the antilog of $\ln(y)$ to get

$$y = be^{mx}$$

In fact, the HP-22 is designed to do this. The circuitries for calculating $\ln(y)$ and e^x are built into the calculator. In this case the keystrokes for fitting an exponential curve to a typical investment earnings (growth is usually exponential) are as follows:

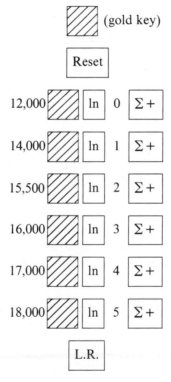

Then to find the forecasted earnings 8 years into the investment, simply stroke

The estimated earnings are found to be \$23,148.48.

A linear estimate of the earnings would be \$21,623.81, which is typical of the "undershoot" of linear estimates of exponential growth.

The Art of Statistical Forecasting

Our discussion of straight line and exponential curve fitting demonstrates that the curve is determined by the number and the particular point pairs input into the calculator. Thus the following decisions must be made:

- How many point pairs should be used?
- Which point pairs should be used?

The science of *data editing* would fill a series of books. Fortunately a businessman's intuition can go a long way in indicating what data to edit. Care must be taken that the rationale for editing data is strong enough to ensure that the counterintuitive behavior of the process that generated the data is not eliminated.

A few common-sense guidelines can be used to select the data for a forecast:

- The range of the historical data should be at least as long as the range of the forecast. For a one-year business plan, the historical data should run to at least a year in the past.
- Obvious "accidents" that give wide, unreasonable variations in the data set should be edited before forecasting.
- Consciously look for "bobbles" in the data that resemble accidents but may have hidden, counterintuitive causes. Stock market chartsmen do this a lot. Often, before *jumps* in the price of a stock, the number of sales of a given stock statistically fluctuate a bit, indicating foreknowledge by profit takers that the stock will move up for some reason. When you think you have found one of these "*statistical indicators*," do not decide on a course of action until you have researched the cause of the bobble and understand what is going on. Paradoxically, statistics, the mathematics of random processes, is an excellent tool for discovering nonrandom or causally related behavior of systems and processes.
- Fit the data with both linear and exponential curves and pick the one that (to the eye) looks best. If the calculator gives the correlation coefficient, pick the curve with the highest correlation coefficient. (The HP-65 has this feature in many of its programs.)

Thanks to the solid-state revolution and pocket calculator manufacturers, businessmen now have useful forecasting techniques only a keystroke away. This advance alone is easily worth the price of a business calculator.

CHAPTER 10

BUSINESS SYSTEMS ANALYSIS

Many business enterprises can be characterized by their cash flow. By definition, business generates cash flow. In the simplest cottage industry businesses, cash flow is often measured in terms of the bank account balance. At the most sophisticated governmental levels, cash flow calculations include concepts of inflation, escalation, inventory (and its overhang), and social value discounts. By its very nature mathematics is used to describe the flow of cash through a business—thus by definition there is a mathematical model of the business. The mathematical model is the set of equations that calculate the flow of money into, through (including transformations into assets or other equivalents of money), and out of the business. In this sense one can *mathematically model* any business.

Within every business money flows through divisions, departments, and other organizational elements. This cash flow can also be mathematically modeled. Service organizations usually track the money flowing in terms of the personnel head-count. In product development organizations cash flow includes head-count and raw materials, inventories, and products in production. Wherever you are in your organization, whether at the top, middle, or bottom, money is flowing and the decisions you make affect the degree to which the total organization is profitable. Each decision maker must responsibly manage the money flowing at his level. He does this by examining his decisions and the money that flows as a consequence of those decisions. A business manager can develop a mathematical model of the cash flow he controls and test his decision alternatives against this model before a final decision. Generally the process is done intuitively. It is the aim of this chapter to present the benefit of preparing more explicit mathematical models that can be studied analytically and numerically. Here the pocket calculator really pays off—**the pocket calculator can improve your *intuitive* business decisions.** How? By allowing tests of intuitive judgment on the mathematics of the cash flow. When your intuition

225

matches the cash flow analysis of a particular venture, it is unlikely that your final decision will have counterintuitive results.

A good business manager responsibly manages the money entrusted to him. Yet it is the author's experience that many managers do not realize the impact of their decisions on the cash flow of the business. We are all familiar with cases of decisions that are deferred. For example, if a process might be carried out more cheaply but involves a complex or tough decision, the tendency is to continue with past methods, not to accept the risk associated with the more aggressive cost reduction approach. Aggressive money management involves the search for new methods and techniques for cash flow generation and control. Applying such techniques involves an element of risk—but it also invloves elements of gain. The trick is to quantify both.

Before continuing, the author would like to add a personal note. Often one reads a "how-to" business book with opinions and advice drawn from an individual's reading and research of the current business literature. The material in this book, however, is written from experience, thus is limited to the extent that other experienced businessmen may have found more and better ways to quantify business decisions. On the other hand the material is not based on ideas read in the literature: it is based on hands-on experience.

At the time of this writing, the author is managing the preparation of a proposal on a $5.7 million contract with an estimated $108 million of follow-on work. To quantify both risk and return in this proposal* extensive math modeling of the key decisions is done to guard against counterintuitive consequences of our decisions. Additionally the author has used these techniques in small businesses for a number of years with very satisfactory results. In short, this chapter is limited to the concepts the author has found useful in his efforts to develop and conduct business; the reader is not being led into using untried techniques.

How then does one quantify both risk and return and use the knowledge in his organization? The answer lies in being able to model the money flowing through the business. This is a mathematicl model of the business, and this chapter deals with (a) the synthesis of mathematical models of business systems, (b) the use of mathematical models tò discover the properties of the business system, and (c) the use of mathematical models for improving the business system.

Before proceeding, an important question must be addressed. Is it worthwhile for a manager to take a few months from his schedule to learn to mathematically model his business? For those graduating from business

*We Won!

schools in the 1970s, the answer is *yes*, because they are trained in this direction. However, the answer may be *no* for the intuitive business manager who *senses* the business cash flow and guides his business by intuition. The intuitionist can take several paths.

- Hire one of the bright young men to assist him in math modeling his business and interpreting the findings.
- Learn to use his pocket calculator to test his "sense" of cash flow in his business; thereby improving his intuition about his business.
- Use a combination of both approaches.

Whatever the choice, math modeling a business will often uncover some surprises and should prove worthwhile, even if it does nothing more than teach you more about your business as you try to develop and understand your math model.

10.1 RISK ANALYSIS

We have previously concerned ourselves with cash flows as a bank might view them, that is, as estimates of the amount of money that would flow in a business enterprise *as a single number*. On the basis of these discrete numbers, an investment decision is made that commits money to the enterprise on the expectation that there will be a reasonable return on investment some time in the future. The key word here is *future*. The business manager or business analyst is constantly faced with forecasting the future outcome of today's decisions. Middle management is characterized by forecasting consequences of decisions associated with either short periods of time or amounts of cash flow that will not individually have a major impact on the overall earnings of the business if a decision is wrong. Executive decisions are usually long-term decisions that are economically significant to the business.

It is the uncertainty associated with forecasting future events that results in risk in business systems. The degree of uncertainty about forecasted results should also be taken into account in a business decision. As pointed out in Chapter 9 (Business Statistics), confidence levels can be specified for estimates of a population based on the statistics computed for a sample. Such confidence levels must be considered as part of the decision-making process. The further ahead one forecasts, the less the confidence can be placed in the forecast. Today's business manager must know how to account for these effects. Merely recognizing that forecasting cash flows should also include calculating the confidence associated with the forecast is important enough to make the intuitive businessman realize the value of quantifying the confidence level in a product development decision involving, say, 3, 4, or 5 years or more, of business operations.

The approach to evaluating risk in business is surprisingly straightforward and éasy to use. First let us examine the business decision process normally encountered for a 5-year investment. Five-year investments are often considered when making capital expenditures, conducting research and development projects associated with a new product line, or engaging in corporation start-up. The first step is to estimate the cash flow associated with the first 5 years of operation. This cash flow projection includes forecasts of revenues from all sources, such as sales and savings, and forecasts of all costs, expenses, and expenditures. In this sense a new venture is said to be *defined* when the forecasted cash flows are defined.

Suppose now that two ways have been identified to begin a new venture and that two cash flows have also been identified. Comparison of the alternatives is to be performed on a net present value basis.* Specifically the net (or accumulated) present value of all the cash flows is computed as discussed in Chapter 3.**

Consider an example of a typical discounted cash flow analysis associated with a new business start up. Table 10-1 illustrates the value of the expected annual sales, the expected annual costs, the resultant cash flow, and the *net present value* associated with the venture. Note that the net present value is a single number. Suppose a different approach were taken to the start-up having the cash flows and net present value listed in Table 10-2. It is apparent that on the basis of this type of analysis, the second alternative is the best. Suppose, however, we have taken into account the probability distributions associated with these alternatives (Figure 10-1). The decision is no longer clear, Although alternative 2 has

---

*For readers who have skipped Chapter 3, the net present value is given

$$NPV = \sum_{n=0}^{N} \frac{CF_n}{(1+i)^n} = CF_0 + \frac{CF_1}{1+i} + \frac{CF_2}{(1+i)^2} + \cdots$$

As mentioned before in Chapter 3, the cash flow values are discounted (the inverse of interest compounding) from future values to present values and the total present value of the alternative is computed. In this equation CF_n is the value of the cash flow in the nth year; i is the discount rate that is usually the **desired** rate of return; NPV is the net present value; and N is the total number of years considered in the analysis. The total number of years is called the *life cycle* or *investment horizon* of the project when all three phases of the project (i. e., development, procurement, and operations) are considered.

**In the past the cash flows were treated as single numbers, not as statistically distributed random variables. Forecasts are based on *estimated business performance* and are variable. If there were no variability, there would be no need for executives to manage the cash flows and see that the business system performs to the forecast.

Table 10-1   Alternative 1—New Business Start-up Cash Flow Analysis (Using "Up-Front" Loading of Costs)

Time (years)	Revenue (then-year $)	Cost (then-year $)	Profit (then-year $)	Discounted[a] Profits (present-value $)
1	0	160,000	− 160,000	− 160,000.00
2	20,000	100,000	− 80,000	− 69,565.22
3	100,000	70,000	+ 30,000	+ 22,684.31
4	200,000	50,000	+ 150,000	+ 98,627.43
5	260,000	50,000	+ 210,000	+ 120,068.18
			150,000	11,814.70
			Apparent value	Net present value

[a] 15% desired rate of return used for discounting.

Table 10-2   Alternative 2—New Business Start-up Cash Flow Analysis (Using Deferred Loading of Costs)

Time (years)	Revenues (then-year $)	Cost (then-year $)	Profit (then-year $)	Discounted[a] Profits (present-value $)
1	0	30,000	− 30,000	− 30,000.00
2	20,000	50,000	− 30,000	− 26,086.96
3	100,000	70,000	+ 30,000	+ 22,684.31
4	200,000	100,000	+ 100,000	+ 65,751.62
5	210,000	160,000	+ 50,000	+ 28,587.66
			120,000	60,936.63[b]
			Apparent value	Net present value

[a] 15% desired rate of return used for discounting.
[b] Note that alternative 2 has a lower apparent value but a higher net present value than alternative 1.

the largest expected net present value, it also has a reasonable probability of resulting in a negative net present value, that is, failure of the system to generate the desired 15% yield. On the other hand, alternative 1 shows virtually no chance of failing, but it has a substantially lower expected net present value. **On the basis of the data given, which alternative would you select?** More important, perhaps, the investment analysis presented in the format of Figure 10-1 gives much more insight into (*a*) the nature of the

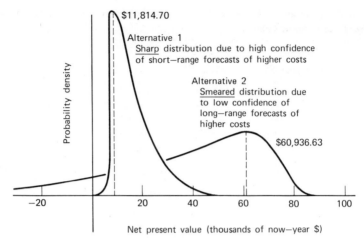

Figure 10-1.   Distributions of the net present value of new business start-up alternatives.

estimate, (*b*) the confidence estimate, (*c*) a visualization of the risk, and (*d*) a quantification of the risk.

10.2   SETTING UP THE BUSINESS MATH MODEL

To set up the math model of a business it is necessary to select one or a number of parameters that describe the business and to compute the relationship between the parameters and the revenues and costs associated with the business. For example,

$$\text{profit} = \text{revenues} - \text{costs}$$

$$P = \Sigma R - \Sigma C$$

Here ΣR represents the sum of the revenues and ΣC represents the sum of the costs. Remember that a "single value" analysis typically carried out by investors in a start-up operation is to make decisions based on the *most likely* (peaks of the cost distributions) estimate of the revenues and costs associated with a venture. Figure 10-2 illustrates an example of the single value measures of

- A single source of revenue.
- Five sources of cost.
- The resulting profit.

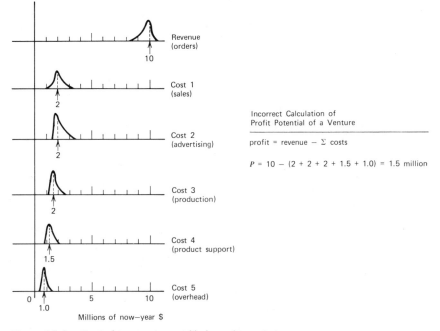

Figure 10-2. Typical incorrect *most likely* profit analysis.

Figure 10-3 shows the *average profit* (expected value of the profit), assuming that the revenues and costs are ·not single valued but are statistically distributed as in Figure 10-2.

An important observation about any business system is that revenues are usually overestimated and costs are usually underestimated (again see Figure 10-2). From the standpoint of cost and revenue distribution, this means that the tail on the revenue distribution is generally longer "to the left" and the tails of the cost distribution are generally longer "to the right."

In this example the most likely value of the profit distribution is not the same as the sum of the expected values (average) of the cash flows. This is a very important point. In statistical analysis, **that which is the most likely value is not the expected value.** Said another way, that which occurs most frequently is not that which can be expected. Subtracting the *expected value* of the costs from the *expected value* of the revenues gives the expected value of the profit. However, the most likely value of the profit, which is defined to be the value of the profit that has the greatest chance of occurring (the value at which the profit frequency distribution achieves

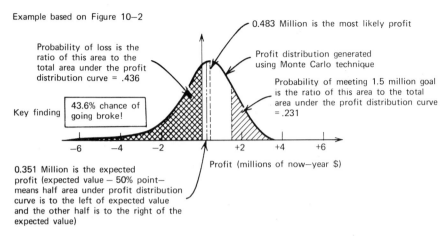

Example based on Figure 10—2

0.483 Million is the most likely profit

Probability of loss is the
ratio of this area to the
total area under the profit
distribution curve = .436

Profit distribution generated
using Monte Carlo technique

Probability of meeting 1.5 million goal
is the ratio of this area to the total
area under the profit distribution curve
= .231

Key finding | 43.6% chance of
going broke!

−6   −4   −2   +2   +4   +6

Profit (millions of now—year $)

0.351 Million is the expected
profit (expected value — 50% point—
means half area under profit distribution
curve is to the left of expected value
and the other half is to the right of the
expected value)

Figure 10-3.   Correct profit analysis. *Step 1*: Using Monte Carlo techniques or correct
analytical procedure, combine all six distributions of revenues and costs to determine the
distribution of profits. *Step 2*: Use the profit distribution to determine (*a*) the most likely
profit, (*b*) the expected profit, (*c*) the probability of meeting your "yield goal" (venture
risk), and (*d*) the probability of incurring a loss (financial legal risk).

its maximum value), cannot generally be computed by simple addition. If a
large number of costs are considered and the most likely values are added,
however, the sum of the most likely values does tend toward the expected
value. This phenomenon is described by the *central limit theorem*, which
says that the sum of a large number of distributions tends toward a
Gaussian distribution regardless of the shape of the individual distributions involved in the sum (within reasonable constraints, of course).
However when we are considering five major cost elements in a cash flow
system (a typical business problem), it is not reasonable to expect the
central limit theorem to apply. This is because the costs are generally
skewed to the right, and the end effects of the distribution do not tend to
cancel.

Summarizing then: **Combining the most likely revenues with the most
likely costs will not compute the expected profits**.

Considering that profits for most businesses are the small differences
between large numbers, estimating a venture's profits on the basis of most
likely values can lead to serious trouble. Summing the expected values of
revenues and costs, on the other hand, yields the correct expected profit.
Generally expected profits are lower than most likely profits!

Thus in risk analysis it is important to consider the exact shape of the
distribution of (*a*) the cash flows involved and (*b*) the measures of
performance of the business system such as NPV, ROI, and profit.

We specify risk by the probability that the measure of performance will exceed precomputed bounds. This requires that all the revenues and costs associated with a business venture be described by a distribution, not just an estimate of the most likely value or the expected value of each of the business revenues and costs. This is the rub—it is usually difficult to calculate these distributions.

Perhaps a way to generate them is simply to guess, recognizing that revenues are skewed to the left and costs are skewed to the right. The consequences of not addressing this problem can be severe, to say the least, if the NPV can have a reasonable probability of slipping into a negative value or if the probable profit margin is small. Said another way, difficulty in specifying the distribution for the revenues and costs is probably due to the analyst's fairly great uncertainty about the actual costs.

Let us now consider the revenues, costs, and annual cash flows computed in Table 10-1. From the distributions we might expect that the cash flows would be drawn as in Figure 10-4, which better represents the distributions of what can be expected from the particular start-up alternative.

A number of techniques can be used to generate these distributions. In the most common, the Monte Carlo technique, the distributions of the revenues and costs are roughly estimated and the profits are computed on the basis of random selection of the distributed revenues and costs. When

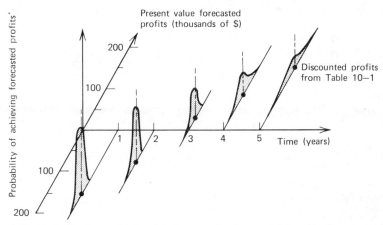

Figure 10-4. Profit forecasts showing the growth of uncertainty with the range of the forecast. Asterisk indicates present value of forecasted profits. From Joel S. Greenberg, "Risk Analysis," *Journal of Aeronautics and Astronautics*, November 1974, by permission of the publisher.

enough random samples have been taken to permit the distribution of profit to be sketched, the Monte Carlo simulation is stopped. The problem lies in establishing the frequency distributions of the revenues and costs.

A number of empirical techniques for establishing the frequency distributions have been developed. One that the author finds useful was reported by Greenberg.* This method is sketched in Figure 10-5. First estimates are of the ranges of uncertainty of the revenues and costs. Each range is then divided into a number of equal intervals. Greenberg suggests the use of five intervals. Then a *relative ranking* of the *relative likelihood* of the variables falling into each of the intervals is developed on the basis of judgment or intuition. This sets the general shape of the frequency distribution and, based on the relative values and knowing that the sum of the five probabilities must be 1, it is possible to solve for the quantitative values and prepare a sketch of the distribution. Then a beta distribution† can be curve fit to the distribution.

This procedure involves much subjective judgment about the revenues and costs. This is not necessarily bad, however, since informed estimates of probability distributions include many subjective factors that relate to the experience of conducting that particular business. Probably because the author is a Bayesian statistical analyst, he favors this subjective approach of establishing the distributions, recognizing that they are not necessarily mathematically developed probability distributions but are based more on judgment. They reflect attitudes, emotions, and intuition about the business—factors that the author has found to be indispensable in effectively conducting business operations.

The cumulative probability distribution can be computed for the NPV associated with a given distribution simply by accumulating the probabilities for each of the five intervals. This is called a risk profile for the NPV,

---

*Joel S. Greenberg, "Risk Analysis," *Journal of Aeronautics and Astronautics*, November 1974.

$$\dagger \text{BETA} = \frac{\Gamma(\alpha+\beta+2)}{\Gamma(\alpha+1)\Gamma(\beta+1)} \, x^{\alpha}(1-x)^{\beta}$$

A method the author uses for setting α and β without the need for a Greenberg-type procedure is based on years of observation that, for most cost and revenue curves, $\alpha = [N \text{ mode}/(1 - N \text{ mode})]^{1/2}, \beta = 1/\alpha, N$ mode = percentage of range of the normalized random variable x, where the mode resides. For the distribution in Figure 10-5:

$$x = \frac{X}{2000 - 1000} = \frac{X}{1000}$$

N mode≈ 0.3

$$\alpha = \left(\frac{0.3}{0.7}\right)^{1/2} = 0.22$$

$$\beta = \frac{1}{0.22} = 4.55$$

$$\text{BETA} = \frac{\Gamma(6.77)}{\Gamma(1.22)\Gamma(5.77)} \, x^{.22}(1-x)^{4.77}$$

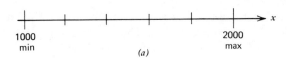

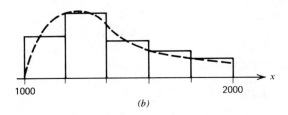

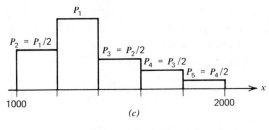

$$P_1 + P_2 + P_3 + P_4 + P_5 = 1$$

(d)

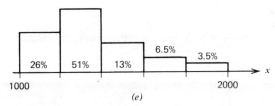

Figure 10-5. A methodology for establishing uncertainty profiles. (a) Specify range of uncertainty. (b) Establish qualitative ranking. (c) Establish relative likelihoods. (d) By substituting from (c), solve for P values ($P_1 + P_2 + P_3 + P_4 + P_5 = 1$). (e) Establish quantitative values. From Joel S. Greenberg, "Risk Analysis," *Journal of Aeronautics and Astronautics*, November 1974, by permission of the publisher.

and it plots the probability of exceeding the indicated NPV as a function of the NPV for the business system. The distribution is usually centered near .5. The significance of this is that the expected NPV distribution becomes more symmetrical and approaches the Gaussian distribution as the numbers of revenues and costs become large.

Another technique for combining the revenues and costs is to assume they are distributed according to a "sketched" beta-type distribution, whereupon approximations for expected value and the standard deviation of the combined distributions can be calculated as in Figure 10-6. Using these relationships and assuming that the central limit theorem applies, it is possible to compute an estimate of the expected value and the standard deviation of the NPV for a venture.

Preparing a similar analysis for a number of alternative ways to conduct a given venture will generate a set of means and variances for the decision alternatives. Then á plot of the mean and variance of the NPV can be made for all the alternatives being considered. An example of such a risk/return plot appears in Figure 10-7. This is the business manager's diagram for comparison of alternatives, since we can usually identify *a boundary of best alternatives*—the boundary of the greatest return for the

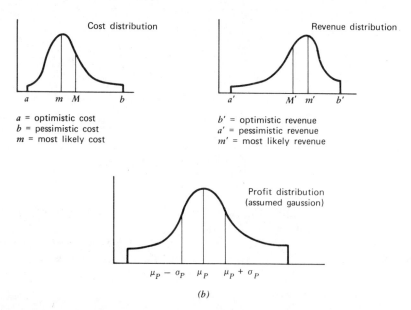

Figure 10-6. Calculating rough estimates of combined revenue and cost distributions. To be used with caution. (*a*) Sketch the revenue and cost distribution. (*b*) Sketch the parameters of profit distribution.

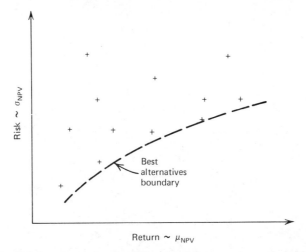

Figure 10-7.   Risk/return plot for visualizing alternative ways to conduct a given venture. The best alternatives boundary is different for different types of ventures and is characteristically of the form $\sigma_{NPV} \cong k\sqrt{\mu_{NPV}}$ (Poisson-type distribution).

least risk associated with a given type of business. All that remains is for the business manager to establish the level of risk at which he is willing to operate and select the alternative that is closest to the boundary of best alternatives. Even more sophisticated decision making is possible on the basis of *utility functions* that express the utility associated with an NPV. This is one transformation further removed from the details of the cash flow associated with the business, but it reflects the business manager's judgment about the significance of the NPV to his corporate operations.

10.3   SPECIFYING CASH FLOW AND LEVEL OF INDEBTEDNESS TO ENSURE THAT GREATER VISIBILITY IS GIVEN TO RISK

The final step in the analysis of business systems from a risk viewpoint is to make plots of the cash flow and level of indebtedness, not as a single curve but as a set of curves having confidence level as a parameter. This provides the business manager with the visibility necessary to establish real funding requirements for a start-up operation or development of a new product, and the information can be used as a tracking chart against which to judge the performance of the managers working in the organization. An example of the cash flows with confidence levels as parameters is given in Figure 10-8. Specifying cash flows in terms of the confidence level helps

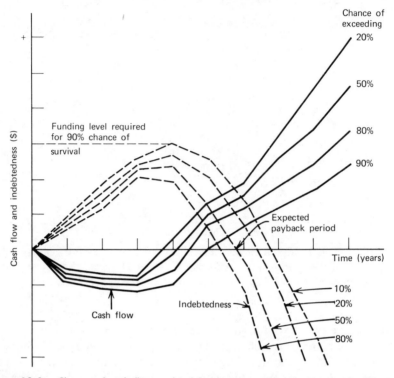

Figure 10-8.   Chance of cash flow and indebtedness exceeding various levels. Illustrates the chance that funding level will be exceeded (i.e., survivability of the venture). From Joel S. Greenberg, "Risk Analysis," *Journal of Aeronautics and Astronautics*, November 1974, by permission of the publisher.

identify the level of indebtedness in such a way that the risk and the consequences of error are clearly visible.

10.4   AN APPROACH TO ALLOCATING NEW BUSINESS FUNDS

In a typical pricing/profit structure for a small engineering business (Figure 10-9), a certain amount of money for new business funds (NBF) is included as part of the pricing structure for any program bid. This is the new business factor just prior to the fee calculation. Whenever a bid is made on a program, the business uses *today's* NBF, expecting to earn it back with the NBF from tomorrow's win. From another viewpoint, every program will pay back the NBF spent to win it (by allowing contractors to

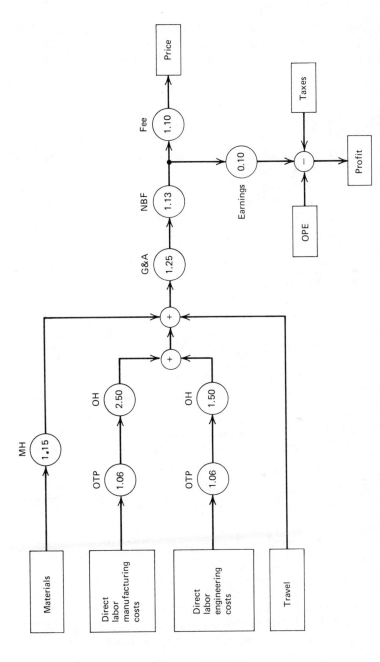

Figure 10-9. Typical pricing/profit structure for a small (less than 100 people) high-technology business. OTP = overtime premium; OH = overhead; MH = materials handling; G&A = general and administrative; OPE = out-of-profit expenditures (entertainment, PR, advertisement, etc.); NBF = new business funds.

include an NBF factor). The government allows a fairly high NBF factor (nominally 13%) for high-technology small businesses. In regular commercial business activities, however, an NBF of 13% is generally not allowed, and the nominal NBF factor is about 1 to 5%.

By way of making clear the NBF pricing relationship, consider the following example. A $100,000 government program has in its budget about $11,700 of NBF to repay competitors for competing on such programs. Actually one competitor will win the entire $11,700; however he must bid on a number of contracts to win one. If the winner has (say) four regular competitors he will win only 20% of the time (all other things being equal). Thus his average NBF earnings for a $100,000 contract are on the order of $11,700/5 = $2340 from each of five $100,000 competitions in which he participates. Another way to think of this is: each competitor can afford approximately $2340 NBF expenditure per $100,000 of contract competition opportunity involving his four major competitors.

A rough estimate of how much NBF a particular competition is worth to all competitors is given by the equation

$$(\text{program value} - \text{fee}) \times 0.13 \sim \text{NBF}$$

If there are N major competitors, the NBF that each can afford is approximately

$$\frac{\text{program value} \times 0.9 \times 0.13}{N} = \text{NBF expenditure per competitor}$$

Now if we further consider the probability that the offerer will be able to fund the program $P(G)$, the NBF that each competitor can afford to spend on each opportunity is on the order of

$$\frac{V \times 0.9 \times 0.13 P(G)}{N} \sim \text{NBF per competitor}$$

Finally, if we use the probability of win per competitor $P(W|G)$ instead of our crude estimate $1/N$, we get

$$\text{NBF per competitor} \sim 0.117 \times V \times P(W|G) \times P(G)$$

Using this formula you can tabulate the characteristics of the new business opportunities being worked in your organization and, applying this reasoning, determine how much each new business opportunity warrants of the NBF investment money. Table 10-3 shows the results of a typical analysis for a small business.

Table 10-3   Typical Small Business Resource Allocation[a]

Opportunity	Program Size (1976 $)	$P(G)$	$P(W\|G)$ (simplified formula = 1/number of competitors)	Expected NBF	Percentage	Resource Allocation $
1	75,000	.1	.3	2,600	3.1	2,170
2	30,000	1	.3	10,500	12.6	8,820
3	15,000	1	.3	5,300	6.3	4,410
4	400,000	.2	.6	56,200	67.3	47,110
5	120,000	.1	.3	4,200	5.0	3,500
6	25,000	1	.15	4,400	5.3	3,710
7	2,000	.5	.25	300	0.4	280
				83,500	100.00	70,000[a]

[a]Assuming $70,000 is allocated to new business fund.

Working out a chart like this is usually helpful for a business manager in planning NBF expenditures and manpower distribution within his organization. What is not covered in this discussion is the distribution of the resources with time. A number of techniques have been tried, including sigmoid curves and half-beta-distribution curves. For small businesses it is sufficient to manually estimate the distribution, making sure that it does not exceed resources or manpower. For large organizations in which hundreds of opportunities are available and fairly large NBF funds are to be distributed, a computer program for distributing the funds to ensure that the resources, people, money, and materials are not exceeded is an iterative task peculiar to the business.

A number of useful advanced resource allocation techniques can be used to apply resources to new business. Occasionally, however, a simple manual procedure that can be worked out on a pocket calculator in minutes is sufficient. A procedure for planning NBF expenditures that the author uses with success is as follows.

1. Compute the expected NBF to be earned by each new business opportunity.

2. Assume that the smallest major opportunity will be the future program whose earnings will replace today's NBF expenditures. This amount can be called a **conservative NBF budget**, which business management should expect to spend on today's major new business opportunities.

3. The fraction of this budget that can be distributed to the new business opportunities can be computed by dividing the expected new

business earnings from each program by the total new business earnings for all the new business opportunities under consideration.

Example:

Suppose three new business opportunities are being considered:

Opportunity	Value
1	$100,000
2	$200,000
3	$300,000

The conservative NBF budget is computed as

$$\$100,000 \times 0.9 \times 0.13 = \$11,700 \qquad \text{for all three opportunities}$$

Now assume you have analyzed each of these opportunities and have assigned to them the following probabilities:

$$P_1(G) = 1$$
$$P_1(W|G) = .5$$
$$P_2(G) = .8$$
$$P_2(W|G) = .25$$
$$P_3(G) = .9$$
$$P_3(W|G) = .2$$

We can now compute the expected NBF (ENBF) as

$$\text{ENBF}_1 = \$100,000 \times 0.117 \times 1 \times 0.5 = \$5850$$
$$\text{ENBF}_2 = \$200,000 \times 0.117 \times 0.8 \times 0.25 = \$4680$$
$$\text{ENBF}_3 = \$300,000 \times 0.117 \times 0.9 \times 0.2 = \$6320$$

From this the total expected NBF may be computed as

$$\text{ENBF}_1 + \text{ENBF}_2 + \text{ENBF}_3 = \$16,850$$

Now we can compute the percentage of the new business funds that will be applied to each of the three new business opportunities as

$$\frac{\mathrm{ENBF}_1}{\text{total ENBF}} = 0.35$$

$$\frac{\mathrm{ENBF}_2}{\text{total ENBF}} = 0.28$$

$$\frac{\mathrm{ENBF}_3}{\text{total ENBF}} = 0.38$$

Applying these percentages to our conservative NBF budget of $11,700, we find that the (rounded off) NBF to be applied to each of the programs is:

$$\text{opportunity } 1 = \$11,700 \times 0.35 = \$4100$$

$$\text{opportunity } 2 = \$11,700 \times 0.28 = \$3280$$

$$\text{opportunity } 3 = \$11,700 \times 0.38 = \$4390$$

In this example the total expected NBF earned is $16,850, more than our conservative $11,700 budget based on the smallest new business opportunity win. In a sense the $16,850 is what a businessman *should* use to budget his NBF expenditure *on the average*. A more conservative businessman might use the $11,700 budget. The high roller would probably budget on the basis of winning the largest new business opportunity.

The expected NBF earnings from any program are given by

$$\mathrm{ENBF} \sim V \times 0.117 \times P(G) \times P(W|G)$$

The ROI on ENBF is

$$\mathrm{ROI} = \frac{V \times 0.117 \times P(G) \times (PW|G)}{\text{B\&P cost}}$$

Here B&P cost is the bid and proposal cost. If V is large but $P(W|G)$ is small, the ROI is usually small because the cost to bid and propose is usually large for large programs. If, however, $P(W|G)$ is so small that a win is unlikely, a businessman might still make a bid if he can get the ROI up to, say, 100 or so. Since all business is a gamble, the high-value programs should be screened to see whether a calculated risk—for example, a bid on the program with a unique low-cost but innovative proposal—is worthwhile.

A few common-sense insights arise from this type of analysis in considering the distribution of NBF funds. The first is an axiom that should be followed by small businesses. However the author has rarely, if ever, heard the concept discussed. New business operations axiom: **new business expenditures must be matched by new business earnings.** The basic idea is that the NBF spent to get new business must be earned back by the way bids are priced *if the business is to continue.* Most of the small-business emphasis in business decisions is based on **profit** analysis. From the standpoint of business systems performance, however, keeping track of NBF expenditures and ensuring that the NBF percentage included in the pricing of new bids is sufficient to earn back the NBF spent is absolutely essential if business is to continue. In this case the focus is on NBF, not on profit. A corollary to the axiom is: **the decision to spend today's NBF must be based on a reasonable expectation that it will result in future NBF earnings of at least an equivalent amount.**

Another corollary of the axiom is: **for the return on investment to ensure business growth, the NBF ROI must be greater than 1.** Notice that the emphasis is on NBF ROI, not on profit ROI. Profit ROI affects the net worth of the corporation through its impact on the stock price-to-earnings ratio. NBF ROI first ensures survival of the business; profits are considered later. Both are of vital importance, but they should be addressed in the proper order—first NBF ROI, then profit ROI.

For each major member of an industry, $P(W|G)$ is a function of how much new business participation the member has in a program. For example, if a program is worth $15 million of NBF participation on the part of *all* industry and there are five principal competitors, each should be spending about $3 million on the opportunity. In a sense, then, $P(W|G)$ is given by the equation

$$P(W|G) \approx \frac{\text{investment by industry member}}{\text{total investment by all industry members}}$$

If each member of industry is spending his $3 million, each will have the probability of win of .2 [same as (number of contractors) $- 1$]. If one contractor spends only $1 million, however, his $P(W|G)$ becomes approximately

$$\frac{1}{3+3+3+3+1} = \frac{1}{13}$$

There is a learning curve effect as well as an investment effect to consider. An equation that probably comes even closer to the actual $P(W|G)$ is*

*The size of the major contract is its total value.

$$P_i(W|G) \sim \frac{\text{INVESTMENT}_i(1 - B_p)(1 - e^{-r_i T_i}) + \Sigma \text{size of major contract}_i(1 - e^{-T_i/5}) B_{p_i}}{\Sigma \text{INVESTMENT}_i(1 - B_p)(1 - e^{-r_i T_i}) + \Sigma \text{size of major contract}_i(1 - e^{-T_i/5}) B_{p_i}}$$

where r_1 = the new business learning curve for the ith industry member
$\quad$ T_1 = the total time the ith member has been working this particular opportunity
$\quad$ T_i = the time since major contract over
$\quad$ B_p = a weighting factor to account for the previous business effect (judgment derived)

Though complicated, this formula does reflect most of the factors involved in complicated business decisions. The mind must juggle the effects in some similar fashion even though we usually do not write them down this way.

CASEBOOK EXAMPLE AND DISCUSSION

Statistically Modeling Risk and Return in a Seminar Business Venture

The binomial distribution is an excellent example of a businessman's distribution. Let us take a few moments to consider this distribution from the viewpoint of evaluating risk and return.

The author was once involved in a business that held nationwide technical seminars. It was an enjoyable venture because it could be modeled fairly precisely with a binomial distribution, thus both the risk and the return could be analyzed to a reasonable degree of accuracy. The only problem was that the math modeling of the venture did not occur until after the business had gone deeply into debt. The case is discussed to illustrate how a little analysis prior to the venture would have ensured success from the start. As it was, the analysis clearly indicated a way out of the difficulties and eventually led to profitable operations.

The Venture

The venture consisted of the presentation of a series of high-technology seminars in the computer and data processing field. The approach was as follows: select a lecturer with a reputation in his field; prepare a three-day seminar on the latest advances in the chosen area; hold the seminar only in the cities that were centers of high technology industry; guard against duplicating seminar topics that might be covered in university courses; advertise the seminar by direct mail, using professional society mailing lists that have a proven "draw;" advertise six weeks prior to the seminar (the average time to make an attendance decision and line up funding); use the "copy-the-leader" approach to advertising.

The Problem

Fifteen thousand flyers were mailed to advertise the first seminar, to be held in Los Angeles. Thirty-eight people attended. The seminar was priced at $235 per person. The revenues were $8930.00. The costs were as follows:

Lecturer's fees	$1500
Advertising	4400
Travel	1000
Facilities	300
Overhead salaries	1000
Total cost	$8200

Thus

$$\text{profit} = \$8930 - \$8200 = \$730$$

This seemed like a reasonable return on the $4400, since the investment horizon was only 23 weeks. The yield for $n = 0.44$ year, $PV = 4400$, FV $= 4400 + 730 = 5130$, is 41.75% (try it on your calculator).

Clearly, if similar results could be achieved with 100 seminars, a very profitable business could be developed. The decision was made to try nine more seminars on a nationwide basis over a period of a year. At the end of that year, the business was in substantial debt. Interestingly, all the indices of incipient failure were before us at the outset of the first seminar. Can you find them?

Analysis of the Problem

The decision to attend a seminar is a binary one. Thus we use a binomial distribution to model the venture. Remember, for a binomial distribution

$\mu = Np =$ expected number of attendees

$q = 1 - p$

$\sigma = \sqrt{Npq}$ = standard deviation in the number of attendees

Now p can be estimated as

$$p \cong \frac{38}{15,000} = .00253$$

$$q \cong 1$$

So

$$\sigma \cong \sqrt{38} \cong 6 \text{ people}$$

In other words, the variance in the average number of attendees is approximately six people for the first seminar. Had six fewer people attended, the profit would have been

$$\text{profit} = \$7520 - \$8200 = -\$680$$

Even worse, the standard error in the mean number of attendees for one sample of the mean (38 in this case) is given by

$$\sigma_{\bar{X}} = \frac{\sigma}{\sqrt{1}} = \sigma \cong 6 \text{ people}$$

Combining the variance of both the estimate of the mean and the variance in the number of attendees to the seminar, we see that

$$\sigma_{\bar{X}} = \text{variance in the attendance based on only one seminar}$$

$$= \sqrt{\sigma^2 + \sigma_{\bar{X}}^2} \cong 9 \text{ people}$$

The impact of the combined incertainly on the profit would have been

$$\text{profit} = \$6815 - \$8200 = -\$1385$$

In short, the earnings from the first seminar were a lucky break. As it turned out, later seminars proved the point.

Solving the Problem

It became clear that in this venture the greatest uncertainty was on the revenues side of the ledger, the costs being fairly well defined. Our conceptual approach to getting the revenues under control was to fix the revenues per seminar and let the costs carry the uncertainty. This approach was implemented by seeking contracts for in-house seminars at a substantially lower (but fixed) price. The costs vary significantly, depending on how much travel and communications are required to obtain a signed contract. The business is more personal, therefore more enjoyable. The overall result was three years of steady profitable business that paid off the debt and now produces a reasonable yield of about 28% per year.

PART 3

BUSINESS AND FINANCIAL ANALYSIS ON THE PROGRAMMABLE POCKET CALCULATOR

CHAPTER 11

THE PROGRAMMABLE
POCKET CALCULATOR

As mentioned in the preface, the premise of this book is that the pocket calculator provides a financial analyst or businessman with new dimensions and capabilities in business systems analysis. The programmable pocket calculator, in the author's opinion, is an *even greater advance* in pocket calculator computing capabilities for the financial analyst. From the analyst's viewpoint, the most significant use of the pocket calculator may turn out to be as a teaching machine. Usually the financial analyst confines his interest in problem solving to the areas for which he is paid. When he studies to develop new insights into finance and business, he uses four techniques:

1. He studies his discipline in textbook fashion.
2. He identifies or develops mathematical tools that are useful for solving problems in his discipline.
3. He works through the "casebook" problems to learn the details and subleties of financial analysis by quantifying the problems.
4. He gains at least two to three years experience in applying the mathematical models of the financial discipline *by working in the discipline itself.*

The process of learning a new discipline is time-consuming. Mastering a financial discipline takes a fairly long period of time—in particular, step 4, which moves from textbook-type knowledge to actual understanding of the discipline. Here the mathematical models are usually more complex, requiring many considerations. For a simple example, the financial analyst usually encounters the difference between ordinary annuities and annuities due by working in business of completely different types. Only then does he identify the "end effects" that are associated with any financial analysis and constitute the fine distinctions that make, for example, leasing different from trusts (even though both deal with annuities). These practical problems, though discussed in textbooks, are rarely given the consideration they require in day-to-day problem solving.

With the advent of the programmable pocket calculator, the analyst has available fairly extensive preprogrammed libraries for many disciplines. These libraries of solved problems (such as the Finance Pac offered by Hewlett-Packard for its HP-65) have been developed by persons having considerable experience in their disciplines. By merely securing the standard library provided by the pocket calculator manufacturers, the analyst who has a programmable pocket calculator can become familiar, in a matter of weeks, with the programs and mathematical tools used in disciplines outside his usual area of experience. Having acquired experience with these practical programs, he can apply the new techniques to his discipline to solve his problems. In a sense the learning process is reversed —the analyst begins with the ability to numerically evaluate problems with which he is only vaguely familiar. These are the practical problems, however, and they involve the mathematical models that have passed the test of time in practical analysis. Under the guidance of a person experienced in this new discipline, the learning process is quite fast.

The programmable pocket calculator thus is a good teaching machine, particularly because it is portable and learning can be conducted in the comfort of one's own home. In the past the numerical evaluation of most practical financial analyses was usually done either on a digital computer (provided the analyst could justify his request for budget time on a computer) or on a desk calculator using extensive mathematical tables, at the analyst's work area or office. Now the financial analyst can study even the most complex aspects of any given financial analysis at home, where most of us do our homework anyway. Furthermore, the analyst learns more quickly now because he spends most of his time *thinking and analyzing*, with a minimum of effort (making the keystrokes) devoted to numerical evaluation.

The most important capability that the programmable calculator brings to the financial analyst is the iterative computation of numbers and the preparation of extensive tables and graphs (involving many point pairs) for a more extensive set of problems than could be handled on the nonprogrammable pocket calculator. For the many financial analysts and small financial organizations that do not have a computer facility, the programmable pocket calculator can bring to each member of the staff tremendous computing power.

Financial analysts usually do not *compute* per se. Rather, they develop formulas that are used to compute and provide insight for problem solving. The pocket calculator allows the analyst to begin with a top-level mathematical model of his process and refine it very quickly by testing the model numerically. Here he develops a system of equations that he thinks will describe a business process or solve a problem and uses the pocket calculator to numerically evaluate the equations, permitting comparison of the results with what is observed about the business system. The analyst judges the degree to which the model can satisfactorily predict the behavior of the business process. Any major discrepancies lend to refining the mathematical model of the business system. Thus while the laws of supply and demand generate the *equations of motion* of a business process (that when solved will predict the behavior of the business system), the numerical comparison between the observed behavior and the predicted behavior may indicate that certain elements have been omitted from the mathematical model. This then lends the analyst to prepare a more comprehensive model of the business system. The new model should improve his ability to forecast business systems dynamics and in particular the response of the business to forcing functions such as advertising, inflation, and losses through defaults.

We see that the pocket calculator does not improve the *method* for generating the equations of motion of a business system, but it helps improve the *mathematical model* to which the methods are applied. This development of mathematical models using *numerical testing* is a convenient and fast operation with the programmable pocket calculator. There is no waiting for batch-processed computer runs to be made to get the data for improving the model. There are no "charge numbers" or budget hurdles to be dealt with before the analyst can use the computer. On the programmable pocket calculator the cost of the run is in the "noise" of the electric bill. Finally, when an acceptable mathematical model is developed, the analyst can transfer the model to a magnetic tape strip to be stored for future use—a convenient means for conserving the energy spent preparing the mathematical model. Furthermore, the key data used in the analysis of a program can also be stored on tape for future reference. Thus the programmable pocket calculator also provides an effective means of documenting an analysis. The analyst can collect at relatively small cost a magnetic tape library that requires minimal storage space.

Finally, the programmable pocket calculator gives the financial analyst portable low-cost computing power for use in the field, in his car, at his client's location, or in his own home.

11.1 HARDWARE CONSIDERATIONS

The programmable pocket calculator has the following parts:

1. The arithmetic unit, that is, the combination of registers that perform the arithmetic.

2. The memory, which stores numbers and instructions as programmed from the keyboard or from stored programs on magnetic tape.

3. The firmware associated with the calculator, that is, its "hard wired" programs and instruction set that are already built into the calculator.

Calculators perform numerical calculations only, as opposed to computers, which are alpha-numeric data processors. Today's programmable calculator, and any that might be expected in the near future, will only be limited in that they perform numerical calculations and not alpha-numeric operations. Apart from this, the pocket calculators are similar to digital computers. Specifically data can be stored in memory, recalled to| the arithmetic registers or arithmetic unit, and processed and restored in memory following the sequence of preprogrammed operations.

An essential and interesting difference between the typical calculator and its digital computer counterpart is that many calculators operate in decimal rather than binary arithmetic. The reason is that decimal arithmetic involves less electronics for the special-purpose calculators than would conversion from decimal to binary and back again, as on general-purpose digital computing machines. Memories therefore are often set up in integer multiples of 10, as is the number of registers in the computing machine. For example, certain pocket calculators have one constant storage register and four arithmetic registers, in which the register arithmetic is performed. Ten additional storage registers are available in an advanced model of the basic calculator. The HP-25 and HP-55 have 49 programmable keystrokes that can be stored in memory. The HP-65 has 100 programmable keystrokes that can be put into memory.

The memory in most programmable calculators can be expected to be a set of registers in conjunction with the operating stack for performing register arithmetic and for scratch-pad storage during the execution of a program. From the standpoint of memory for storing numbers, there are only the registers in the stack plus the scratch-pad registers for number storage and manipulation. For example, if there are nine scratch-pad registers and four stack registers, there are thirteen storage locations for storing numbers generated by a program. There is, however, memory for integer multiples of ten keyboard instructions. For example, in the HP-65, 100 instructions can be stored in the calculator for sequential operations. That is, a program of 100 *keystrokes* on the keyboard of the machine can be stored and executed automatically. Though numbers can be programmed into the calculator, using the 100 storable keystrokes is relatively inefficient. Instead, the numbers can be input into the scratch-pad memory directly as opposed to inputting a 13-digit number into memory with as many keystrokes. This is perhaps the only important distinction between programmable pocket calculators and the standard digital computer. The typical programmable pocket calculator can be expected to store between 50 and 1000 *keystrokes* (not 13-*digit numbers*). Thus when we say that a digital computer has $32k$ 16-bit words or that a desk-top calculator has $4k$ 12-bit words, for the pocket calculator we say that it can store 100 or so *keystrokes*. This might seem somewhat limiting, but actually many pocket calculator problems involve fewer than 100 keystrokes. With a 100-stroke memory capability we can evaluate rather advanced mathematical functions and program fairly sophisticated iterative procedures for solving difficult problems.

11.2   FIRMWARE

The firmware consists of the instruction set built into the pocket calculator and "*called*" from its keyboard. The basic instruction set usually contains all functions on the keyboard of the scientific calculator and a set of special functions associated with the programming aspect of the programmable pocket calculator. These include the following:

1.   The GO-TO instruction. This instructs the calculator to perform the instruction at the nth step in the stored program. Thus GO-TO 50 would tell the calculator to perform the instruction at the fiftieth step in the program.

2.   The JUMP instruction. This instructs the calculator to jump the next two steps. It is expected that this instruction will be a natural part of many programmable calculators. The two steps that are skipped are usually GO-TO type instructions. Thus the JUMP instruction with the GO-TO instruction permits the calculations to be looped iteratively in the computer program.

3.   The DECREMENT AND JUMP ON ZERO instruction. This instruction, which can reasonably be expected in programmable calculators, examines the contents of one of the scratch-pad storage registers. If the register is not zero, it decrements the register by 1 and continues. When the register is zero, it will perform the JUMP operation.

4.   The LOGICAL or TEST FLAG instruction. The flag can be set equal to 1 or zero, thus controlling the data flow in a calculator program, based on whether the flag is 1 or zero. Usually the test flags or Booleans can be set manually on the keyboard or, since it is a keyboard instruction, with the program.

5.   The STOP instruction. This is an instruction to stop the program.

6.   The TEMPORARY STOP or RUN/STOP instruction (R/S). The

calculator is told temporarily to stop, usually for the purpose of data input or data output.

Other keyboard instructions that can be expected to be found on the typical programmable pocket calculators are the DELETE function, the NO-OP function, and the SINGLE-STEP function. The SINGLE-STEP function permits the program to be processed or reviewed a single step at a time. This allows debugging the program and examining or modifying the program by stepping up to the location in the instruction sequence that is to be modified or changed and the DELETE function instruction used to delete the previously programmed instruction, leaving it available for reprogramming. Finally, the NO-OP function can be used to fill memory with an instruction not to perform an operation. In this way, the remaining steps of a program can be safeguarded against accidental programming of the instruction sequence with undesirable program steps.

The firmware in a programmable pocket calculator can also include a keyboard for performing user-defined functions—functions that are programmed in a normal manner by a sequence of keystrokes telling the calculator how to execute the function. Of the firmware just discussed, only the latter uses part of the programmable memory; the former functions are part of the keyboard sequence, thus are designed into the electronics of the calculator.

11.3 SOFTWARE

The software in programmable calculators is usually a magnetic tape strip, a magnetic card strip, or a tape cassette that is used to read in and read out data and instructions from or to the memory of the calculator. It can be expected that manufacturers will provide preprogrammed software for performing analysis for many disciplines. In fact, it is precisely this software that permits a single pocket calculator to be programmed to perform special-purpose calculations in many disciplines. In a discussion with the Chief Engineer on the HP-65 Program, Chung Tung, the author was informed that it was precisely this motivation that led Hewlett-Packard to develop the HP-65, the first of the programmable pocket calculators.

The software associated with any pocket calculator is usually developed so that problems involving more than 100 instruction sets and requiring more than the scratch-pad storage provided by the stacks plus scratch-pad memory can be programmed on a series of magnetic tapes or magnetic card strips. In attempting to see how far this process could be carried, the author programmed an eleven-card sequence on the HP-65 for conducting a fairly sophisticated analysis of a dynamic process. The process included numerical integration of a fourteenth-order differential equation featuring saturation limits and hard-stop nonlinearities. Though somewhat impractical to use, the program developed points out the flexibility of this method when general-purpose computing machines are not available—when the calculation is required in the field or when important analyses are being conducted away from the computer center.

11.4 PROGRAMMABLE POCKET CALCULATOR TECHNIQUES

The basic procedure for solving a problem on the programmable pocket calculator is as follows:

1. *Definition of the problem.* The generic types of problems that are conveniently solved on the pocket calculator are data processing (which includes interpolation, extrapolation, and filtering), the numerical evaluation of functions, the solution to systems of equations (whether algebraic or differential), the simulation of continuous processes, and the statistical analysis of data. The problem is defined when the equations to be solved are identified.

2. *Preparation of a math flow of the sequence of keystrokes required.* For this the equations for solving the problem must be determined and the sequence of keystrokes to numerically evaluate the equation must be worked out in a form that can be solved explicitly and/or implicitly. The preparation of the math flow will, by definition, identify the control operations for automatic execution of the keystrokes.

3. *Programming of the calculator by keying in the keystroke sequence, including control operations.* Once the program is stored in memory, it is useful to load it onto a magnetic-tape strip to prevent inadvertent destruction of the program. It is reasonable to expect that programmable calculators will have an ERASE BEFORE WRITE tape load function. Thus reprogramming or redefining the program or modifying the program can be restored on the same magnetic-tape strip or cassette by simply reloading the program on the magnetic-tape strip.

4. *Verification and checking of the program* by tests with all numerical values set equal to zero, 1, or a single sequence of numbers that permits testing the program and its loops.

5. *Running the sequence automatically* with the actual problem data.

As an example, consider the problem of analyzing continuously compounded interest on a principal. Figure 11-1 shows the three steps in the

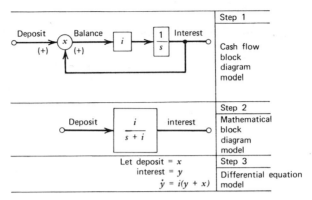

	Step 1
	Cash flow block diagram model
	Step 2
	Mathematical block diagram model
Let deposit = x	Step 3
interest = y	
$\dot{y} = i(y + x)$	Differential equation model

Figure 11-1.   Continuously compounded interest mathematical model; $s =$ Laplace transform operator.

mathematical modeling process. First the physical block diagram model is drawn, including all the cash flow inputs, and cash flow outputs. In this case we have a simple bank savings account that is being compounded continuously. Money is given to the bank, and the bank compounds the interest continuously. The interest is computed in the computer and added to the balance in the savings account. The mathematical block diagram of this process in Laplace transform notation is the second step in modeling the process, as shown. The savings account balance can be computed from the time-domain response of this process to the forcing function, the deposits into the savings account. It is necessary to prepare the differential equation that models this cash flow system—the third step in modeling the process (bottom of Figure 11-1). The next step is to prepare a math flow for the savings account balance mathematical model.

The math flow visualizes the way in which the program is intended to be solved on the programmable pocket calculator. As Figure 11-2 indicates, the first task is to initialize the problem with the cash flows and parameters of the problem, together with the coefficients involved in the numerical integration process for solving the differential equations of motion of the continuously compounded savings account. Also included in the initialization are the control variables that are used to determine the computing path within the math flow. In this case the initial cash flow is the initial deposit made into the account, and the other parameter is the interest rate paid by the bank in its continuous compounding of the interest. The parameter associated with numerical integration processes is the integration step size, and the control variable is the number of steps that we will

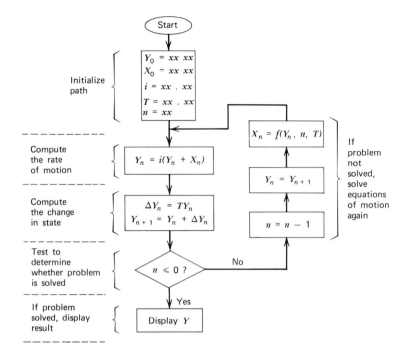

Figure 11-2. Math flow of the continuously compounded bank savings account mathematical model; $T=1$ year divided by the number of compounding periods per year.

take through the system of differential equations to compute the bank account at time $t = nT$.

After traversing the initialization path, the calculator is programmed to compute the time rate of change of the bank account balance. The next step in the math flow is to compute the new value of the bank account balance and this calculation is followed by a test to determine whether the calculations are to be stopped. In this example we ask whether 100 passes through the system of equations have been taken. When the answer is yes, the results are displayed in the display register. If the answer is no, another pass is made through the system of equations (after renaming the variables and computing the input cash flow for the next step, of course). In this example we simplify the situation by examining only the response of the bank account balance to a single deposit into the account. Thus the calculation of the bank account deposit in a closed-loop feedback process is not necessary. This has no effect on our general discussion, since computing of the bank account deposits is a straightforward process when the payments into the bank account are preknown.

Table 11-1 illustrates the third step in the problem-solving procedure—preparing a keystroke sequence that can be performed on the pocket calculator. In this example the HP-65 calculator was used, and some attention must be given to the details of its implementation to understand this step in the preparation of problems on a programmable pocket calculator. This keystroke sequence programmed on the HP-65 is nevertheless typical of the keystroke sequences one can expect to encounter on most programmable pocket calculators.

Table 11-1   Preparation of a Keystroke Sequence

| Math Flow | Math Flow | |
	Keystroke	Function
Initialization path	LBL-A	Label the initialization path A
	R/S	Stop then input and store y_0
	STO-1	
	R/S	Stop then input and store x_0
	STO-2	
	R/S	Stop then input and store i
	STO-3	
	R/S	Stop then input and store T
	STO-4	
	R/S	Stop then input and store n
	STO-8	
Identify loop closure points	LBL-1	Label this step "1"
Compute rate	RCL-2	Recall x
Compute rate	RCL-1	Recall y
	+	$x+y$
	RCL-3	Recall i
	×	$i(x+y)$
Compute state	RCL-4	Recall T
	×	$\Delta y = T\dot{y}$
	RCL-1	
	+	$x = y + \Delta y$
	STO-1	$y_n = y_{n+1}$
Test for problem being solved	DSZ[a]	Test register 8 for zero. If zero, skip next step and proceed
Go through equations of motion again if not solved	GO-TO	If R-8 not zero then go to step "1" and decrement R-8 by one and go to 1
Display results	R/S	Display y

[a]Decrement and skip on zero.

The first eleven steps in Table 11-1 are the steps taken along the initialization path. The sequence begins by labeling the initialization path A to distinguish it from the normal feedback path, which begins at step 12 and is labeled 1 (it identifies the point at which the feedback·path loop closure occurs). The steps 2 through 11 involve automatically stopping to input a number on the keyboard and then manually starting the program again to store the keyboard number in memory. For example, step 2 stops the automatic program sequence so that the variable Y_0 can be input on the keyboard and then stored in location 1 (step 3) when the RUN-STOP key is again stroked (step 2). When operating, the computer will automatically progress to the first RUN-STOP (which is step 2) and stop; the variable Y_0 is manually input through the keyboard into the display register, and when the RUN-STOP key is stroked, the variable Y_0 will be stored in memory register 1 (step 3). The computer will then automatically proceed to step 4, where it will stop to await keyboard input of X_0 and the associated RUN-STOP keystroke to allow the program to proceed to step 5, which is to store the contents of the display register in memory register 2. This procedure of initializing the program continues until step 11, where the loop closure point is identified by labeling that particular step as step 1.

The next five steps compute the time rate of change of the bank account balance according to the differential equation in Figure 11-2. Updating the bank account balance output is done in the next five steps of the program. Then we test to see whether 100 steps through the equations of motion have been completed. This is the step beginning with keystroke DSZ, which means "decrement and skip on zero." The function of the DSZ is to test register 8 for zero. If register 8 is zero, the next step in the program will be skipped. In this example if register 8 is zero, the calculator will jump over the GO-TO instruction and go immediately to the RUN-STOP instruction, where the program will stop and the latest value of Y will be displayed in the display register. If, however, the contents of register 8 are not zero, the program will not skip the GO-TO instruction—it will go to the step labeled 1 and simultaneously the contents of register 8 will be decremented by 1. In Hewlett-Packard's implementation of the DSZ function, register 8 is used for the contents of the number of steps to be made in an iterative procedure. For other pocket calculators, it can be expected that other implementations of this DSZ function can be made. They will have one thing in common, however: the decrementing of *some* register and skipping the next step if the register's contents are zero. If the contents are not zero, the next step will not be skipped; however, the contents of the test register will be decremented by 1.

The author recommends terminating an iterative procedure based on a test of the number of iterations if at all possible. This is because for many iterative procedures an estimate of the number of steps to solve the problem is usually possible. This solution often gives insight into the convergence properties of the problem, which is helpful in establishing confidence in any result. For these problems, where estimates of steps that should give the solution are known, the DSZ function is a "natural" test procedure and thus is particularly important in pocket calculator analysis.

Table 11-2 shows three *static check cases* used to check this program. Simple static tests of a program can often be made with numbers that are quite unlike the physical characteristics of the process being studied. In this set of check cases only zeros and/or 1 were used in the first two cases and zero through 2 for the third. It is important to develop dynamic check cases by using either an alternate means to solve the problem or a predetermined analysis of a simplified version of the problem. This is not shown as our straightforward example.

Table 11-3 illustrates the fifth step in the problem-solving procedure in which the calculator makes 100 passes through the equations to compute

Table 11-2   Preparation of a Check Case

Check Case 1	Check Case 2	Check Case 3
Let $Y_0=0$	$Y_0=1$	$Y_0=1$
$X_0=1$	$X_0=1$	$X_0=0$
$i=0$	$i=1$	$i=2$
$T=1$	$T=1$	$T=2$
$n=1$	$n=1$	$n=1$
Then $\dot{Y}=0$	$\dot{Y}=2$	$\dot{Y}=2$
$\Delta Y=0$	$\Delta Y=2$	$\Delta Y=4$
$Y_n=0$	$Y_n=3$	$Y_n=5$
Display $Y_n=0$	Display $Y_n=3$	Display $Y_n=5$

Table 11-3   Running of the Automatic Sequence to Compute the Bank Account Balance[a]

Three Sample 100-Step Solution Cases at $T=1/365$ year and Deposit $=\$1000$			
Time	$i=0.06$	$i=0.07$	$i=0.08$
100 days	$y=\$16.5728$	$y=\$19.3613$	$y=\$22.1573$

[a]This problem is specially set up to compute interest based on daily compounding of the interest for easy comparison with interest tables the reader may have at hand.

the account's response at 1 year, varying the other financial parameters. The material for the example was developed and programmed and the sequence of solutions was run in approximately 17 minutes. The static check cases were run in 20 seconds and the three 100-step solutions were run in approximately 3 minutes.

It is worth pointing out that as the calculator is programmed, the keystrokes are displayed according to their row-column location on the keyboard. For example, if the key that is at the intersection of the third column of keys and the second row of keys is depressed, a "32" is displayed in the register window. In this way, the programmer can monitor the programming of the process to ensure that the desired program is being stored in memory. This feature is also used in conjunction with the single-step key to review a program that is already in memory and, when necessary, to single-step up to the point at which a change is to be made.

Relational tests that are not used in this example but can be expected in programmable pocket calculators include determinations of whether a register is greater than, equal to, or less than the contents of another register. In the Hewlett-Packard 65 implementation, the relational tests are conducted in conjunction with the ninth memory register. As with the DSZ function, it can be expected that other implementations will be available in other programmable pocket calculators.

Finally, in the preparation of any computer program on any programmable calculator (where there is more than enough memory for the problem), it is advisable to include additional RUN-STOP operations in long programs to display intermediate results while writing and checking the problem. When the program is finally checked out, the unwanted stops can be deleted. The deletion procedure is simply to single-step to the RUN-STOP and then use the DEL instruction to eliminate the RUN-STOP instructions used for checkout purposes.

11.5 METHODS OF ANALYSIS ON THE PROGRAMMABLE POCKET CALCULATOR

The three basic types of numerical methods for solving problems on the programmable pocket calculator are as follows

- Explicit methods.
- Implicit methods.
- Simple search methods.

In the explicit method the equations to be numerically evaluated are simply programmed on the calculator, thus eliminating the need for manually working out the sequence of keystrokes to solve the problem. A manual optimization problem is a good example. Assume that the top-level cost model for a satellite program takes the form

$$C = n\underbrace{\left[30 + \left(\frac{M-1}{1.5}\right)30\right]}_{\text{procurement}} + 4\underbrace{\left[30 + \left(\frac{M-1}{1.5}\right)30\right]}_{\substack{\text{research,}\\\text{development}}}$$

$$+ 0.4\underbrace{\overbrace{\left[30 + \left(\frac{M-1}{1.5}\right)30\right]}^{\text{refurbishment}}\frac{T}{M}}_{\substack{\text{tests and}\\\text{engineering}}} + \underbrace{2T}_{\text{ground support}} + \overbrace{\frac{22T}{M}}^{\text{launch costs}}$$

where

$n =$ number of satellites

$M =$ satellite mean mission duration

$T =$ total program lifetime

$C =$ total program cost~millions of dollars

The model involves 69 keystrokes for numerical evaluation and the use of four scratch-pad storage locations.

It is clear from the cost model that the mean mission duration of the satellite plays a dominant role in the cost equation. If the mean mission duration is small, the number of launches (T/M) is large, and the cost associated with each launch results in high total program cost. If the mean

Table 11-4   Total Program Cost for the XYZ Satellite Program

Number of Satellites	Program Duration (years)	Mean Mission Duration (years)	Total Program Cost (millions $)
2	5	0.25	650
2	5	0.50	453
2	5	0.75	401
2	5	1.00	385
2	5	1.25	383
2	5	1.50	389
2	5	1.75	399
2	5	2.00	411
2	5	2.25	425
2	5	2.50	440

mission duration is large, the cost associated with the design and develop-ment of the satellite is large, which also leads to a high total program cost. Clearly, somewhere in between is a minimum total program cost. To determine it, we use a sequence of solution values for the cost equation, as shown in Table 11-4. It is apparent that a satellite mean mission duration of ∼1.25 years minimizes the total program cost.

The preparation of Table 11-4 on the programmable pocket calculator involved 61 keystrokes to program the calculator and 100 keystrokes for data entry and manual program iteration. The entire procedure took 14 minutes, including checkout. When the table was manually prepared without using the programming feature of the calculator, approximately 45 minutes was required for preparation. The time saving shown here is typical of pocket calculator analysis, yet what is not shown (but is equally important) is that if the total program cost model had given unexpected or unexplained results calling for its modification, the cost model modifica-tions could have been incorporated and a new Table 11-4 prepared in only 3 minutes. With the programmable calculator, the modification would have been reprogrammed only for the part of the program at which it was required. The entire program need not necessarily be rewritten. Then only an additional 100 keystrokes would have been needed to prepare another version of Table 11-4.

The second method of problem solving is the implicit method. An implicit equation is prepared and solved implicitly. The procedure is to program the iterative procedure so that the solution to the implicit equa-tion satisfies error criteria established by the analyst.

The final procedure is neither implicit nor explicit. It is simply a brute-force search for the solution to an equation or system of equations by systematically testing regions in which the solution is expected to exist and retaining only the value (or values) in the region that best satisfies the equation to be solved. Of the three methods, the latter is the most systematic, involving the fewest calculations and taking maximum advan-tage of the programmability feature of the pocket calculator. The only test that needs to be done is to determine whether, when a solution is computed at a test point, the equation is better satisfied with the test solution currently being used than with any previous test solutions. If the current solution is best, the new test point is stored in memory and the old one is erased (or retained if it is desirable to monitor the convergence of the process). Otherwise the systematic search algorithm proceeds to the next test point, retaining the best previous test point. Of the iterative implicit and systematic search methods, the latter is the least efficient but involves the fewest programming steps, whereas the former method is more sophisticated, requiring logical tests and search algorithms.

From the analyst's viewpoint, the explicit mode of computer solution, which involves the analyst in selecting the conditions to substitute into the computer program (manual iteration), is at best a gross procedure but requires only a few quick iterations, since the manual interaction will lead to a closing in on the gross solution fairly rapidly. The implicit method results in solutions that are difficult to develop with man-machine interaction because the precision with which the solution is to be determined is beyond the level at which the manual interaction can easily guess a better solution than a preprogrammed solution search algorithm.

Finally, the third method, while systematic and simple to program, results in the least efficient and least accurate solution to the problem. The accuracy can be improved through refined grids of possible solution values. It is a very practical and useful method when only a rough answer is required for a problem that takes many keystrokes to evaluate. Also, it is mentioned here as an example of the simplest form of problem solving available on the pocket calculator at a low programming overhead penalty.

Note

Much of the material in the foregoing chapter was drawn from "Scientific Analysis on the Pocket Calculator," J. M. Smith, 1975, by permission of John Wiley & Sons, Inc.

CONCEPTS OF TIME AND MONEY

The Hewlett-Packard Corporation has graciously provided a clearly written summary of the concepts of time and money, which is reproduced here with only a few minor modifications.

It is well known that the Hewlett-Packard Corporation has a series of high-quality business pocket calculators. Less well known outside the calculator industry is the fact that the company has outstanding product support and marketing organizations. These organizations work together to provide the owners of their calculators with guides and user manuals that are second to none in the calculator industry. This appendix illustrates this point.

* * *

Essentially, there are two things you can do with money: spend it or invest it. A savings account in a bank is considered an investment. Yet whether you spend money or invest it, you need to receive something worthwhile in return.

This appendix looks at the nature of cash, how it flows, and how time and money relate to each other. And time *does* influence the value of money: $1000 today does not have the same value that $1000 had in 1945. Likewise, $1000 in 1945 had a different value from the same amount in 1930.

The formulas for solving time and money problems are presented here in the context in which they arise and are used. The emphasis is on understanding the concepts of time and the value of money. The formulas are included for the sake of completeness.

A-1 PERCENT: THE UNIVERSAL YARDSTICK

Percentage is the universal yardstick—the common standard of measurement—in the financial world. If your money increases or decreases, the gain or loss is measured in percent as well as in dollars. Taxes, interest rates, discounts, inflation, appreciation, depreciation, even the last raise you got, or the typewriter you bought last week for 40% off—all are expressed in terms of percent.

Percent, denoted by the symbol %, simply means hundredth. When you see 25%, it's the same as 25/100 or 0.25 or 1/4. Percentage is a dynamic relationship, a comparison or ratio of two numbers that often signifies that a change has taken place. "third-quarter earnings are down 27% from last year" may be cause for concern, while "a 12% raise effective today" may be cause for celebration.

Likewise, when you start with a given amount of money and receive money in return, the difference—whether it's a gain or loss—is viewed in relation to the original amount and expressed as a percentage. If you start out with one share of stock worth $100 and sell it for $125, you have earned 25/100 or a 25% return.

When you superimpose that gain or loss against time, it's called the **rate of return**. The time period most commonly used in business is one year. So if you earned that $25 in one year, that's a 25% annual rate of return.

A-2 INTEREST

Percent is also used to calculate interest. **Interest** is a charge for the use of money. In a sense, you "rent" the money to someone or someone "rents" it from you. Interest is based on three things:

1. The amount of money borrowed or saved.
2. The length of time.
3. The interest rate (a percentage).

This makes sense because the longer you rent something, the more you pay for it. If you rent a car for a week, it will cost more than if you rent it one day.

You can charge for money by the day, the week, or the month, but usually money is loaned or borrowed at a yearly rate. This annual interest rate is called the annual percentage rate or APR and is expressed as a percent. If a certain investment pays 9% yearly, that means $9 per year for every $100 invested.

But there are other considerations, too, when you pay or receive interest —namely, what *type* of interest and how often it is paid.

A-3 SIMPLE INTEREST

With **simple interest**, only the principal (i.e., the original amount of money) earns interest for the entire life of the transaction. For example, suppose you put $1000 in the bank at 8% simple interest for 3 years. The formula for calculating simple interest is

$$\text{interest}_{simple} = \text{principal} \times \text{interest rate} \times \text{time}$$

So, you would earn: $I = \$1000 \times 8\% \times 3 = \$240$ during that time period (Figure A-1). In essence, you receive $80 in interest at the end of the first year. Since only the principal ($1000) earns interest, you would receive another $80 at the end of the second year, and another $80 at the end of the third year. Could you earn more than $240 in those three years with the same $1000? Yes, by adding the interest to the principal each year.

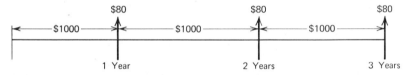

Figure A-1. Simple interest.

A-4 COMPOUND INTEREST

Suppose at the end of the first year, you withdraw the $1080, go to another bank, and deposit a balance of $1080. The second year you will earn $I = \$1080 \times 8\% \times 1$ or $86.40. You do the same thing again and, at the end of the third year, earn $I = \$1166.40 \times 8\% \times 1$, or $93.31 (Figure A-2). Instead of $240, you receive $259.71. By adding the simple interest to the

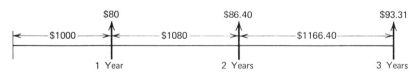

Figure A-2. Compound interest.

principal each year, you increased the earning power of your money by $19.71.

Fortunately, you don't have to run all over town withdrawing and depositing money. Banks have an efficient way of handling that for you. With **compound interest**, each time the interest is paid, it is added to the balance or principal. Compound interest is usually stated as an annual rate, although it may be paid (compounded) daily, monthly, quarterly, or semiannually.

So if you have $1000 at present, before you invest you can calculate how much money you will receive in the future. This is called **future value**. The formula for computing the future value of money with compound interest is:

$$FV = PV \times (1 + i)^n$$

or:

future value = present value

$$\times \left(1 + \frac{\text{interest rate}}{\text{per compounding period}}\right)^{\text{number of compounding periods}}$$

Or perhaps you want $1000 in the future—to take a trip to Acapulco next year—and want to know how much you have to invest to reach that goal. Since you have established the desired future value, you are solving for the money required right now or the **present value**. The formula for computing present value with compound interest is:

$$PV = \frac{FV}{(1 + i)^n}$$

or:

$$\text{present value} = \frac{\text{future value}}{\left(1 + \dfrac{\text{interest rate}}{\text{per compounding period}}\right)^{\text{number of compounding periods}}}$$

Notice that both formulas use compounding "period" as the time element. If interest is compounded annually, then one year is the period of time. But when interest is compounded more often, the time element or compounding period affects the value of your money.

Compounding Periods

Let's go back to your original $1000, invested at 8% compounded annually for 3 years. Using the future value formula, you can calculate what you will receive at the end of those 3 years:

$$FV = \$1000 \times (1 + 0.08)^3 = \$1259.71$$

Is there a way to earn more money with that $1000 at the same 8% interest rate? Yes, by compounding or adding the interest to the principal more than once a year. Suppose you put that money into an account where the 8% interest is compounded quarterly. How much do you have at the end of a year? (Note: in the formula, you *must* use "interest rate per period" for *i*. Since 8% is the annual rate, you have to divide by the number of compounding periods, in this case, 4.)

$$FV = \$1000 \times (1 + 0.02)^4 = \$1082.43$$

How much will you have after 3 years?

$$FV = \$1000 \times (1 + 0.02)^{4 \times 3} = \$1268.24$$

Now, instead of $240 or $259.71, you earned $268.24 in interest. It becomes apparent that the more often interest is compounded, the more money you receive in return.

Try figuring $1000 at 8%, compounded monthly for 3 years:

$$FV = \$1000 \times \left(1 + \frac{0.08}{12}\right)^{12 \times 3} = \$1270.24$$

Try the same problem again, compounded daily this time:

$$FV = \$1000 \times \left(1 + \frac{0.08}{365}\right)^{365 \times 3} = \$1271.22$$

Just by more frequent compoundings, you have increased your earnings. Notice, in the foregoing problems, that *interest rate per period MUST correspond with the compounding period interval.* Don't mix monthly interest with quarterly period or daily interest with semiannual compounding periods.

Is there a limit to the amount of money you can earn by increasing the frequency of compounding? Of course, and it's called **continuous compounding**. We've seen that compounding more and more frequently increases your earnings. If you compound continuously (more often than daily or hourly or every second), you earn the maximum mathematical limit. In other words, you reach the point where you just can't compound any more often.

A-5   EFFECTIVE ANNUAL RATE

Something interesting is emerging here. Even though 8% is stated as the annual rate, you actually receive more than 8% interest with compounding more than once a year.

Table A-1 $1000 at 8% for 1 Year

Compounded	Return	% Interest
Quarterly	$1082.43	8.243%
Monthly	$1083.00	8.300%
Daily	$1083.28	8.328%
Continuous	$1083.29	8.329%

When interest is compounded more often than once a year, the stated annual rate (8% in Table A-1) is called the **nominal rate**. The rate of interest actually earned in one year (8.328%) is called the **effective rate**.

Many savings institutions quote both the nominal rate and the effective rate. Your calculator can quickly convert one to the other. As Table A-1 shows, the effective rate may differ considerably from the nominal rate, so. it pays (literally!) to know what it is.

* * *

So far, we have been dealing with four basic elements: the amount of money you have, right now, to invest (present value), the interest rate i, the number of compounding periods n, and the amount of money you will get back (future value). Notice that these four elements correspond to four out of the top five keys on any business pocket calculator.

The fifth key (PMT) stands for payment. We just used an example where money sat in the bank. Now, let's look at a few situations where you are required to make payments.

A-6   ANNUITIES

An **annuity** is a series of equal payments made at regular intervals. Your paycheck is an example of an annuity—also your monthly rent or mortgage payment, the premiums on an insurance policy, the installments on a car loan, or regular deposits into a savings account.

The time between annuity payments is called the **payment interval** or payment period. If your payment is due at the *end* of each payment period, it's called an **ordinary annuity** or payments in arrears. Examples of ordinary annuities are a car loan (where you drive away now and pay later) or a mortgage (where the payments start one month after you get your loan).

The time/money relationship for an ordinary annuity with monthly payments for a year—a loan, for example—would look as in Figure A-3.

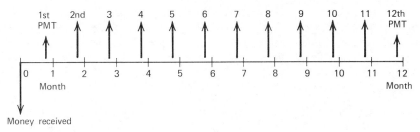

Figure A-3.   Ordinary annuity.

But with some annuities—like insurance premiums or a lease—the payment is due at the beginning of the month. This is called an **annuity due** because the payment falls at the beginning of the payment period. Other terms are payments in advance or anticipated payments.

An annuity due with monthly payments for a year—say, a car insurance policy—looks like Figure A-4. Notice that with an annuity due, you have a payment right away at the beginning of the first interval. With an ordinary annuity, your payment isn't due until the end of the first period, but you also have a payment at the end of the entire term.

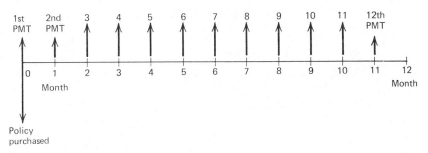

Figure A-4.   Annuity due.

What difference does it make whether you pay at the beginning of the month or at the end of the month? It's still 12 payments so it's all the same, right? WRONG! It does make a difference.

Suppose you are undecided whether to buy or lease a car. Either way it will cost you $165 a month for 24 payments at 12% interest. So you check it out to see whether the loan or lease would be less expensive.

The formula for the present value of an ordinary annuity (loan) is

$$PV = PMT \frac{1-(1+i)^{-n}}{i}$$

Substituting the known values, you calculate the present value of that series of payments (i.e., if you paid a cash lump sum instead of making payments, you'd pay $3505.16). The formula for the present value of an annuity due (lease) is:

$$PV = PMT \left[\frac{1-(1+i)^{-n}}{i} \right] (1+i)$$

Substituting the values for PMT, i and n, you discover that the present value of the lease payment would be $3540.21. An annuity due will cost you $35.05 more.

That was a borrowing example. Now, look at a savings situation or money in the bank. The sooner you make a deposit, the sooner you start collecting interest. If you wait a month before making a deposit, you will lose a month's interest.

Consider a saving plan in which you deposit $100 a month and earn 8% interest compounded monthly. The formula for future value of an ordinary annuity is

$$FV = PMT \times \frac{(1+i)^n - 1}{i}$$

So, if you deposit the money at the end of each month, after a year you will have

$$FV = \$100 \times \frac{\left(1 + \frac{0.08}{12}\right)^{12} - 1}{\frac{0.08}{12}} = \$1244.99$$

The formula for future value of an annuity due is

$$FV = PMT \times \left[\frac{(1+i)^n - 1}{i} \right](1+i)$$

So, if you deposit at the beginning of each month, after a year you will have more:

$$FV = \$100 \times \left[\frac{\left(1 + \frac{0.08}{12}\right)^{12} - 1}{\frac{0.08}{12}} \right]\left(1 + \frac{0.08}{12}\right) = \$1253.29$$

Although it's the same number of payments, the same amount, and the same interest rate, as you can see, investing at the beginning of the payment period does make a difference: you earn more money!

It's important to remember that if you are *borrowing* or paying money, an *ordinary annuity* is to your advantage because it will cost you less. If you are *investing* or receiving money, an *annuity due* is preferable because it is more profitable.

A-7 LOANS AND AMORTIZATION

Many of the annuities that you will encounter are loans, so here's a word or two concerning interest on loans.

Annual Percentage Rate

The federal "Truth-in-Lending" Law requires a lender to state interest in terms of the annual percentage rate or APR.

If previously an interest rate was quoted as "$1\frac{1}{2}$% a month" now it is quoted as "$1\frac{1}{2}$ % a month or 18% annual percentage rate." Whenever you encounter a daily, monthly, or add-on rate—anything other than the annual interest rate—for your own protection, you should also know the APR.

Add-On Interest

Frequently you will encounter a loan that has add-on interest. This means that simple interest is computed for the life of the loan and added to the loan.

Add-on interest can be deceptive, so be sure you also know the annual percentage rate. Add-on interest sounds attractive because the rate quoted is usually low. However, a 5% add-on loan of $1500 for 18 months actually comes to 9.27% APR.

With add-on interest, you pay interest on the entire loan amount for the entire term. As you will learn in the next discussion, with a direct reduction loan you pay only on the unpaid loan balance, which gradually decreases.

Amortization

If a loan or interest-bearing debt is discharged by (usually) equal payments, then it is said to be **amortized**. The word amortization comes from the French "*à mort*" meaning "at the point of death." Likewise, you are "killing" a loan by paying it off.

Most simple mortgages and installment loans are called **direct reduction loans**. The debt is discharged by equal periodic payments, although varying portions of each payment are applied toward principal and interest.

The interest is paid first, then the remainder of the payment is used to reduce the debt. The time frame over which you make payments is called the **schedule of payments**. The breakdown of payments into interest portions and principal portions is called an **amortization schedule**.

Suppose you find your dream house. If you take out a $35,000 mortgage for 30 years at $8\frac{3}{4}\%$, your monthly payments are $275.35. Your payment schedule would resemble Figure A-5. At the end of the first month, interest is calculated on the entire $35,000:

$$\frac{8.75\%}{12} \times 35,000 = \$255.21$$

and is added to the balance

$$\$35,000 + \$255.21 = \$35,255.21$$

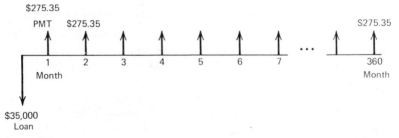

Figure A-5

Then your first payment is deducted to obtain your new balance:

$$\$35,255.21 - \$275.35 = \$34,979.86$$

The next month and every month thereafter, the same procedure is followed; that is, interest is calculated first and added to the balance before your payment is subtracted.

The amortization of your mortgage would look as in Figure A-6. As you reduce the size of the loan, the interest decreases... and a gradually higher percentage of each payment goes toward the debt itself or outstanding principal. By the time you reach your last payment, very little is deducted for interest.

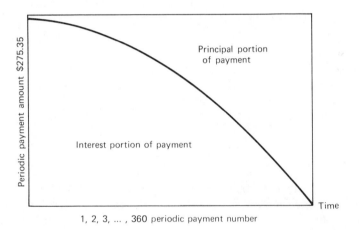

Figure A-6

Balloon Payments

In real life, cash flows (money in and money out) are not always so simple that they can be divided neatly into equal amounts of money or equal periods of time. A common financial occurrence is an annuity that has a large payment at the end (Figure A-7). The last payment—usually considerably larger, although it could also be smaller than the others—is called a **balloon payment** or balloon. For example, if you inherit a windfall and pay off your mortgage before the 30 years of the loan have elapsed, that's a balloon. In some instances, when your money is tied up elsewhere, it is to your advantage to make small installment payments, then later pay the major portion of the debt when money is available.

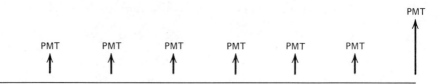

Figure A-7

In the leasing and real estate industries, this large amount at the end is often called the **residual value**. Even after several years of use or depreciation, a building (and especially the land that it is on) still has some cash value. For example, an owner can lease an office building for 25 years and then still sell it. The cash flow for residual value fits a similar pattern to the balloon payment (Figure A-8).

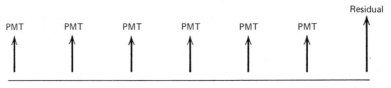

Figure A-8

There are other financial situations that fit the same pattern. For example, you lease a piece of capital equipment—say, a computer—for 5 years. At the end of the leasing period, the equipment still has a certain residual or fair market value.

Regardless of the specific name, just remember the concept of a balloon payment: a different amount, usually larger, at the end of the term.

A-8   SINKING FUNDS

Another method of discharging a debt is called the sinking fund method and is commonly used with bond issues.

Put yourself in the position of a bond issuer. Since millions of dollars are often borrowed by the sale of bonds, that amount of money just can't be plucked out of thin air when the bonds mature. In order to be able to meet the redemption price of the bonds, the bond issuer creates a separate fund into which he makes equal periodic deposits over the term so that just after the last deposit, the fund amounts to the debt (the face values or redemption prices of the bonds). This is called a **sinking fund** because its purpose is to sink—or shrink—the debt. Usually the sinking fund itself earns interest but not necessarily the same rate of interest that the bond issuer is paying.

How does this differ from putting money aside in a regular savings account? Mainly because a sinking fund is an ordinary annuity—not annuity due—and payments into the fund are made at the *end* of each payment period.

Let's look at an example: a 10-year bond of $100,000 is to be discharged by the sinking fund method. If 20 semiannual deposits, the first due in 6 months, are made into a fund that pays 5% compounded semiannually, find out how much you have to deposit into the fund each time.

To solve this, consider a sinking fund to be the same as the future of an ordinary annuity.

$$FV = PMT \times \frac{(1+i)^n - 1}{i}$$

$$\$100,000 = PMT \times \frac{(1+0.025)^{20} - 1}{0.025}$$

$$PMT = \$3914.71 \left(\begin{array}{l} \text{your semiannual deposit} \\ \text{into the sinking fund} \end{array} \right)$$

The bond issuer's deposits into the sinking fund look as in Figure A-9. In summary, using a sinking fund means that you discharge a debt by accumulating funds.

Figure A-9

A-9 DISCOUNTED CASH FLOW ANALYSIS

By now, you have a good grasp of several financial terms and concepts. But we haven't answered the questions you will ask over and over again: "What should I invest in?" "Is investment A better than investment B?"

"Where will I make the greatest profit?" "Should I buy securities or a shopping center?" Your calculator can help you evaluate future cash demands and returns to see which scheme or investment best meets your **profit objectives**.

One method of evaluation is called **discounted cash flow analysis**. There are two ways to use discounted cash flow analysis: the net present value approach or finding the discounted rate of return.

Solving for Net Present Value (NPV)

Suppose you invest a large amount of money (INV) into a scheme that generates a cash flow (cf_1) the first year, cf_2 the second year, and so on, up to cf_n in the nth year when the cash flow ends. You could write it down like this:

$$-INV + \text{cash flow first year} + \text{cash flow second year} + \cdots$$

$$+ \text{cash flow } n\text{th year}$$

or:

$$-INV + cf_1 + cf_2 + \cdots + cf_n$$

INV, the original investiment, is negative because it represents a cash outlay. A diagram of the cash flows might look as in Figure A-10. Notice that the cash flows may not necessarily be positive. Maybe, in a new business, you have a loss the first year. Or perhaps after you've been in business a while, a recession causes you to have a bad year.

You also have to consider the *time* value of money, not just the dollar value. (Would you rather have someone give you $10,000 today or 5 years from today?) The cash flows (cf_1, cf_2, etc.) are minifuture values that you are going to receive. But realistically they have to be translated back (discounted) to present value in order for you to accurately assess the investment.

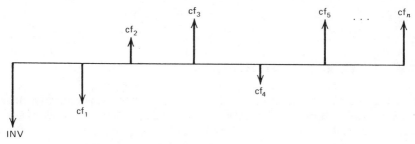

Figure A-10

In the compound interest discussion, you learned the formula for present value:

$$PV = \frac{FV}{(1+i)^n}$$

You can translate the future cash flows to present values:

$$NPV = -INV + \frac{cf_1}{(1+i)^1} + \frac{cf_2}{(1+i)^2} + \cdots + \frac{cf_n}{(1+i)^n}$$

This method of analysis is called solving for **net present value** because you are comparing the sum of the present values of all the future cash flows (all the cfs) to the initial investment ($-INV$). **For i substitute the rate of return that you want to achieve with the investment.**

At the start, the net present value (NPV) is negative because you've put out a large amount of money (INV). As the cash returns flow in, NPV will increase. Eventually – hopefully–NPV will turn positive. When $NPV = 0$, you have reached the break-even point on the investment.

If you have a specified period of time in mind and NPV is still negative after that time has elapsed, then forget that investment scheme and move on to another.

It's a simple, clear-cut analysis: if NPV is negative, the net present value is less than the investment and the investment is NOT profitable. Assuming a desired minimum yield, if NPV is positive, the investment does meet your **profit objectives**.

For example, you are thinking of buying an apartment building for $100,000. Based on the anticipated cash flows below, will this investment return 10% a year?

Year	Cash Flow
1	$7,000
2	$8,500
3	$9,000
4 (You intend to sell it.)	$120,000

Simply substitute these values into the equation

$$NPV = -\$100,000 + \frac{\$7000}{(1+0.10)^1} + \frac{\$8500}{(1+0.10)^2} + \frac{\$9000}{(1+0.10)^3}$$

$$+ \frac{\$120,000}{(1+0.10)^4} = \$2111.88$$

The net present value after the fourth year is positive, so the investment does return 10% or greater per year.

Suppose you sell the building in the second year for $110,000. Would that be more profitable?

$$NPV = -\$100,000 + \frac{\$7000}{(1+0.10)^1} + \frac{\$110,000}{(1+0.10)^2} = \$-2727.27$$

Answer: no. The net present value is negative so you won't even meet your desired 10% rate of return.

Solving for Internal Rate of Return (IRR)

Sometimes if you know your initial investment and can predict the periodic cash flows, you want to find the rate of return that you will earn. This is also called **yield, discounted rate of return, or internal rate of return (IRR)**. The same formula applies, only NPV = 0.

$$NPV = -INV + \frac{cf_1}{(1+i)^1} + \frac{cf_2}{(1+i)^2} + \cdots + \frac{cf_n}{(1+i)^n} = 0$$

Solving for i gives you the rate of return on your investment.

The easiest way is to estimate the rate of return you are looking for. Substitute that percentage for i, then solve the equation. *When NPV is 0, your "guesstimate" is the actual IRR.* If NPV is negative, your estimated percentage is higher than the actual IRR—try a lower interest rate. If NPV is positive, the actual IRR is even better or higher than your desired rate. For example, what is the estimated rate of return for a restaurant costing $200,000 that produces the following cash flows?

Year	Cash Flow
1	− $4,000
2	$20,000
3	$27,000
4	$42,000
5	$56,500
6 (You sell it.)	$230,000

If you try 12%, the NPV after the sixth year is $6867.05 so the actual IRR is higher than 12%.

Next, try 13%. This time the NPV is negative (− $2265.95), so the IRR must be less than 13%.

As a result of these two iterations, the IRR must be between 12 and 13%. Since the NPV for 13% is closer to zero than the NPV for 12%, the IRR must be closer to 13%. The actual yield or IRR on this restaurant investment is approximately 12.75%.

* * *

When you have finished reading this book, you should be able to work the following casebook decisions and examples in a few minutes. Give them a try to see how you do.

CASEBOOK DECISION

Your production manager wants to buy a new machine for $25,000. He estimates that over the next four years it will save $48,000 in labor and materials and will cost $5100 to maintain. Considering your company's 15% APR objective, should you buy the machine? Answer: yes.

CASEBOOK DECISION

You want to expand into another building selling for $100,000. Two banks each offer a 20-year, 90% mortgage. One will charge 8% interest plus 4 points, and the other 8.25% interest plus 1 point. Which is the better deal? Answer: 8.25% interest plus 1 point.

CASEBOOK DECISION

You decide to give your assistant a bonus paying him $5000 now or $480 per month for the next year. Which alternative would benefit your company, considering the current interest rate on your money is 15%? Answer: $480 per month.

CASEBOOK DECISION

You have just ordered $10,000 worth of inventory, and your supplier will allow you 90 days if you will pay $10,200. If capital costs 1% per month, should you pay now or in 90 days? Answer: 90 days.

CASEBOOK EXAMPLE

You have been making payments for 7 years on your $25,000, 30-year, 6% mortgage. The lender offers you a $2000 discount if you will pay the remaining balance. Given today's 10.5% interest rates, should you? Answer: no.

CASEBOOK EXAMPLE

You want to invest $12,000 in remodeling your store. If you place $200 per month in a savings account earning at the rate of 5% compounded monthly, how long will it take to save the money? Answer: 4.46 years.

CASEBOOK EXAMPLE

You are a real estate salesmen who has closed a sale on a $42,000 house. Your commission rate is 6% on the first $25,000, 5% on the next $15,000, and 4% on the remainder. How much will you earn? Answer: $2330.

CASEBOOK EXAMPLE

You want to start saving for the college education of your 10-year old son. If you are guaranteed 6% interest compounded quarterly, how much would you have to save per month to amass $12,000 by the time he is eighteen? Answer: 98.31.

CASEBOOK EXAMPLE

Five years ago you paid $34,000 for a home. If you were to sell it today for $50,000, what would be your annual rate of appreciation? Answer: 8.02%.

BINOMIAL PROBABILITIES

BINOMIAL PROBABILITIES

n	x							P						
		0.05	0.1	0.2	0.25	0.3	0.4	0.5	0.6	0.7	0.75	0.8	0.9	0.95
2	0	0.902	0.810	0.640	0.563	0.490	0.360	0.250	0.160	0.090	0.063	0.040	0.010	0.002
	1	0.095	0.180	0.320	0.375	0.420	0.480	0.500	0.480	0.420	0.375	0.320	0.180	0.095
	2	0.002	0.010	0.040	0.063	0.090	0.160	0.250	0.360	0.490	0.563	0.640	0.810	0.902
3	0	0.857	0.729	0.512	0.422	0.343	0.216	0.125	0.064	0.027	0.016	0.008	0.001	
	1	0.135	0.243	0.384	0.422	0.441	0.432	0.375	0.288	0.189	0.141	0.096	0.027	0.007
	2	0.007	0.027	0.096	0.141	0.189	0.288	0.375	0.432	0.441	0.422	0.384	0.243	0.135
	3		0.001	0.008	0.016	0.027	0.064	0.125	0.216	0.343	0.422	0.512	0.729	0.857
4	0	0.815	0.656	0.410	0.316	0.240	0.130	0.062	0.026	0.008	0.004	0.002		
	1	0.171	0.292	0.410	0.422	0.412	0.346	0.250	0.154	0.076	0.047	0.026	0.004	
	2	0.014	0.049	0.154	0.211	0.265	0.346	0.375	0.346	0.265	0.211	0.154	0.049	0.014
	3		0.004	0.026	0.047	0.076	0.154	0.250	0.346	0.412	0.422	0.410	0.292	0.171
	4			0.002	0.004	0.008	0.026	0.062	0.130	0.240	0.316	0.410	0.656	0.815
5	0	0.774	0.590	0.328	0.237	0.168	0.078	0.031	0.010	0.002	0.001			
	1	0.204	0.328	0.410	0.396	0.360	0.259	0.156	0.077	0.028	0.015	0.006		
	2	0.021	0.073	0.205	0.264	0.309	0.346	0.312	0.230	0.132	0.088	0.051	0.008	0.001
	3	0.001	0.008	0.051	0.088	0.132	0.230	0.312	0.346	0.309	0.274	0.205	0.073	0.021
	4			0.006	0.015	0.028	0.077	0.156	0.259	0.360	0.396	0.410	0.328	0.204
	5			0.001	0.002	0.010	0.031	0.078	0.168	0.237	0.328	0.590	0.774	
6	0	0.735	0.531	0.262	0.178	0.118	0.047	0.016	0.004	0.001				
	1	0.232	0.354	0.393	0.356	0.303	0.187	0.094	0.037	0.010	0.004	0.002		
	2	0.031	0.098	0.246	0.297	0.324	0.311	0.234	0.138	0.060	0.033	0.015	0.001	
	3	0.002	0.015	0.082	0.132	0.185	0.276	0.312	0.276	0.185	0.132	0.082	0.015	0.002
	4		0.001	0.015	0.033	0.060	0.138	0.234	0.311	0.324	0.297	0.246	0.098	0.031
	5			0.002	0.004	0.010	0.037	0.094	0.187	0.303	0.356	0.393	0.354	0.232
	6					0.001	0.004	0.016	0.047	0.118	0.178	0.262	0.531	0.735
7	0	0.698	0.478	0.210	0.134	0.082	0.028	0.008	0.002					
	1	0.257	0.372	0.367	0.312	0.247	0.131	0.055	0.017	0.004	0.001			
	2	0.041	0.124	0.275	0.312	0.318	0.261	0.164	0.077	0.025	0.012	0.004		
	3	0.004	0.023	0.115	0.173	0.227	0.290	0.273	0.194	0.097	0.058	0.029	0.003	
	4		0.003	0.029	0.058	0.097	0.194	0.273	0.290	0.227	0.173	0.115	0.023	0.004
	5			0.004	0.012	0.025	0.077	0.164	0.261	0.318	0.312	0.275	0.124	0.041
	6				0.001	0.004	0.017	0.055	0.131	0.247	0.312	0.367	0.372	0.257
	7						0.002	0.008	0.028	0.082	0.134	0.210	0.478	0.698
8	0	0.663	0.430	0.168	0.100	0.058	0.017	0.004	0.001					
	1	0.279	0.383	0.336	0.267	0.198	0.090	0.031	0.008	0.001				
	2	0.051	0.149	0.294	0.312	0.296	0.209	0.109	0.041	0.010	0.004	0.001		
	3	0.005	0.033	0.147	0.208	0.254	0.279	0.219	0.124	0.047	0.023	0.009		
	4		0.005	0.046	0.087	0.136	0.232	0.273	0.232	0.136	0.087	0.046	0.005	
	5			0.009	0.023	0.047	0.124	0.219	0.279	0.254	0.208	0.147	0.033	0.005
	6			0.001	0.004	0.010	0.041	0.109	0.209	0.296	0.312	0.294	0.149	0.051
	7					0.001	0.008	0.031	0.090	0.198	0.267	0.336	0.383	0.279
	8						0.001	0.004	0.017	0.058	0.100	0.168	0.430	0.663

From Donald F. Koosis, *Business Statistics*, Wiley, New York 1972, pp. 279–283.
Copyright © 1972. Reprinted by permission of John Wiley & Sons, Inc.

								P						
n	x	0.05	0.1	0.2	0.25	0.3	0.4	0.5	0.6	0.7	0.75	0.8	0.9	0.95
9	0	0.630	0.387	0.134	0.075	0.040	0.010	0.002						
	1	0.299	0.387	0.302	0.225	0.156	0.060	0.018	0.004					
	2	0.063	0.172	0.302	0.300	0.267	0.161	0.070	0.021	0.004	0.001			
	3	0.008	0.045	0.176	0.234	0.267	0.251	0.164	0.074	0.021	0.009	0.003		
	4	0.001	0.007	0.066	0.117	0.172	0.251	0.246	0.167	0.074	0.039	0.017	0.001	
	5		0.001	0.017	0.039	0.074	0.167	0.246	0.251	0.172	0.117	0.066	0.007	0.001
	6			0.003	0.009	0.021	0.074	0.164	0.251	0.267	0.234	0.176	0.045	0.008
	7				0.001	0.004	0.021	0.070	0.161	0.267	0.300	0.302	0.172	0.063
	8						0.004	0.018	0.060	0.156	0.225	0.302	0.387	0.299
	9							0.002	0.010	0.040	0.075	0.134	0.387	0.630
10	0	0.599	0.349	0.107	0.056	0.028	0.006	0.001						
	1	0.315	0.387	0.268	0.188	0.121	0.040	0.010	0.002					
	2	0.075	0.194	0.302	0.282	0.233	0.121	0.044	0.011	0.001				
	3	0.010	0.057	0.201	0.250	0.267	0.215	0.117	0.042	0.009	0.003	0.001		
	4	0.001	0.011	0.088	0.146	0.200	0.251	0.205	0.111	0.037	0.016	0.006		
	5		0.001	0.026	0.058	0.103	0.201	0.246	0.201	0.103	0.058	0.026	0.001	
	6			0.006	0.016	0.037	0.111	0.205	0.251	0.200	0.146	0.088	0.011	0.001
	7			0.001	0.003	0.009	0.042	0.117	0.215	0.267	0.250	0.201	0.057	0.010
	8					0.001	0.011	0.044	0.121	0.233	0.282	0.302	0.194	0.075
	9						0.002	0.010	0.040	0.121	0.188	0.268	0.387	0.315
	10							0.001	0.006	0.028	0.056	0.107	0.349	0.599
11	0	0.569	0.314	0.086	0.042	0.020	0.004							
	1	0.329	0.384	0.236	0.155	0.093	0.027	0.005	0.001					
	2	0.087	0.213	0.295	0.258	0.200	0.089	0.027	0.005	0.001				
	3	0.014	0.071	0.221	0.258	0.257	0.177	0.081	0.023	0.004	0.001			
	4	0.001	0.016	0.111	0.172	0.220	0.236	0.161	0.070	0.017	0.006	0.002		
	5		0.002	0.039	0.080	0.132	0.221	0.226	0.147	0.057	0.027	0.010		
	6			0.010	0.027	0.057	0.147	0.226	0.221	0.132	0.080	0.039	0.002	
	7			0.002	0.006	0.017	0.070	0.161	0.236	0.220	0.172	0.111	0.016	0.001
	8				0.001	0.004	0.023	0.081	0.177	0.257	0.258	0.221	0.071	0.014
	9					0.001	0.005	0.027	0.089	0.200	0.258	0.295	0.213	0.087
	10						0.001	0.005	0.027	0.093	0.155	0.236	0.384	0.329
	11								0.004	0.020	0.042	0.086	0.314	0.569
12	0	0.540	0.282	0.069	0.032	0.014	0.002							
	1	0.341	0.377	0.206	0.127	0.071	0.017	0.003						
	2	0.099	0.230	0.283	0.232	0.168	0.064	0.016	0.002					
	3	0.017	0.085	0.236	0.258	0.240	0.142	0.054	0.012	0.001				
	4	0.002	0.021	0.133	0.194	0.231	0.213	0.121	0.042	0.008	0.002	0.001		
	5		0.004	0.053	0.103	0.158	0.227	0.193	0.101	0.029	0.012	0.003		
	6			0.016	0.040	0.079	0.177	0.226	0.177	0.079	0.040	0.016		
	7			0.003	0.012	0.029	0.101	0.193	0.227	0.158	0.103	0.053	0.004	
	8			0.001	0.002	0.008	0.042	0.121	0.213	0.231	0.194	0.133	0.021	0.002
	9					0.001	0.012	0.054	0.142	0.240	0.258	0.236	0.085	0.017
	10						0.002	0.016	0.064	0.168	0.232	0.283	0.230	0.099
	11							0.003	0.017	0.071	0.127	0.206	0.377	0.341
	12								0.002	0.014	0.032	0.069	0.282	0.540

n	x	0.05	0.1	0.2	0.25	0.3	0.4	P 0.5	0.6	0.7	0.75	0.8	0.9	0.95
13	0	0.513	0.254	0.055	0.024	0.010	0.001							
	1	0.351	0.367	0.179	0.103	0.054	0.011	0.002						
	2	0.111	0.245	0.268	0.206	0.139	0.045	0.010	0.001					
	3	0.021	0.100	0.246	0.252	0.218	0.111	0.035	0.006	0.001				
	4	0.003	0.028	0.154	0.210	0.234	0.184	0.087	0.024	0.003				
	5		0.006	0.069	0.126	0.180	0.221	0.157	0.066	0.014	0.005	0.001		
	6		0.001	0.023	0.056	0.103	0.197	0.209	0.131	0.044	0.019	0.006		
	7			0.006	0.019	0.044	0.131	0.209	0.197	0.103	0.056	0.023	0.001	
	8			0.001	0.005	0.014	0.066	0.157	0.221	0.180	0.126	0.069	0.006	
	9				0.001	0.003	0.024	0.087	0.184	0.234	0.210	0.154	0.028	0.003
	10					0.001	0.006	0.035	0.111	0.218	0.252	0.246	0.100	0.021
	11						0.001	0.010	0.045	0.139	0.206	0.268	0.245	0.111
	12							0.002	0.011	0.054	0.103	0.179	0.367	0.351
	13							0.001	0.010	0.024	0.055	0.254	0.513	
14	0	0.488	0.229	0.044	0.018	0.007	0.001							
	1	0.359	0.356	0.154	0.083	0.041	0.007	0.001						
	2	0.123	0.257	0.250	0.180	0.113	0.032	0.006	0.001					
	3	0.026	0.114	0.250	0.240	0.194	0.085	0.022	0.003					
	4	0.004	0.035	0.172	0.220	0.229	0.155	0.061	0.014	0.001				
	5		0.008	0.086	0.147	0.196	0.207	0.122	0.041	0.007	0.002			
	6		0.001	0.032	0.073	0.126	0.207	0.183	0.092	0.023	0.008	0.002		
	7			0.009	0.028	0.062	0.157	0.209	0.157	0.062	0.028	0.009		
	8			0.002	0.008	0.023	0.092	0.183	0.207	0.126	0.073	0.032	0.001	
	9				0.002	0.007	0.041	0.122	0.207	0.196	0.147	0.086	0.008	
	10					0.001	0.014	0.061	0.155	0.229	0.220	0.172	0.035	0.004
	11						0.003	0.022	0.085	0.194	0.240	0.250	0.114	0.026
	12						0.001	0.006	0.032	0.113	0.180	0.250	0.257	0.123
	13							0.001	0.007	0.041	0.083	0.154	0.356	0.359
	14								0.001	0.007	0.018	0.044	0.229	0.488
15	0	0.463	0.206	0.035	0.013	0.005								
	1	0.366	0.343	0.132	0.067	0.031	0.005							
	2	0.135	0.267	0.231	0.156	0.092	0.002	0.003						
	3	0.031	0.129	0.250	0.225	0.170	0.063	0.014	0.002					
	4	0.005	0.043	0.188	0.225	0.219	0.127	0.042	0.007	0.001				
	5	0.001	0.010	0.103	0.165	0.206	0.186	0.092	0.024	0.003	0.001			
	6		0.002	0.043	0.092	0.147	0.207	0.153	0.061	0.012	0.003	0.001		
	7			0.014	0.039	0.081	0.177	0.196	0.118	0.035	0.013	0.003		
	8			0.003	0.013	0.035	0.118	0.196	0.177	0.081	0.039	0.014		
	9			0.001	0.003	0.012	0.061	0.153	0.207	0.147	0.092	0.043	0.002	
	10				0.001	0.003	0.024	0.092	0.186	0.206	0.165	0.103	0.010	0.001
	11					0.001	0.007	0.042	0.127	0.219	0.225	0.188	0.043	0.005
	12						0.002	0.014	0.063	0.170	0.225	0.250	0.129	0.031
	13							0.003	0.022	0.092	0.156	0.231	0.267	0.135
	14								0.005	0.031	0.067	0.132	0.343	0.366
	15									0.005	0.013	0.035	0.206	0.463

APPENDIX C

GAUSSIAN DISTRIBUTIONS

AREAS UNDER THE NORMAL CURVE

An entry in the table is the proportion under the entire curve which is between $z = 0$ and a positive value of z. Areas for negative values of z are obtained by symmetry.

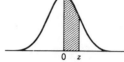

z	.00	.01	.02	.03	.04	.05	.06	.07	.08	.09
0.0	.0000	.0040	.0080	.0120	.0160	.0199	.0239	.0279	.0319	.0359
0.1	.0398	.0438	.0478	.0517	.0557	.0596	.0636	.0675	.0714	.0753
0.2	.0793	.0832	.0871	.0910	.0948	.0987	.1026	.1064	.1103	.1141
0.3	.1179	.1217	.1255	.1293	.1331	.1368	.1406	.1443	.1480	.1517
0.4	.1554	.1591	.1628	.1664	.1700	.1736	.1772	.1808	.1844	.1879
0.5	.1915	.1950	.1985	.2019	.2054	.2088	.2123	.2157	.2190	.2224
0.6	.2257	.2291	.2324	.2357	.2389	.2422	.2454	.2486	.2517	.2549
0.7	.2580	.2611	.2642	.2673	.2703	.2734	.2764	.2794	.2823	.2852
0.8	.2881	.2910	.2939	.2967	.2995	.3023	.3051	.3078	.3106	.3133
0.9	.3159	.3186	.3212	.3238	.3264	.3289	.3315	.3340	.3365	.3389
1.0	.3413	.3438	.3461	.3485	.3508	.3531	.3554	.3577	.3599	.3621
1.1	.3643	.3665	.3686	.3708	.3729	.3749	.3770	.3790	.3810	.3830
1.2	.3849	.3869	.3888	.3907	.3925	.3944	.3962	.3980	.3997	.4015
1.3	.4032	.4049	.4066	.4082	.4099	.4115	.4131	.4147	.4162	.4177
1.4	.4192	.4207	.4222	.4236	.4251	.4265	.4279	.4292	.4306	.4319
1.5	.4332	.4345	.4357	.4370	.4382	.4394	.4406	.4418	.4429	.4441
1.6	.4452	.4463	.4474	.4484	.4495	.4505	.4515	.4525	.4535	.4545
1.7	.4554	.4564	.4573	.4582	.4591	.4599	.4608	.4616	.4625	.4633
1.8	.4641	.4649	.4656	.4664	.4671	.4678	.4686	.4693	.4699	.4706
1.9	.4713	.4719	.4726	.4732	.4738	.4744	.4750	.4756	.4761	.4767
2.0	.4772	.4778	.4783	.4788	.4793	.4798	.4803	.4808	.4812	.4817
2.1	.4821	.4826	.4830	.4834	.4838	.4842	.4846	.4850	.4854	.4857
2.2	.4861	.4864	.4868	.4871	.4875	.4878	.4881	.4884	.4887	.4890
2.3	.4893	.4896	.4898	.4901	.4904	.4906	.4909	.4911	.4913	.4916
2.4	.4918	.4920	.4922	.4925	.4927	.4929	.4931	.4932	.4934	.4936
2.5	.4938	.4940	.4941	.4943	.4945	.4946	.4948	.4949	.4951	.4952
2.6	.4953	.4955	.4956	.4957	.4959	.4960	.4961	.4962	.4963	.4964
2.7	.4965	.4966	.4967	.4968	.4969	.4970	.4971	.4972	.4973	.4974
2.8	.4974	.4975	.4976	.4977	.4977	.4978	.4979	.4979	.4980	.4981
2.9	.4981	.4982	.4982	.4983	.4984	.4984	.4985	.4985	.4986	.4986
3.0	.4987	.4987	.4987	.4988	.4988	.4989	.4989	.4989	.4990	.4990

Second decimal place of z

From Donald F. Koosis, *Business Statistics*, Wiley, New York 1972, pp. 279–283. Copyright © 1972. Reprinted by permission of John Wiley & Sons, Inc.

CRITICAL POINTS OF THE t DISTRIBUTION

The first column lists the number of degrees of freedom (v). The headings of the other columns give probabilities (P) for t to exceed the entry value. Use symmetry for negative t values.

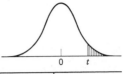

P df	.10	.05	.025	.01	.005
1	3.078	6.314	12.706	31.821	63.657
2	1.886	2.920	4.303	6.965	9.925
3	1.638	2.353	3.182	4.541	5.841
4	1.533	2.132	2.776	3.747	4.604
5	1.476	2.015	2.571	3.365	4.032
6	1.440	1.943	2.447	3.143	3.707
7	1.415	1.895	2.365	2.998	3.499
8	1.397	1.860	2.306	2.896	3.355
9	1.383	1.833	2.262	2.821	3.250
10	1.372	1.812	2.228	2.764	3.169
11	1.363	1.796	2.201	2.718	3.106
12	1.356	1.782	2.179	2.681	3.055
13	1.350	1.771	2.160	2.650	3.012
14	1.345	1.761	2.145	2.624	2.977
15	1.341	1.753	2.131	2.602	2.947
16	1.337	1.746	2.120	2.583	2.921
17	1.333	1.740	2.110	2.567	2.898
18	1.330	1.734	2.101	2.552	2.878
19	1.328	1.729	2.093	2.539	2.861
20	1.325	1.725	2.086	2.528	2.845
21	1.323	1.721	2.080	2.518	2.831
22	1.321	1.717	2.074	2.508	2.819
23	1.319	1.714	2.069	2.500	2.807
24	1.318	1.711	2.064	2.492	2.797
25	1.316	1.708	2.060	2.485	2.787
26	1.315	1.706	2.056	2.479	2.779
27	1.314	1.703	2.052	2.473	2.771
28	1.313	1.701	2.048	2.467	2.763
29	1.311	1.699	2.045	2.462	2.756
30	1.310	1.697	2.042	2.457	2.750
40	1.303	1.684	2.021	2.423	2.704
60	1.296	1.671	2.000	2.390	2.660
120	1.289	1.658	1.980	2.358	2.617
∞	1.282	1.645	1.960	2.326	2.576

THE HUD GUIDE TO REAL ESTATE SETTLEMENT COSTS*

You are planning to buy a home. When you do, you will probably make a downpayment and finance the balance of the purchase price with a loan secured by a mortgage on your home.

Before you take possession of your home, *a closing or settlement will occur at which ownership of the property will be transferred to you*, and your obligation to repay the mortgage loan will become effective (emphasis added). The terms and conditions of the loan—interest rate, monthly payment, and the repayment period—are specified in the documents signed by you. These include a note evidencing the loan for the unpaid purchase price, a mortgage placing a lien on your home, and other documents.

In some states, it is the custom for the buyer and seller to attend the settlement in person; in others it is handled automatically by an escrow agent when all papers and funds have been deposited with him.

At the closing or settlement, both you and the seller will have to pay certain charges incident to transferring title to real estate and obtaining the mortgage loan. These charges are called "settlement costs" or "closing costs."

This booklet has been prepared to inform you, the buyer, about the nature and costs of the settlement process. As required by law, this booklet is given to you by a lending institution at the time you apply for a mortgage loan to finance the purchase of a one- to four-family residential dwelling. At this stage, you have selected the home you want to buy. You may have already reached informal agreement with a seller or even signed a sales contract and made a deposit ("earnest money deposit") indicating

*"Settlement Costs-A HUD Guide," U.S. Department of Housing and Urban Development, 1975.

your serious intention to buy—a deposit which could be forfeited should you fail to complete your purchase.

This booklet is intended to acquaint you with the appropriate procedures and charges for settlement services which you will encounter in closing your home purchase transaction.

For answers to specific questions or for information on mortgage lending and settlement practices in your locality, you may want to consult a state or local consumer affairs agency, an attorney, a legal aid society, or the local real estate board.

D-1   HOME LOAN FINANCING

The home purchase loan is evidenced by your signature on a note or bond, and the loan (your debt) is secured by a mortgage (or deed of trust) which you must sign, which pledges the home as security for repayment of the loan. If you fail to repay the loan or comply with the terms and conditions of the mortgage, the lender can initiate foreclosure of the loan, which would lead to sale of your home at a public auction to satisfy the debt.

In a home mortgage transaction, you promise to repay the loan and interest in monthly installments at the interest rate and over the period of time specified in the mortgage contract. In the early years when your debt is largest, most of the monthly payment goes for interest. The amount applied to the outstanding debt gradually increases so that in the final years of the mortgage most of the payment goes to principal and less to interest. This is known as an amortized mortgage, and most mortgages are written this way.

In some states, the security instrument instead of being a mortgage is a deed of trust under which the borrower deeds the property to a trustee. Normally, the terms of a deed of trust are substantially the same as those of a mortgage.

Husband and wife often take title to their home as joint tenants with right of survivorship. You may wish to seek legal advice on this and other matters. The manner in which you take title to the home you buy can have important income tax, estate planning, and other consequences.

D-2   DISCLOSURE/SETTLEMENT STATEMENT

The Real Estate Procedures Act of 1974 (Public Law 93-533) requires use of a standard form for advance disclosure of settlement costs and to record actual charges incurred at settlement in all mortgage transactions involving federally related loans.

The same form is used for both advance disclosure and settlement and is reproduced on the following pages to acquaint you with it. **Settlement cost items are numbered to correspond with the accompanying explanation of each item.** The listing of these items on the form does not imply that any particular charge listed is or should be made in a given geographic area. Even in a given geographic area, you may find that different lenders and providers of settlement services vary as to whether they make certain charges and as to the amount of the charge. You may wish to "shop around."

Some settlement costs typically are charged to the buyer. Others usually are the responsibility of the seller. Although local custom and practices often dictate which are the buyer's and which the seller's costs, there are no hard and fast rules that apply, and in most cases the buyer and seller can negotiate as to who will pay specific settlement charges. You can also negotiate with providers of settlement services as to whether each charge will be made and the amount. You should be charged only for services actually performed, as required by settlement practices in a particular locality.

1. *Contract Sales Price*. This is the price of the home agreed to in the sales contract between buyer and seller.

2. *Personal Property*. Those items, such as carpets, drapes, or appliances, which the seller transfers with the home, may be paid for by the buyer at settlement. When the sales contract is made, you should make sure that items to be transferred are described. The sales contract should state whether such items are included in the sales price.

3. *Settlement Charges*. This is the total amount of the settlement charges to be paid by the buyer. These charges are itemized on page 2 of the form [Figure D-1].

4,9. *Adjustments or Pro-rations*. These amounts represent pro-rated adjustments of certain costs, such as real estate taxes, utilities, and fuel. Such adjustments are often made in order to charge the seller for the period he owned the property (up to settlement) and to charge the buyer for the period after settlement. Item 4 states amounts for which the buyer compensates the seller. Item 9 states amounts for which the seller compensates the buyer. As an example, where settlement occurs October 1, 1975, and the seller has paid the real estate taxes in advance for the entire year, a typical adjustment would be for the buyer to compensate the seller for one-fourth of the real estate taxes for 1975, that is, the period from October 1 through December 31. That amount would be shown at item 4.

5. *Gross Amount Due from Borrower*. This is the total amount of all charges to the buyer included in items 1, 2, 3 and 4.

6. *Deposit or Earnest Money*. This is the amount of money deposited by the buyer under the contract of sale, usually at the time it was signed.

7. *Principal Amount of Loan(s)*. This is the amount of mortgage money loaned to the buyer to purchase his home.

8. *Existing Loan(s) Taken Subject To....* This space is used for cases in which the buyer is assuming or taking title subject to an existing loan or other lien on which he is expected to make the payments.

10. *Total Amounts Paid By or In Behalf of Borrower*. This amount is the sum of items 6, 7, 8, and 9 which will be applied to reduce the amount of charges to the buyer in item 5.

11. *Cash Required from (Payable to) Borrower*. This is the total amount of cash which the buyer will need at settlement (subtract item 10 from item 5). At time of advance disclosure this is the estimated amount.

12. *Real Estate Broker's Sales Compensation*. This charge compensates the real estate broker or brokers for services involved in listing and selling the property, and is normally the seller's obligation to pay. This commission or fee may be split among more than one broker if each performed services in connection with the transaction, but no person may accept any portion, split, or percentage of such commission or fee other than for services actually performed.

13. *Loan Origination Fee*. This compensates the lender for expenses incurred in originating the loan, preparing documents, and related work. When such a fee is charged, it is usually a percentage of the face amount of the mortgage. In FHA-insured or VA-guaranteed mortgage transactions involving existing structures, the fee charged the borrower can be no more than 1% of the mortgage amount. For example, if you are approved for a VA-guaranteed loan of $30,000, the origination fee charged to you may not exceed $300. However, when the lender makes inspections and partial disbursements during construction of a new home, both FHA and VA permit a higher origination fee, but not more than $2\frac{1}{2}$% for FHA-insured loans or 2% for VA-guaranteed loans. The Farmers Home Administration does not permit a loan origination fee.

14. *Loan Discount Points*. Discounts or "points" are a one-time charge made by the lender to increase its yield (the effective interest return or income) on the mortgage loan. Each "point" is 1% of the mortgage amount.

In FHA and VA transactions, the buyer may not be charged a discount by the lender, but the seller may volunteer to pay points in order to help the buyer obtain financing. For example, if a lender charges 4 points on an FHA-insured loan of $30,000, this amounts to a discount of $1200. You, the buyer, may pay only the loan origination fee described in item 13 if it is a VA or FHA transaction. Discounts are not permitted on Farmers Home Administration loans.

15. *Appraisal Fee.* This charge compensates the lender for a property appraisal made by an independent appraiser or by a member of the lender's staff.

16. *Credit Report.* The buyer's credit history is often obtained by the lender, and a charge paid to a credit bureau for ascertaining the status of the buyer's credit may be collected, usually from the buyer.

17. *Lender's Inspection Fee.* This charge covers only inspections made by personnel of the lending institution at its discretion. Pest or other inspections made by companies other than the lender are described in item 31.

18. *Mortgage Insurance Application Fee.* This covers the cost of an FHA or VA appraisal, which in an FHA loan is included in a mortgage insurance application fee. For conventional loans it may cover application fees when charged by private mortgage insurers. In the case of an FHA-insured mortgage, the amount of this charge is set by HUD Regulations and may be charged to the buyer. The buyer in a VA-guaranteed loan may not be charged an appraisal fee unless identified by name in the request for VA's appraisal.

19. *Assumption Fee.* In a case where the buyer assumes the seller's existing mortgage on the property, the lender's charges for processing the assumption are entered here.

20. *Prepaid Interest.* This charge covers interest which will accrue from the date of settlement to the beginning of the period covered by your first monthly payment. For example, if your mortgage payment is due on the first of each month, but settlement occurs on April 20, the prepaid interest at settlement will cover the period from April 20 to April 30 if your first monthly mortgage payment is due on June 1. Thus your June 1 payment will not have to include an extra amount of interest for the period before May 1.

21. *Prepaid Mortgage Insurance Premium.* This is the portion of the premium prepaid by the buyer at settlement for mortgage insurance. This type of insurance is required when FHA or a private mortgage insurance company covers the lender against loss if the buyer fails to meet the mortgage obligation. Mortgage insurance premiums are required for all FHA-insured loans (but not for VA loan guarantees), and may be required on a conventional loan.

This type of insurance should not be confused with mortgage life, credit life, or disability insurance designed to pay off a mortgage in the event of physical disability or death of the borrower. Such insurance is available but usually not required by lenders.

22. *Prepaid Hazard Insurance Premium.* This is the portion of the premium prepaid by the buyer at settlement for purchase from a private company of insurance against loss due to fire, windstorm, and natural hazards. This coverage may be included in a homeowner's policy which insures against possible additional risks, such as personal liability and theft.

A hazard insurance or homeowner's policy does not protect you against loss caused by flooding. In special flood-prone areas identified by HUD, you must carry flood insurance on your home. Such insurance may be purchased at low federally subsidized rates in communities eligible under the National Flood Insurance Act. Contact a local hazard insurance agent concerning eligibility in your case.

23. *Reserves Deposited with Lender.* These funds are placed by the buyer in an "escrow" or "impound" account maintained by the lender to assure an adequate accumulation of funds to meet charges for real estate taxes and hazard insurance when they become due; and also, if applicable, for mortgage insurance, annual assessments, homeowners' association fees, or flood insurance. (These reserves are explained in more detail later.)

These reserves may be held in non-interest-bearing accounts. However, certain states now require lenders to pay interest on this money, and lenders in other states may be willing to do this voluntarily.

24. *Settlement, Closing, or Escrow Fee.* This charge may be made for handling and supervising the settlement transaction. The settlement may be conducted by the lender, a real estate broker, a title company in some states, an escrow agent in some states, or an attorney. The seller and buyer may negotiate regarding who pays or whether the charge is shared between them. The amount of the charge may be negotiated with the provider of the service. In a VA-guaranteed loan, this fee cannot be charged to the buyer when the buyer is assessed the 1% origination fee.

25. *Title Charges.* These charges cover the costs of title search and examination of public records of previous ownership and sales to establish the right of the seller to convey the property to the buyer. A search and examination are performed to determine whether the seller has good title to the property that he can transfer to the buyer, and to disclose any matters on record that could adversely affect the buyer, the lender, or others with an interest in the property. Examples of these problems are unpaid mortgages, judgments, or tax liens, a power line easement, or a road right-of-way that could limit use and enjoyment of the real estate by the buyer.

In some parts of the nation, a title search customarily takes the form of an "abstract," which is a compilation including copies of pertinent documents that provides a condensed history of property ownership and related matters. In other places, title searches are performed by extracting related information from the public record without assembling abstracts. Either way, it then is necessary for an expert examination to be made of the evidence accumulated in the search in order to determine status of title as shown by the public record.

Depending on local custom, title examinations normally are made by attorneys or title company employees. Through a title search and examination, land title problems of record are disclosed in advance so they can be cleared up, when possible, before a transaction is completed.

26. *Notary Fees.* This charge may be made for the services of a notary in authenticating signatures to the various documents in the transaction. In a VA-guaranteed loan, this fee cannot be charged to a buyer in the event the buyer is charged a 1% origination fee.

27. *Attorney's Fees.* These include charges which the lender may require the buyer to pay for legal services to the lender in connection with the transaction. The buyer should not assume that he is represented by an attorney hired by the lender who prepares the documents and handles the settlement. In a VA-guaranteed loan, this lender's attorney fee cannot be charged if the buyer is charged the 1% origination fee.

The buyer and seller may each retain attorneys to represent them and may pay the fees at the settlement, in which case these fees also appear on this part of the form.

In some states, attorneys provide bar-related title insurance as part of their services to the buyer for transfer of title. The attorney's fee in this case may include the title insurance premium.

28. *Title Insurance.* A one-time premium may be charged at settlement for a policy which protects the lender's interest in the property against land title problems including those that might not be disclosed by a title search and examination. Whether the buyer or seller pays for this varies with local custom.

The buyer must request and pay for an additional owner's policy if he wants this protection for his interest in the property. There are many areas where an owner's policy can be obtained at a modest additional charge if issued simultaneously with a lender's policy. In some areas, the seller pays for the owner's title insurance policy.

29. *Government Transfer Taxes and Charges.* The fees and taxes in this section are generally levied by state and/or local governments when property changes hands or when a mortgage loan is made. Depending on local custom, these charges may be paid by the buyer, seller, or otherwise split between them.

30. *Survey.* The lender or a party to the transaction may require a survey showing the precise location of the house and lot lines.

31. *Inspections.* This part of the form records charges for various inspections required by the lender or a party to the transaction, such as those for termite and other pest infestation. In a VA-guaranteed loan, the buyer may not be charged for the pest inspection.

There may also be presale inspections for the buyer's benefit to evaluate heating, plumbing, and electrical equipment and overall structural soundness. The charge for such an inspection may include a fee for insurance or warranty services to back up the inspection.

D-3 ADVANCE DISCLOSURE*

The Settlement-Disclosure Statement itemizes each settlement cost charged to the buyer and each charged to the seller. Advance disclosure serves a twofold purpose: (1) to provide notice of the cash you will need at settlement and (2) to make possible "comparison shopping" of settlement charges so that you can arrange terms most favorable to you. If you don't "shop around" you will not save money if the same services are offered elsewhere for less.

It is important to realize that advance disclosure provides for earlier and more systematic information about the costs of the settlement transactions but does not affect any contractual agreement which may already have been made between buyer and seller. Try to obtain as much of this information as possible prior to signing a sales contract for the house you intend to buy. Or, if the seller is agreeable, you may want to make the sales contract contingent upon your approval of the advance disclosure statement. Once you have signed, you may not be able to rescind the contract in the event that you are dissatisfied with some aspect of the transaction revealed by disclosure. It is in your interest to condition your purchase contract on your ability to obtain a mortgage loan on specified terms.

The law requires the lender to give you a copy of the completed advance disclosure statement at the time of loan commitment. In most circumstances this should be not later than 12 calendar days before the settlement date. Normally, the loan commitment and advance disclosure occur several weeks prior to settlement. In the case of a long-term commitment, such as that obtained by a buyer of a new home under construction, disclosure should be made shortly after signing the contract to buy the house. Typically, this might be in the range of 60 to 90 days before settlement.

If the exact cost of any settlement service is not known in time to meet the deadline, the lender must provide a good faith estimate of the charge.

*See note on page 313

Form Approved
OMB No. 63–R1501

A. U.S. DEPARTMENT OF HOUSING AND URBAN DEVELOPMENT

DISCLOSURE/SETTLEMENT STATEMENT

B. TYPE OF LOAN:

1. ☐ FHA 2. ☐ FMHA 3. ☐ CONV. UNINS.
4. ☐ VA 5. ☐ CONV. INS.

6. FILE NUMBER   7. LOAN NUMBER

8. MORTG. INS. CASE NO.

If the Truth-in-Lending Act applies to this transaction, a Truth-in-Lending statement is attached as page 3 of this form.

C. NOTE: This form is furnished to you prior to settlement to give you information about your settlement costs, and again after settlement to show the actual costs you have paid. The present copy of the form is:

☐ ADVANCE DISCLOSURE OF COSTS. Some items are estimated, and are marked "(e)". Some amounts may change if the settlement is held on a date other than the date estimated below. The preparer of this form is not responsible for errors or changes in amounts furnished by others.

☐ STATEMENT OF ACTUAL COSTS. Amounts paid to and by the settlement agent are shown. Items marked "(p.o.c.)" were paid outside the closing; they are shown here for informational purposes and are not included in totals.

D. NAME OF BORROWER

E. SELLER

F. LENDER

G. PROPERTY LOCATION

H. SETTLEMENT AGENT

PLACE OF SETTLEMENT

I. DATES

LOAN COMMITMENT   ADVANCE DISCLOSURE

SETTLEMENT   DATE OF PRORATIONS IF DIFFERENT FROM SETTLE-MENT

Figure D-1

J. SUMMARY OF BORROWER'S TRANSACTION

100. GROSS AMOUNT DUE FROM BORROWER:

101.	Contract sales price	①
102.	Personal property	②
103.	Settlement charges to borrower	③
	(from line 1400, Section L)	
104.		
105.		

Adjustments for items paid by seller in advance:

106.	City/town taxes	to	
107.	County taxes	to	
108.	Assessments	to	
109.		to	
110.		to	④
111.		to	
112.		to	

120. GROSS AMOUNT DUE FROM BORROWER: ⑤

200. AMOUNTS PAID BY OR IN BEHALF OF BORROWER:

201.	Deposit or earnest money	⑥
202.	Principal amount of new loan(s)	⑦
203.	Existing loan(s) taken subject to	⑧
204.		
205.		

K. SUMMARY OF SELLER'S TRANSACTION

400. GROSS AMOUNT DUE TO SELLER:

401.	Contract sales price	
402.	Personal property	
403.		
404.		

Adjustments for items paid by seller in advance:

405.	City/town taxes	to
406.	County taxes	to
407.	Assessments	to
408.		to
409.		to
410.		to
411.		to

420. GROSS AMOUNT DUE TO SELLER

NOTE: The following 500 and 600 series sections are not required to be completed when this form is used for advance disclosure of settlement costs prior to settlement.

500. REDUCTIONS IN AMOUNT DUE TO SELLER:

501.	Payoff of first mortgage loan	
502.	Payoff of second mortgage loan	
503.	Settlement charges to seller	
	(from line 1400, Section L)	
504.	Existing loan(s) taken subject to	

Figure D-1 (*Continued*)

302

Credits to borrower for items unpaid by seller:

206. City/town taxes	to	
207. County taxes	to	
208. Assessments	to	
209.	to	⑨
210.	to	
211.	to	
212.	to	
220. TOTAL AMOUNTS PAID BY OR IN BEHALF OF BORROWER		⑩
300. CASH AT SETTLEMENT REQUIRED FROM OR PAYABLE TO BORROWER:		
301. Gross amount due from borrower *(from line 120)*		
302. Less amounts paid by or in behalf of borrower *(from line 220)*	( )	
303. CASH (☐ REQUIRED FROM) OR (☐ PAYABLE TO) BORROWER:		⑪

505.	
506.	
507.	
508.	
509.	

Credits to borrower for items unpaid by seller:

510. City/town taxes	to	
511. County taxes	to	
512. Assessments	to	
513.	to	
514.	to	
515.	to	
520. TOTAL REDUCTIONS IN AMOUNT DUE TO SELLER:		
600. CASH TO SELLER FROM SETTLEMENT:		
601. Gross amount due to seller *(from line 420)*		
602. Less total reductions in amount due to seller *(from line 520)*	( )	
603. CASH TO SELLER FROM SETTLEMENT		

HUD-1 (5–75)

Figure D-1 (*Continued*)

		PAID FROM BORROWER'S FUNDS	PAID FROM SELLER'S FUNDS
L. SETTLEMENT CHARGES			
700. SALES BROKER'S COMMISSION based on price $ @ %			
701. Total commission paid by seller	⑫		
Division of commission as follows:			
702. $ to			
703. $ to			
704.			
800. ITEMS PAYABLE IN CONNECTION WITH LOAN.			
801. Loan Origination fee %	⑬		
802. Loan Discount %	⑭		
803. Appraisal Fee to	⑮		
804. Credit Report to	⑯		
805. Lender's inspection fee	⑰		
806. Mortgage Insurance application fee to	⑱		
807. Assumption/refinancing fee	⑲		
808.			
809.			
810.			
811.			

Figure D-1 (*Continued*)

900. ITEMS REQUIRED BY LENDER TO BE PAID IN ADVANCE.

901.	Interest from	to	@ $ /day	⑳
902.	Mortgage insurance premium for	mo. to		㉑
903.	Hazard insurance premium for	yrs. to		㉒
904.		yrs. to		
905.				

1000. RESERVES DEPOSITED WITH LENDER FOR: ㉓

1001.	Hazard insurance	mo. @$	/mo.
1002	Mortgage insurance	mo. @$	/mo.
1003.	City property taxes	mo. @$	/mo.
1004.	County property taxes	mo. @$	/mo.
1005.	Annual assessments	mo. @$	/mo.
1006.		mo. @$	/mo.
1007.		mo. @$	/mo.
1008.		mo. @$	/mo.

1100. TITLE CHARGES:

1101.	Settlement or closing fee to	㉔
1102.	Abstract or title search to	㉕
1103.	Title examination to	
1104.	Title insurance binder to	
1105.	Document preparation to	
1106.	Notary fees to	㉖
1107.	Attorney's Fees to	㉗

(includes above items No.

Figure D-1 (Continued)

304

1108.	Title insurance to		
	(includes above items No.:)		
1109.	Lender's coverage $		
1110.	Owner's coverage $		
1111.			
1112.			
1113.			

(28)

1200. GOVERNMENT RECORDING AND TRANSFER CHARGES

1201.	Recording fees: Deed $	, Mortgage $	Releases $
1202.	City/county tax/stamps: Deed $	; Mortgage $	
1203.	State tax/stamps: Deed $	; Mortgage $	
1204.			

(29)

1300. ADDITIONAL SETTLEMENT CHARGES

1301.	Survey to	
1302.	Pest inspection to	
1303.		
1304.		
1305.		

(30)
(31)

1400. TOTAL SETTLEMENT CHARGES *(entered on lines 103 and 503, Sections J and K)*

NOTE: Under certain circumstances the borrower and seller may be permitted to waive the 12-day period which must normally occur between advance disclosure and settlement. In the event such a waiver is made, copies of the statements of waiver, executed as provided in the regulations of the Department of Housing and Urban Development, shall be attached to and made a part of this form when the form is used as a settlement statement.

Figure D-1 (Continued)

305

Lenders are prohibited from charging a specific fee for the preparation and submission of disclosure and settlement costs statements or for the information they must provide under the Truth-in-Lending Act.

If your circumstances are such that you want to settle and take title to your new home before the lender can meet his 12-day advance disclosure deadline, you may sign a waiver of that requirement. Advance disclosure is intended to protect your interests, not hamper or delay your plans, so you should carefully consider before signing a waiver. Even if you agree to waive, HUD Regulations require the lender to provide the disclosure statement to you at least three days prior to the date of settlement.

Except in the case of a waiver, the lender must meet the advance disclosure requirement or be liable to you for actual damages or $500, whichever is greater. If court action is necessary to enforce this liability, the lender may be ordered to pay court costs and your attorney's fees as set by the court if the lender loses the case. You would pay attorney's fees in the event that you lose the case. A lender will not be held liable for a violation if he can show that it was not intentional and resulted from a bona fide error in spite of maintenance by the lender of procedures adopted to avoid such error.

D-4 UNFAIR PRACTICES AND UNREASONABLE OR UNNECESSARY CHARGES TO AVOID

A principal finding of Congress in the Real Estate Settlement Procedures Act of 1974 is that consumers need protection from "...unnecessarily high settlement charges caused by certain abusive practices that have developed in some areas of the country." The potential problems discussed below may not be applicable to most loan settlements, and the discussion is not intended to deter you from buying a home. Most professionals in the settlement service business will give you good service. Nevertheless, you may save yourself money or worry by keeping the following considerations in mind.

Illegal Practices

Practices specifically prohibited by this act fall into two categories.

1. *Kickbacks.* Kickbacks and referral of business for gain most often are tied together, so the law prohibits anyone from giving or taking a fee, kickback, or anything of value under an agreement that business related to real estate settlements will be referred to a specific person or organization.

This requirement does not, of course, prevent agents for lenders and title companies, attorneys, or others actually performing a service in connection with the mortgage loan or settlement transactions, from receiving compensation for their work.

The prohibition is aimed primarily at eliminating the kind of arrangement in which one party agrees to return part of his fee in order to obtain a volume of business from the referring party. The danger is that some settlement fees can be inflated to cover this additional party, resulting in a higher total cost to you. For example, a title company might pay a fee to another party for bringing it title insurance business even though the other party performs no work and provides no service in connection with issuance of the title insurance policy. As another example, a lawyer might give a part of his fee to another party to the transaction in exchange for the referral of business.

It is also illegal to charge or accept a fee or portion thereof other than for services actually performed.

There are criminal penalties of both fine and imprisonment for any violation of these provisions of law. There are also provisions for you to recover three times the amount of the fee involved or a portion thereof. In any successful action to enforce your right, the court may award you court costs together with a fee for your attorney.

2. *Title Companies.* Another abuse prohibited by law is any requirement by the home seller that title insurance be purchased from a particular company. Under the law, sellers may not require, as a condition of sale, that title insurance be purchased by the buyer from any particular title company. A violation would make the seller liable to you in an amount equal to three times all charges made for the title insurance.

Choices Open to the Buyer and Other Points to Remember

Because the various parties to the settlement transaction have different interests, there will be many steps in the process of buying a home which call for caution on your part. As a home buyer, you have a number of choices open to you concerning settlement costs and services. Some points to keep in mind are as follows.

1. *Understand the Role of the Real Estate Broker.* Although the real estate agent or broker usually provides helpful advice to you on many aspects of home buying and may in some areas supervise the settlement, he normally serves as agent of the seller. While the real estate licensing laws of most states require that the broker treat both buyer and seller fairly, you

should not expect the broker to represent your interests to the exclusion of those of the seller.

The broker's basic objectives are to obtain a signed contract of sale which properly expresses the agreement of the parties and to complete the sale and earn a commission or fee. Before you sign, make sure that the sales contract correctly expresses your agreement with the seller on such important details as method of paying the sales price of the home, the time set for your move-in, and the status of fixtures and other property in the home.

A broker may recommend that you deal with a particular lender, title company, attorney, or provider of settlement services. Although this recommendation may be based on the broker's up-to-date knowledge of rates and quality of service, you should feel completely free to consider alternatives, compare rates and fees, and make your own decision on these matters.

It is up to you to review the documents carefully. Although the broker may offer helpful advice, keep in mind that you are the one who is spending the money to buy a home and you are entitled to a full understanding of the costs. The broker's principal interest at settlement is to get the transaction closed and his fee or commission disbursed.

2. *Settlement Attorneys, Escrow and Closing Agents.* In some parts of the country, settlements are often conducted by attorneys who specialize in real estate transactions. In other parts of the country, the settlement may be conducted by an escrow or closing agent or by the lender or broker. Their primary concern is orderly completion of all the details called for in the sales contract and in the mortgage commitment.

Because mortgage lenders, unlike borrowers, go through settlement often, they often will not be present at the settlement, preferring to spell out in detail in a letter of instruction to the person conducting the closing that which they expect to be done before loan funds can be released.

You, the buyer, will not have a letter of instructions. You will be asked at settlement to make a number of decisions in areas with which you may have had little previous experience.

Before settlement, you should ask the broker, the settlement attorney, or an attorney retained by you what questions will probably come up. Write them down so that you may have time to think about decisions that are important to you.

Settlement attorneys do not mind answering your questions—that is a part of their job—but at the same time they may not invite questions. If you have doubts, ask questions. Don't let anyone rush you. There are likely to be lengthy documents to sign at settlement. If you or your attorney asks, you can usually get copies of the forms in advance.

3. *Legal Representation.* If you feel unfamiliar or unsure with real estate settlements, and many people do, consider hiring your own attorney to represent you. If you hire an attorney, be certain that there is a clear understanding in advance about what services he is to perform and what his fee will be for those services. Some will quote a flat fee, others an hourly rate or one based on a percentage of the sales price. The important point is that you should know in advance how much you should expect to pay for his services. If you do not know an attorney who is well versed in real estate transactions, many local bar associations may be able to refer you to one who is.

4. *Discuss with Lenders Their Requirements for Settlement Services.* The lender's legitimate business interest is in making a loan on terms which will provide a good yield with little risk. In selecting a lending institution, ask about requirements for property surveys, appraisals, escrows for taxes and insurance, and other settlement services. You may compare these requirements with those of other lenders. Some lenders will give you the discretion to shop among different providers of settlement services. But most lenders deal regularly with certain title companies, attorneys, appraisers, surveyors, or others in whom they have confidence, and usually want to arrange for provision of all settlement services through these parties as a convenience to the buyer and lender. If you wish to bargain directly to reduce rates for settlement services, discuss this with various lenders.

Remember to compare also the mortgage interest rates and other mortgage terms quoted by different lenders. A lender may gain through higher mortgage interest over the repayment term what it gives up at the "front end" in reducing requirements for loan origination fees, discount points and other one-time charges which must be paid in cash at settlement. Other features of available loans should also be compared as you shop.

Feel free to select a lender other than the one recommended by the broker or seller. It is entirely possible that you may find financing which is more advantageous to you.

5. *Title Insurance Required by the Lender Protects the Lender: You May Buy a Separate Owner's Title Insurance Policy for Your Own Protection.* Title insurance is often required to protect the lender against loss if a flaw in title is not found by the title search made when a home is purchased. The lender's title insurance policy will be paid for by you or by the seller according to local custom or the sales contract.

You and the lender have different interests in the property you are buying, and there are many kinds of title defects that can trouble you without creating problems for the lender. You may buy a separate owner's title insurance policy for your own protection in areas where this policy is not furnished by the **seller** as a matter of custom.

6. *Try to Minimize the Performance and Cost of Repetitive or Excessive Settlement Requirements.* Some settlement costs are beyond your control, such as government transfer charges. Other items may be negotiable, however, such as certain services which the lender requires but which you pay for.

a. *Title Search.* There may be no need for a full historical title search "back to the year one" each time title to a home is transferred. If you are buying a home which had recently changed hands, inquire at title companies about a "reissue rate." If the policy of the previous owner is available, take it to a title insurer before settlement. It may help you obtain a "reissue rate." Generally this rate, when permitted by state law or regulations, allows a reduction of the usual charge for a new policy if the previous policy was issued by the same title insurer or by another reputable company within a recent period.

Title search requirements are sometimes set by agencies which insure or guarantee the loan, or by investors who purchase mortgages originated by other lending institutions. The lender you deal with may not have discretion on eliminating or reducing these requirements.

b. *Survey.* The survey of the property may be simplified and the cost reduced if a full professional survey was performed recently. A new survey may not be needed to show that no recent changes have occurred which affect the validity of the last survey. A surveyor may be able to avoid the cost of a repetitive complete survey of the property if he has access to a recent survey which he can "update." Here again, the requirements of investors who buy loans originated by your lender may limit the lender's discretion to negotiate this point.

c. *Settlement Agent.* Settlement practices vary from locality to locality, and even within the same county or city. In various areas settlements are conducted by the lending institutions, title insurance companies, escrow companies, real estate brokers, and attorneys for the buyer or seller. By investigating and comparing practices and rates, you may find that the first suggested settlement agent may not be the least expensive. You might save money by taking the initiative in arranging for settlement and selecting the firm and location which best meets your needs.

d. *Escrows.* The Real Estate Settlement Procedures Act of 1974 has placed limits on the amount of money which the lender can require you to place in escrow at settlement for later payment of property taxes and insurance.

Know your rights under this new Section 10 provision of the act, as explained in the next subsection.

D-5   ESCROW ACCOUNTS

Item 23 (p. 297) covers payments your lender may require you to make to an "escrow," "reserve," or "impound" account for insurance premiums, real estate taxes, and unpaid assessments.

Many lenders require that each monthly payment on the mortgage include amounts for taxes and hazard insurance. When applicable, lenders will also collect mortgage insurance premiums and assessments payable to homeowner and other associations as well as to special assessment districts. These funds are set aside each month in escrow accounts and are accumulated to pay the taxes and other bills when they are due.

By law, the amount you pay into an escrow at settlement may not exceed your share of taxes and insurance accrued prior to settlement, **plus** one-twelfth of the estimated amount which will come due for taxes and insurance in the 12-month period beginning at settlement. If taxes or insurance costs go up periodically over the life of your mortgage, the lender will need to collect more money for the escrow accounts to cover these increased costs, resulting in a larger monthly housing payment for you. Should these costs decline periodically, the lender should reduce the monthly escrow collection accordingly.

The escrow service provided by your lender is designed to meet ongoing expenses of homeownership. By spreading payments over the year it eliminates the prospect of being faced with large annual bills, perhaps at an inopportune time. On the other hand, you may want to manage your own payment of taxes and/or insurance, instead of paying into an escrow held by the lender. Discuss this point when shopping among lenders. Be aware, however, that certain escrow accounts are required by federal regulation, and in some states by laws affecting state-chartered savings and loan associations.

D-6   PREVIOUS SELLING PRICE DISCLOSURE

The lender is required by law before making a commitment to finance a mortgage on a house, which was completed more than 12 months prior to settlement, to confirm that the seller or his agent has disclosed in writing to the buyer the following information:

- The name and address of the present owner.
- The date the property was acquired by the present owner (the year only of acquisition need be given if the property was acquired more than two years previously).
- If the seller has not owned the property for at least two years prior to the date of your loan application and has not used the property as a place of residence, the date and purchase price of the last "arm's length transfer" of the property, a list of subsequent improvements other than maintenance, and the cost of the improvements.

The purpose of this requirement is to inform you whether the house is being sold by an owner-occupant or by someone who has acquired the house and prepared it for resale. Many investors make a livelihood by investing in existing housing, making repairs and improvements, and reselling at a fair profit. However, abuses have occurred in which only superficial repairs have been made and homes have been sold at prices greatly in excess of their values. As a buyer, your knowledge of the previous selling price may help you determine the present value of the property.

The lender's obligation is considered met if he receives a copy of the written statement from the seller to you giving the information described above. At that time, the lender may make the mortgage loan commitment.

To back up your right to full disclosure concerning existing property, any person (or persons) who knowingly and willingly provides false information or fails to comply with disclosure requirements may be subject to criminal penalties of fine and imprisonment, and civil damages.

D-7 JURISDICTION OF COURTS

If you have suffered damages through violations of the Real Estate Settlement Procedures Act of 1974 as described in the preceding pages, action may be brought in the United States District Court for the district in which the property involved is located or in any other court of competent jurisdiction, within one year from the date of the occurrence of the violation. You may also have rights under other federal or state laws.

D-8 TRUTH IN LENDING DISCLOSURE

At the time of advance disclosure, you will receive a Truth in Lending statement as part of the standard settlement cost disclosure form. This

Truth in Lending information will also appear on the standard settlement statement given to you upon completion of the settlement. The Truth in Lending statement discloses the annual percentage rate (APR) which you will pay on your mortgage loan. This rate may be higher than the contract interest rate quoted on your mortgage. This is because the contract rate includes only interest, but the APR expresses the total finance charge including certain credit costs besides interest on the loan.

* * *

Author's Note: Law requiring advance disclosure of house closing costs repealed.

Many Congressmen were surprised when prospective home purchasers started complaining about a recent law requiring lenders to disclose all settlement costs at least 12 days before the closing of a real estate transaction. This law, after all, was supposed to give buyers time to shop around for lower priced services and guard them against unexpected charges.

But what the law did, buyers told Congress, was delay the time between the making of an offer and the closing of a deal. This delay caused hardships to transferred executives who wanted to move their families to new locales as quickly as possible.

Congress repealed the advance disclosure provisions of the Real Estate Settlement Procedures Act. A new provision was substituted that provides that buyers must be given a good faith estimate—at the time they apply for a loan—of the charges likely to be incurred. And the buyer can request a list of all charges one business day before the closing. But only the charges that are known then need be disclosed.

INDEX